Helion & Company Limited
Unit 8 Amherst Business Centre
Budbrooke Road
Warwick
CV34 5WE
England
Tel. 01926 499 619
Email: info@helion.co.uk
Website: www.helion.co.uk
Twitter: @helionbooks
Visit our blog https://helionbooks.
wordpress.com/

Text © Michal A. Piegzik 2024
Photographs © as individually credited
Artworks Jean Marie Guillou and
    Gregorz Nowak © Helion & Company 2024
Map drawn by George Anderson
    © Helion & Company 2024

Typeset by Oliver Barstow, Milan, Italy
Cover design by Paul Hewitt, Battlefield
    Design (www.battlefield-design.co.uk)

ISBN 978-1-804514-62-7

British Library Cataloguing-in-Publication
    Data
A catalogue record for this book is available
    from the British Library

We always welcome receiving book
proposals from prospective authors.

CONTENTS

Note: In order to simplify the use of this book, all names, locations and geographic
designations are as provided in *The Times World Atlas*, or other traditionally accepted
major sources of reference, as of the time of described events.

We have these garrisons all over the world and in many of the posts they have not only a great deal of loneliness to combat and lack of action, but extreme discomforts of heat and cold, or wind and rain, as in the Aleutians. The men across the ice cap of Greenland, with literally no diverting facilities and Arctic winter darkness to combat, have a very hard role to play. There are others manning air look-out towers in the peaks of the Himalayan Mountains between India and China who have a fearfully trying task to perform. It makes a very moving picture to one who is aware of the conditions.[1] – **from General Marshall's letter to Private Allen, 17 December 1942.**

1
AUTUMN CAMPAIGN OF 1942 IN THE ALEUTIANS

アリューシャンにおける１９４２年の秋の作戦
Aryūshan ni okeru 1942-nen no Aki no Sakusen

After establishing a fully operational airfield on Adak, the Americans returned to the strategy of a war of attrition to prevent the Japanese from consolidating their positions in the Aleutian Islands. On 13 September, a LB-30 bomber escorted by two P-38 fighters took off from the 'Fireplace' (Adak) and headed to Kiska to carry out a photographic mission. Upon arrival over the island, the reconnaissance flight encountered three float planes, which attacked the intruders, slightly damaging the LB-30 and severely damaging a Lightning. Despite one damaged engine and a blown-off wheel in the landing gear, the fighter pilot skidded in on his belly at Adak.[2] One Japanese fighter was reported shot down that day, but the *5th Kaigun Kōkūtai* (5th Air Group) action report does not include information about any losses. The Japanese document also correctly indicates the number and type of aircraft that took part in the action on the enemy's side.[3] The Americans, on the other hand, remembered this mission as follows:

> Two Zeroes were laying for us at the base of the overcast. They were flushed out and engaged by our escort [a P-38 shot one Zero down in flames]. Coming out of our bomb-photography run, one Zero paralleled our course until a few bursts of our waist gun dissuaded his attempts to cut in on us. Shortly after, we saw two fighters flying under a cloud base at 3 o'clock. Captain Wernick turned to a head-on course to them, thinking they were our escort.
>
> It turned out they were Zeroes. One Zero, completely surprised, pulled up and fled into the overcast. The other attacked, put one explosive 20mm shell through our left bomb-bay door, cutting a fuel line and just missing the nose fuses of our 500lb. bombs.[4]

The 11 AF (Eleventh Air Force) still felt helpless against the enemy on Kiska, but in the late afternoon of 13 September, 31 fighters (15 P-38s and 16 P-39s) and 16 bombers (15 B-25s and one B-17) landed on Adak.[5] Thus, the next day, the Americans were able to launch their first massive strike on enemy positions from the 'Fireplace'. Twelve B-24s, escorted by 14 P-38s and 14 P-39s, carried out a coordinated raid that B. Garfield later described as the first Second World War bombardment 'from zero ceiling'.[6] Due to the need to maintain complete radio silence at the Adak airbase, the Alaska Defense Command did not know what damage had been inflicted on the enemy. However, Japanese documents clearly show that the attack resulted in one seriously damaged and two missing floatplane fighters, a damaged periscope of the *RO-68* submarine, a strafed *RO-63*, flooded compartments of the *Nojima Maru* transport ship, three buildings set on fire and several men killed.[7]

American landing on Adak, 30 August 1942. (NH&HC)

Seabees' tents on Adak. (Dmitri Kessel/Life Pictures)

A P-38 over the Aleutians. (Dmitri Kessel/Life Pictures)

Rear Admiral Akiyama Katsuzō. (NDL)

Just before completing the evacuation of the Attu garrison, on 15 September, the Japanese reorganised their forces in the Aleutians. As part of the AO Defence Unit (*AO Bōbi Butai*), they established the 51st Naval Base Force,[8] which also included the 5th Garrison Unit, the 5th Submarine Chaser Squadron, the Submarine Base Unit, the *5th Kaigun Kōkūtai*, the minesweeper *Shin'ei Maru No. 10* and five patrol boats. Rear Admiral Akiyama Katsuzō, who arrived in Kiska with his staff aboard the seaplane tender *Kimikawa Maru* on 25 September, was appointed the new commander of the 51st Base Unit.[9]

Along with the significant shortening of the day, the Japanese were convinced that the Americans would not decide to launch a landing operation on Kiska in September. Thus, they intended to strengthen their positions on the island until the spring thaw. Unexpectedly, the Guadalcanal campaign became a major issue for the Navy General Staff, which expected that most American warships would be diverted from the North to the South Pacific. However, the 14 September raid, especially the number of escort fighters that appeared over Kiska, alarmed the Fifth Fleet headquarters. During a staff meeting

five days later, the Japanese discussed reasons for the sudden change in the enemy's air raid tactics. Although no one believed that the 11 AF had a well-developed air base west of Umnak, some officers urged for carrying out additional reconnaissance missions in Nazan Bay and Kuluk Bay in the next few days.[10]

Regardless of the questions about numerous American escort fighters over Kiska, the Japanese decided to use floatplane fighters to defend Kiska, as they proved effective in deterring enemy bombers or flying boats. According to a report presented by the *5th Kaigun Kōkūtai* on 15 September, the unit had only one operational Rufe, and the further defence of Kiska depended on sending additional aircraft. Four days later, the Fifth Fleet replied that although the domestic aircraft industry produced only 12 floatplane fighters a month, it had already sent six Rufes and two additional reconnaissance seaplanes to the North Pacific.[11] Fortunately for the Japanese, the Americans did not repeat air raids in the following days, and the reinforcements for the *5th Kaigun Kōkūtai* finally arrived on 24 September. During the staff talks in the second half of September and early October, the Fifth Fleet also acceded to the proposal of hasty construction of the Kiska airfield. Also, the Japanese decided to speed up organising the convoys, which would deliver to the Aleutians additional supplies for the garrison, ammunition for anti-aircraft guns and spare parts for planes.[12]

The opening of the new airfield on Adak coincided with the deterioration of weather conditions in the Aleutian Islands. Thick clouds and fog prevented the Americans from bombing Kiska and significantly hampered routine reconnaissance missions. As late as 24 September, three B-17s attempted to attack enemy positions on Attu.[13] However, due to encountering a Japanese floatplane fighter, they were unable to drop bombs on the abandoned base.[14] On the same day, the *5th Kaigun Kōkūtai* received the six new Rufes mentioned above, which soon became a valuable reinforcement during the American air raids in the following days.[15]

On 25 September, the 11 AF launched another mission against Kiska. Nine B-24s, escorted by 11 P-39s and 17 P-40s headed for the Japanese base in the Aleutians.[16] The attacking group encountered seven Rufes, which tried to distract the bombers but were forced to engage with the American fighters.[17] Eventually, bombs fell on the anti-aircraft guns' ammunition depot, destroying part of the

Nakajima A6M2-N Type 2 Rufe. (Pacific Eagles)

Japanese supplies intended for further defence. During the dogfight, the raiders shot down one floatplane fighter and lost two fighters. The Americans also believed that they had scored several direct hits on a transport and set her on fire. They only slightly damaged the submarine *RO-67* in reality.[18]

The Americans made the next move on 27 September. Eight B-24s and one B-17 took off from Adak, escorted by 14 fighters. Due to the worsening weather conditions, 13 fighters returned to the base. The bombers and their remaining P-38, however, continued the flight and encountered five enemy floatplane fighters waiting for them over the bay.[19] Thick clouds obscured the harbour and the main Japanese camp so much that the group decided to abort the mission. Rufes usually avoided chasing the intruders, but this time, they harassed the Americans for several minutes, reporting that several bombers had been shot up and set on fire.[20]

On 28 September, 11 AF made three strikes against Japanese positions in the Aleutian Islands. First, one B-17 and one LB-30 dropped incendiary bombs on the abandoned Attu camp, destroying all buildings except the church. Less than an hour later, five B-24s escorted by 16 fighters conducted a raid on Kiska harbour. According to the TF-8 report, the group encountered no enemy resistance.[21] However, the Japanese accounts argue that five Rufes took off and tried to prevent the Americans from dropping the bombs at all costs.[22] A moment later, three more B-24s appeared over the Japanese base and decided to attack the anchored vessels. Without confirmation of any hits, all American aircraft returned to base.[23] Based on the Japanese documents, it can be assessed that several reconnaissance seaplanes, a signal post, and other garrison buildings were slightly damaged.[24] One bomb also struck directly on the deck of the transport ship *Hiryō Maru* and caused some

damage.[25] In the dogfight over the island, the *5th Kaigun Kōkūtai* lost two floatplane fighters and one pilot.[26]

On the last day of September, nine B-24s returned to Kiska and conducted a horizontal bombing from an altitude of approximately 5,000m. They targeted ships in the anchorage and the ground facilities. The Japanese reacted by sending four Rufes and bringing into action their anti-aircraft artillery, but all bombers returned to Adak intact.[27] The transport ship *Kanō Maru* suffered minor damage from the near miss. Despite Liberator crews' claims about setting the camp afire,[28] the Japanese did not suffer additional losses.

On 30 September, the Japanese also conducted long-awaited reconnaissance flights over Nazan Bay and Kuluk Bay. The *5th Kaigun Kōkūtai* finally sent one seaplane in each direction, each armed with two 60kg bombs. As the crews expected, in Nazan Bay, they spotted two enemy surface vessels, probably destroyers or seaplane tenders. However, the result of the scouting run over Kuluk Bay shocked equally the Aleutians Defense Command, the Fifth Fleet and the Naval General Staff. Suddenly, the Japanese discovered that the Americans had secured Adak and were in an advanced stage of building a new airport. The crews estimated its dimensions at 2,000 by 300m and noticed approximately 20 bombers and 30 fighters with air personnel on the ground. There were also smaller transport vessels in Kuluk Bay, which were believed to have delivered supplies and equipment to the local garrison.[29]

As a first reaction to the unexpected American occupation of Adak, the *5th Kaigun Kōkūtai* responded with a night attack by three reconnaissance seaplanes, which took off armed with eight 30kg bombs in total. After dusk on 1 October, planes attacked the enemy base at Kuluk Bay, but the results of this raid were unknown.[30] Even if the Japanese managed to hit runways or other facilities, their bombs

Consolidated B-24D Liberator. (AF MIL)

were too small to cause damage that the engineering battalion could not repair within a few hours. The ineffective tactics of bombing ground targets by seaplanes not adapted for this purpose, repeated several times in the following days, was noticed by the Naval General Staff. At the end of September, the officers in Tokyo started to develop a comprehensive plan for the defence of Kiska during the winter season. The commander of the 51st Base Force also presented his suggestions on this matter, and on 2 October, he sent to his superiors a telegram consisting of three points:

> 1. The Kuluk Bay airfield must be captured.
> 2. If it is impossible to capture the airfield, the *Kidō Butai* [Mobile Force] should destroy it.
> 3. The local air and submarine forces should be reinforced if the second point proves impossible.[31]

Undoubtedly, the capture of the American airfield on Adak was beyond the Japanese capacities. The *Kidō Butai*'s involvement in the North Pacific also seemed a bad idea, especially considering the simultaneous struggle for Guadalcanal and the recent defeat of the Combined Fleet in the Battle of the Eastern Solomons. However, the Chief of Staff of the Fifth Fleet wrote in his notes from 18 October that Vice Admiral Hosogaya supported the 51st Base Force's demands in general. He also understood that apart from the suggestion to seize the airfield on Adak and deploy the *Kidō Butai* from the South to the North Pacific, the Japanese staff needed to prepare the Kiska garrison for the upcoming winter and ask for additional planes and warships.[32] General Marshall was right when he wrote to Lieutenant General DeWitt on 2 October that 'the occupation of Adak and the rapid development of the airfield have had a devastating effect on the Japanese.'[33]

At this stage, the defence of the Aleutian Islands became the subject of detailed discussion and analysis involving all levels of the command, including the 51st Base Force, the AO Defence Unit, the Fifth Fleet, the Combined Fleet, and the Navy General Staff. Army representatives also took part in talks, as they were responsible for deploying additional troops to the North Pacific area to build-up the Japanese positions on Kiska in preparation for the American advance.

Based on the Japanese documents, it is difficult to determine who had the primary initiative in developing the concept of defending the Aleutians. The commander of the 51st Base Force presented his proposals to the Fifth Fleet, which also had its vision for the North Pacific area. Despite slight differences in views, Rear Admiral Akiyama and Vice Admiral Hosogaya had the same interest – to persuade the Combined Fleet and the Navy General Staff to send additional surface and air forces to the Aleutians. Also, the Japanese initiated the discussion to obtain consent to start the construction of a new airfield on Kiska and possibly occupy one of the nearby islands in case it was necessary to establish a spare runway for fighters. Rear Admiral Akiyama, in his dispatch from 4 October (Tokyo time), estimated that if the construction of the Kiska airport began in October, it would be completed in March of the following year at the earliest, also considering the break in aerial action caused by bad weather in winter. However, the Combined Fleet issued Operational Order No. 321 the same day, which said that securing the garrison camp, ammunition, food, and other supplies on Kiska against American air raids should be the most significant task. The decision on the airfield construction was suspended until a separate order was issued.

The Combined Fleet's reluctant attitude towards the Fifth Fleet and the 51st Base Force's suggestions to build a new airfield in the Aleutians was dictated by several factors. Firstly, in the strategic situation of autumn 1942, sending heavy equipment to Kiska and materials necessary for the construction took a lot of trouble. Since the Navy planners focused on the Guadalcanal campaign, they felt that organising additional convoys with escort to the North Pacific seemed a waste of the already limited navy potential. Secondly, the construction of an air base on Kiska was assessed as a long-term and expensive undertaking that would be exposed to American air attacks from neighbouring Adak. Thirdly, even if construction work could be completed according to the initial schedule, the airfield still needed its air force. The decision to allocate the planes, however, could only be made by the Navy General Staff. Despite giving consent to constructing an airfield on Kiska, the staff officers at Tokyo were convinced that sending the planes to the North Pacific would mean accepting the war of attrition and repeating the same mistake from the Guadalcanal campaign. This time, the Japanese Navy fully knew its logistical and material limitations. This opinion was supported, among others, by Lieutenant Commander Miyo Kazunari, one of the leading naval aviation planners at the Navy General Staff. Although he argued that constructing an airfield on Kiska was advisable and should be completed by April 1943, he underlined that the entire project would rely on close cooperation with the Army.[34]

The construction of the Kiska airfield aroused great interest in the Army. Even General Tōjō Hideki spoke on this matter, arguing that the work could be completed within half a month with the appropriate involvement of engineering units. Despite the unreality of this statement, the Japanese Army considered the defence of the western part of the Aleutian Islands one of its priority tasks. During talks at the Imperial Headquarters on 15 October, which was attended by the Fifth Fleet, the Navy General Staff and the Army General Staff representatives, the latter argued that in addition to building an airfield on Kiska, Amchitka and the Semichi Islands should be secured, or at least, investigated by the reconnaissance party. It should be noted that the Japanese realised that the American occupation of Adak and the construction of a new airbase significantly reduced the chances of holding Kiska until the spring thaw of 1943 without deploying additional forces in the Aleutians. Even though the North Pacific campaign seemed of secondary importance, especially compared to the struggle for Guadalcanal, the Army and Navy could not let the enemy recapture Kiska. Where

Prime Minister and Army Minister, General Tōjō Hideki. (NDL)

the advanced positions in the Aleutian Islands were lost, the home islands, Tokyo and the industrial heartland of Japan around its capital would become utterly defenceless against American aircraft carrier raids by mid-1943. This fear led to a simple conclusion – a fully operational airfield should be built on Kiska, and the local air, naval and ground forces should be significantly reinforced.

Additionally, the Japanese planned to capture positions in the western Aleutians to build a buffer zone between Kiska and the American bases. Although the Army advocated the defence of Kiska at all costs, it also agreed with the Navy that the single island could be easily isolated. The Aleutians would fall into the enemy's hands if this stronghold collapsed in the decisive battle. Thus, the occupation of additional positions in the chain was considered within the available resources: Amchitka, the Semichi Islands and the recently abandoned Attu. Finally, on 17 October, the Imperial Headquarters adopted a new plan for the defence of the Aleutians. Apart from confirming the existing arrangements for constructing an airfield on Kiska and the Semichi Islands at an unspecified date (considering the Navy's transport capacities) and sending additional air forces and supplies for the local garrison, it did not bring any revolutionary changes. This decision proved that staff officers in Tokyo still believed that the Americans would stop their advance by securing Adak and that the Japanese victory in the Guadalcanal campaign would also solve the Army and Navy's problems in the North Pacific.

The *Nippon Kaigun* (Imperial Japanese Navy) was more sceptical about the general plans of the Imperial Headquarters. On 17 October, it organised a separate meeting of the Fifth Fleet's staff and the 1st Section (Strategic Planning) of the Navy General Staff. Its main topic was a discussion of the Attu reoccupation. The

Japanese agreed that the island was a crucial station in the rear of the Kiska garrison and a convenient place to establish a transit base for seaplanes and convoys. Since all officers shared the same view, they prepared a memorandum, which was sent to Tokyo and soon influenced the decision to return to Attu in the following days.

Planning at the strategic level did not change the fact that the Fifth Fleet had to constantly support the garrison on Kiska, which the Americans had increasingly bombed in the last few weeks. After the transfer of the garrison from Attu, the Japanese spent most of September and the first half of October to organise convoys with equipment and supplies. Table 1 presents the runs to Kiska involving transport ships, destroyers, and seaplane tenders.[35]

American Air Offensive in October
１０月の米空襲
10-gatsu no Beikūshū

October marked the increased activity of the American bomber wing, which aimed to inflict the most tremendous possible losses on the Kiska garrison. On the first day of the month, seven B-24s dropped 60 500kg bombs on the hangars and ramps of the Japanese seaplane base.[36] Four floatplane fighters tried to prevent this attack, and after the clash, they claimed to have damaged several Liberators and shot down one bomber.[37] The Americans, however, did not lose a single aircraft and succeeded in burning 600 barrels of aviation gasoline stored on the ground. The raid also resulted in the killing of one Japanese soldier, but the base remained largely intact.[38] On the same day, two B-24s took off from Adak to destroy a surface vessel spotted by Catalina north of Kiska. However, the bombers could not find the target and returned to the base.[39]

Table 1: Japanese convoys to Kiska from mid-September to 15 October 1942			
Date	Route	Ships	Supplies
12–25 September	Ōminato – Muroran – Kiska	*Tōei Maru Nr 2*	food supplies for the garrison
13–17 September	Shimushu – Kiska	*Hinata Maru*	food supplies for the garrison
17–24 September	Yokosuka – Ōminato – Kiska	*Kimikawa Maru, Hatakaze*	6 Rufes and 2 reconnaissance seaplanes
22–24 September	Paramushiru – Kiska	*Hiryō Maru, Hatsuharu*	winter equipment for the garrison
22 September – 1 October	Ōminato – Kataoka Bay – Kiska	*Nittei Maru*	2,000 barrels of aviation fuel
24 September – 2 October	Ōminato – Kataoka Bay – Kiska	*Wakaba*	102,000 rounds for 7.7mm machine guns (102 chests) 7 chests of ammunition belts 10,000 rounds for 13mm machine guns (40 chests) 150 rounds for 8cm coastal guns The destroyer evacuated 13 wounded soldiers and took 18 damaged telegraph poles
26 September – 5 October	Otaru – Kiska	*Borneo Maru*	22nd Independent Anti-Aircraft Company 39th Signal Unit 3rd Engineering Company (38th Engineering Regiment) food supplies and hard coal for the garrison
11–15 October	Kataoka Bay – Kiska	*Wakaba*	150,000 rounds for the machine guns 150 rounds for 8cm coastal guns 12 chests of medications jackhammer for drilling heavy stones

American soldiers in their barracks. (Dmitri Kessel/Life Pictures)

Table 2: Summary of American air operations against the Japanese positions in the Aleutians from 13 September to 3 October 1942

Date	Forces	Target/Details
14 September	12 B-24s 14 P-38s 14 P-39s	Kiska harbour and military facilities photographic mission
15–24 September	-	-
24 September	3 B-17s	Attu military facilities
25 September	9 B-24s 11 P-39s 17 P-40s	Kiska harbour and military facilities
26 September	-	-
27 September	8 B-24s 1 B-17 1 P-38	planes returned from Kiska without bombing the base
28 September	1 B-17 1 LB-30 5 B-25s 16 fighters 3 B-24s	Attu military facilities Kiska harbour and military facilities
29 September	-	-
30 September	9 B-24s	Kiska
1 October	7 B-24s	Kiska
2 October	11 B-24s 6 P-39s	Kiska
3 October	6 B-24s 4 P-38s 8 P-39s	Kiska

On the morning of 2 October, 11 AF raided Kiska with 11 B-24s escorted by six P-39s. The Liberators dropped 25 454kg bombs from an altitude of just over 3,000m, targeting two transport ships in the harbour. In addition, 71 227kg HE bombs fell on the ground facilities. No hits were scored on enemy ships, but the crews believed that several buildings and a hangar south of the seaplane ramp were set on fire.[40] As the Americans emphasised, the group was welcomed by a fierce anti-aircraft fire, which killed two B-24 crew members. Japanese floatplane fighters also took part in the island's defence. Four Rufes claimed two victories (including one unconfirmed), but one was shot down and crashed during the dogfight in return.[41] The Japanese action report does not mention the attack on 2 October, but it can be assumed that the raid did not cause any significant damage to the garrison.

The American raid on 3 October had much worse consequences for the Japanese. 11 AF sent six B-24s over Kiska, escorted by four P-38s and eight P-39s. In the early afternoon, the bombers dropped almost 100 HE bombs on targets located in the harbour and the main camp. Thick and low clouds made it challenging to observe the effects of the attack, but it was known that during the clash with Rufes, they managed to shoot down one enemy aircraft, which exploded in the air.[42] The *5th Kaigun Kōkūtai* report and the Aleutian Islands combat diary confirm this claim and mention serious damage to another two floatplane fighters. Out of three Rufes that had taken off to prevent the enemy from bombing Kiska, none of them were operational after the dogfight.[43] Although the raid had not hit the Japanese base and the defenders managed to shoot down one P-38, on the evening of 3 October, the *5th Kaigun Kōkūtai* had only two fully operational reconnaissance seaplanes and no floatplane fighters.[44]

The summary of the 11 AF raids against the Japanese positions on Kiska and Attu from establishing the Adak airfield to 3 October was as shown in Table 2.[45]

An inspection of the *5th Kaigun Kōkūtai* seaplanes carried out on the evening of 3 October revealed the dire situation of the Japanese air forces in the Aleutian Islands. All Rufes, damaged in recent days, could not be repaired without spare parts from Japan. The Kiska garrison had no fighters to provide cover and had to wait until a convoy with the necessary equipment or additional aircraft arrived. Although the defenders still enjoyed the support of the well-positioned anti-aircraft artillery, its effectiveness strongly depended on the weather conditions and the altitude of the American bombers. Theoretically, the reconnaissance seaplanes could also support the air defence, but they were relatively easy prey for the enemy's fighters. Thus, the Japanese placed their hope in thick clouds preventing 11 AF from conducting regular raids on Kiska.

In the following days, bad weather conditions impacted the American strategy in the North Pacific. As late as 6 October, nine B-24s and one B-17, escorted by eight P-38s and 10 P-39s, took off from Adak. The striking group reported that it did not encounter any floatplane fighters. Moving at an altitude of 3,300m to 4,000m, the bombers dropped incendiary and high-explosive bombs on military facilities on the island and two transport ships – one in the harbour and the other further south. The crews confirmed at least one hit on the vessel off Kiska. They also claimed to have destroyed one of the five Rufes in the seaplane base.[46] The Japanese report admitted that the transport ship *Akebono Maru* (*Borneo Maru* in reality) and one reconnaissance seaplane were damaged that day. This meant that

The peaks of Attu covered in snow. (Dmitri Kessel/Life Pictures)

Lieutenant Tominaga's Jake remained the only operational Japanese aircraft in the Aleutians. Additionally, the bombs killed five and injured nine Army soldiers.[47]

The Americans quickly realised that the Kiska garrison no longer had any operational floatplane fighters, and they wanted to take advantage of this situation by harassing the island with massive bombing raids. The enemy's positions were attacked between 8–11 and 14–19 October by Liberators, Flying Fortresses, and Marauders, which arrived on Adak mid-month. The 11 AF felt confident enough not to assign fighter escorts for bombers on some days.[48] The raid on 8 October damaged submarine chaser No. 13 and seriously injured its commander. The following day, the bombs fell on submarine chaser No. 14. On 11 October, the Americans destroyed the main power generator on the island, and on 14 October, they burned a

significant part of the food supplies and seaplane ammunition.[49] The Japanese could defend only with their anti-aircraft artillery, which managed to shoot down a B-26 on 15 October. Although it was an ordinary operational loss, the Americans later noted that if the enemy managed to recover the wreckage, they could obtain confidential information – code books and detailed maps of the area, with marked military facilities and expansion plans.[50]

Of all the October raids, the bombing on 16 October was particularly painful for the Japanese when a convoy heading towards Kiska was destroyed. A group comprising the destroyers *Oboro* and *Hatsuharu*, transporting mainly ammunition for the garrison, set off from Yokosuka on 11 October and headed for the Aleutian Islands via Shimushu. On the afternoon of 16 October, it was attacked by six B-26s approximately 30 miles northeast of Kiska. Despite the anti-aircraft fire, the Marauders conducted a low-level approach. Five of them dropped 20 136kg high-explosive bombs. One of them struck *Oboro* and jammed her rudder.[51] In a short time, the flames spread throughout the vessel and led to the tragic explosion of stored ammunition.

The fate of the destroyer was sealed and it sank rapidly at about 1635 hours. Only 17 crew members, including her commander, Lieutenant Commander Yamana Hirō, abandoned the ship. The survivors were taken on board by *Hatsuharu*, which also fell victim to the Marauders. One direct hit caused the explosion of the transported ammunition stored behind the depth charge launchers. The blast put main artillery turrets No. 2 and 3 out of action and damaged part of the engine room. Crew losses accounted for two killed, seven seriously wounded and seven slightly wounded men.[52] The crew struggled to control the ship and extinguish the flames on board. They also occasionally responded to American planes with 40mm anti-aircraft guns and even claimed to shoot down a bomber. The 11 AF reports confirm that one B-26 was lost. The Japanese interrupted the convoy mission when the enemy planes disappeared over the horizon. The damaged *Hatsuharu* set course for Kataoka Bay, arriving just over a week later.[53] The failure of the convoy was a painful defeat for the Fifth Fleet, which lost *Oboro* – the recently assigned destroyer after numerous requests to the Navy General Staff, intended to support operations in the North Pacific.[54]

A summary of the 11 AF raids against Japanese positions on Kiska and Attu from 6 to 19 October is shown in Table 3.[55]

The destroyer *Oboro*. (Kure Maritime Museum)

The destroyer *Hatsuharu*. (Kure Maritime Museum)

Table 3: Summary of American air operations against the Japanese, 4–19 October 1942

Date	Forces	Targets/Details
6 October	9 B-24s 1 B-17 10 P-39s 8 P-38s	Kiska harbour and military facilities
7 October	-	-
8 October	6 B-24s 3 B-17s 12 P-38s	Kiska harbour and military facilities
9 October	10 B-24s 7 B-17s 12 P-38s	Kiska harbour and military facilities
10 October	7 B-17s 8 P-38s	Kiska harbour and military facilities
11 October	10 B-24s	Kiska military facilities and vessel off the island
12–13 October	-	-
14 October	9 B-24s 1 B-17 3 B-26s 12 P-38s	Torpedo attack on the vessels off Kiska Kiska military facilities
15 October	3 B-26s	Surface vessels off Kiska
16 October	6 B-26s 1 B-17 4 P-38s 1 PBY	Convoy off Kiska Kiska military facilities
17 October	5 B-24s	Kiska military facilities
18 October	4 B-24s	Surface vessels off Kiska Kiska military facilities
19 October	3 B-24s 3 B-17s 6 P-38s	Kiska military facilities

The Japanese Return to Attu
日本がアッツ島に戻る
Nihon ga Attsu-tō ni Modoru

On 18 October, the Imperial Headquarters received a dispatch warning that the Americans had secretly secured Amchitka. Although this information was completely incorrect and its source still needs to be discovered, it resulted in Army Operational Order No. 706 regarding the reoccupation of Attu, which was issued two days later. On 21 October, the Navy quickly detached the 1st Torpedo Squadron for the future task force. Soon after, on 24 October, the North Sea Garrison Force (*Hokkai Shubitai*) was established, and it became part of the Fifth Fleet as an Army unit responsible for defending Kiska and Attu. Its organisation was as follows:

North Sea Garrison Force, commander: Major General Mineki Toichirō
- Force HQ
- 301st, 302nd, 303rd Independent Infantry Battalions
- infantry detachment from the Northern Kurils Fortress Battalion
- 22nd, 24th, 32nd, 33rd Independent Anti-Aircraft Artillery Companies
- 301st, 302nd, 303rd Independent Infantry Construction Companies
- 11th Independent Signal Platoon, 39th Base Signal Unit
- medical units[56]

One of the first decisions the Army and Navy staff made concerning the reoccupation of Attu was the hasty organisation of a convoy to secure the island by the end of the month. Under Navy General Staff Order No. 13 of 21 October, the Fifth Fleet issued Secret Operational Order No. 37, which designated the cruisers *Nachi, Kiso, Tama* and the 1st Torpedo Squadron as the vessels responsible for screening the landing party. The dispatch also specified the movements of each ship and ordered a preliminary scouting of the island by 100 Army soldiers before the planned landing. In addition, one day before and during the landing at Attu, the Navy planned to use reconnaissance seaplanes to scout the nearby waters. To accomplish this task, the seaplane tender *Kimikawa Maru*, screened by the destroyer *Usugumo*, was ordered on 23 October to deliver five floatplane fighters and three reconnaissance seaplanes to Kiska.

Retaking Attu, a seemingly simple undertaking, involved enormous operational risk considering the new American airfield on Adak. The Chief of Staff of the Combined Fleet fully understood

Major General Mineki Toichirō. (NDL)

the possible threats. On 21 October, he instructed the Fifth Fleet that the convoy should take advantage of weather conditions whenever possible on the day of landing to avoid losses resulting from American air attacks. Four days later, Vice Admiral Hosogaya issued Operational Order No. 1, establishing the so-called Volunteer Convoy Force (*Teishin Yūsō Butai*) responsible for the landing on Attu. Its organisation was as shown in Table 4.[57]

On the same day, the Japanese started to embark the Army unit on the vessels gathered in Paramushiru. In addition to the infantry soldiers, the cruisers carried eight heavy machine guns, two anti-tank guns, three radio stations and about 90 tons of ammunition.[58] The Transport Force was to set off from Paramushiru the following day and proceed directly to Attu. The remaining part of the Fifth Fleet was to take up appropriate positions to screen the convoy along the route. The Japanese planned that the convoy would arrive just after midnight on 29 October. The landing was to be carried out without issuing additional orders to speed up the operation and minimise the risk of American intervention.

Despite numerous warnings about a violent storm in the northern part of the Kuril Islands, at 1800 hours on 26 October, the Screening Force set off from Paramushiru. It quickly became apparent that this was not a good decision, and the group was forced to reduce speed to get through the storm unscathed. Nine sailors from the destroyer *Hatsushimo* fell overboard and could not rescued. The ships were eventually forced to return to base, and the commander of the Fifth Fleet allowed a possible 24-hour delay of the Attu landing operation. The atmosphere in the Army and Navy was exceptionally gloomy at that time. In addition to this setback, late in the evening of 26 October, the staffs of armies and fleets gradually received various dispatches concerning the unsuccessful assault of the Seventeenth Army on Guadalcanal. Reports from 48 hours earlier said that

Henderson Airfield had been captured. Eventually, it turned out that the joy was far too premature, and the Japanese troops on the 'hell island' were decimated.

Unfavourable weather conditions only slightly thwarted the Japanese plans in the North Pacific. The next day at 1300 hours, the convoy, screened by the forces indicated in the Fifth Fleet order issued on 21 October, set off for the Kuril Islands, trying to avoid American submarines at all costs.[59] During the route northeast, the convoy received a report from the 51st Base Force, whose reconnaissance floatplane from the *5th Kaigun Kōkūtai* was conducting a reconnaissance patrol over Attu. Its crew reported no enemy presence, thick clouds, and a calm sea.[60] Less than 24 hours later, favourable conditions for landing in Holtz Bay and Chichagof Bay were also confirmed by the commander of the 26th Submarine Squadron. According to the expectations, his vessels did not encounter any American aircraft or surface forces off Attu. Therefore, late in the evening of 28 October, the Transport Forces were detached and entered the local bay under the cover of darkness. Before dawn on 29 October, the message about the successful landing on Attu was sent to the Fifth Fleet.[61] The unloading of men and equipment took about four hours. Then, based on Vice Admiral Hosogaya's orders, the ships departed the island and joined the Screening Force. In the afternoon of 31 October, all groups returned safely to Paramushiru and reported the successful completion of the mission.[62]

While the landing operation on Attu was still ongoing, on 27 October (Tokyo time), the Imperial Headquarters issued an order which required the Army and Navy to cooperate closely to implement the plan of the Aleutian Islands' defence. Shortly after that, on 1 November, Navy Operational Order No. 154 gave more specific guidance, highlighting new tasks for the upcoming months. In addition to the principle that defending the Aleutian Islands would be the responsibility of the Fifth Fleet and the North Sea Garrison Force, the Japanese agreed that holding the entire area would focus on three key positions – Kiska, Attu and Semichi Islands. The order repeated the need to construct the air bases on Kiska and Semichi, expand seaplane bases on Kiska and Attu, and, most importantly, send reinforcements and additional supplies to the Aleutians. It also suggested capturing Amchitka, yet the specific purpose of this proposal was not indicated.[63]

Against Difficult Weather Conditions
困難な気象条件と戦う
Kon'nan na Kishō Jōken to Tatakau

The lack of Japanese floatplane fighters on Kiska and intelligence reports indicating possible increased enemy convoy traffic towards Attu prompted the Americans to use their naval forces. On 11 October, TG-8.7, comprising the cruisers *St. Louis*, *Nashville*, the destroyers *Bailey*, *Bancroft*, and the minesweeper *Long*, departed Kodiak and headed for the area north of Kiska. On 13 October, the group closed to within 100 miles of the island and operated north of

Table 4: Organisation of the Volunteer Convoy Force responsible for Attu landing operation

Unit	Commander	Forces	Task
Transport Force	Commander of the 1st Torpedo Squadron	light cruisers *Abukuma*, *Tama*, *Kiso*	transporting the Army detachment
Screening Force	Commander of the 21st Destroyer Division	21st Destroyer Division (minus *Hatsuharu*)	screening the convoy
'Yonekawa' Unit	Lieutenant Colonel Yonekawa	about 600 men	securing Attu

Attu in the following three days to hunt down the Japanese transport ships. During that time, *St. Louis* and *Nashville* catapulted seaplanes to conduct several reconnaissance patrols of the nearby waters. The Americans also monitored the area through radar equipment. At midnight on 17 October, TG-8.7 passed Attu from the west and headed south of Agattu over the next 36 hours. By then, no Japanese vessels had been found, so after refuelling the destroyers, the decision was made to change the course to east. Another 'loop' was executed south of Amchitka, and the destroyers were again fuelled. Finally, at 1900 hours on 19 October, the Americans decided to return to Kodiak, where they arrived less than three days later.[64]

While 11 AF was conducting intensive air strikes against Japanese positions on Kiska and TG-8.7 was hunting Japanese convoys, CINCPAC (Commander-in-Chief Pacific) decided to hastily redeploy some surface forces from the North to the South Pacific. Since the battle for Guadalcanal had entered a decisive phase and the US Navy command agreed that heavy cruisers were unnecessary in the Aleutians, *Louisville* left Kodiak and headed south on 12 October.[65] Less than two weeks later, *St. Louis* and seaplane tender *Thornton* was detached from TF-8 to replace the *McFarland* damaged by Japanese dive bombers. Soon after, the Americans also planned to send *Indianapolis* and *Nashville* to the South Pacific. They were to be replaced by the obsolete light cruisers *Raleigh* and *Detroit*. Besides these naval forces, the recently received 12 Wildcats that the Navy believed would provide critical reinforcement in the Solomon Islands were also withdrawn from the Alaska area. On 30 October,

based on the CINCPAC order, five surface vessels borrowed from the Canadians were returned to them, including three auxiliary cruisers.[66] The transfers ordered at that time meant that further action against the Japanese in the Aleutian Islands rested on the shoulders of the USAAF (US Army Air Forces).[67] In addition to the Army planes, Catalinas from Patrol Wing 4 were also involved in the search for enemy ships. For example, on 22 October, eight flying boats set off from the area around Unimak and Akutan to hunt for a Japanese submarine that had attacked its American counterpart, *Dolphin*. Although the intruder could not be found, the enemy knew it would not be so easy to approach Dutch Harbor without the severe risk of punishment.[68]

In the last 10 days of the month, unfavourable weather conditions typical of the Aleutian Islands were again present. Due to heavy clouds and strong wind, 11 AF could only attack Kiska with a small number of aircraft on 23, 24, 28 and 31 October. Reconnaissance missions often ended without taking photos of critical value for intelligence, and thus, the Fifth Fleet's reoccupation of Attu completely escaped American notice. The situation was not much better with the arrival of the new month. November began with strong gusts of wind and heavy rainfall, which caused the Adak airfield to be flooded with water up to four inches deep.[69] Waiting for its removal and improvement of the weather conditions, by 7 November, 11 AF had minimal opportunities to conduct air raids on Attu and Kiska. However, on 3 November, several B-24s appeared over the latter island, forcing the Japanese submarines to disperse

The light cruiser *St. Louis*. (NARA)

TG-8.7 sortie against Japanese convoys off Attu and Kiska, 13–19 October 1942. (NARA)

from their base. The crew of the hurriedly submerging *RO-65* did not have time to secure the hatch, causing the unexpected and sudden flooding of the stern. The submarine settled on the bottom at an angle of approximately 40 degrees. Nineteen sailors drowned in compartments that were deliberately closed to stop water from entering the entire ship. The rest of the crew evacuated through the torpedo tube compartments. Immediately after that, *RO-65* lost stability, rolled over and sank.[70]

On 7 November, a B-17 bomber on a weather reconnaissance mission over Attu unexpectedly discovered six floatplane fighters and one seaplane in Hotz Bay. The crew dropped eight bombs on the spotted aircraft but scored no hits. Information about the presence of Japanese planes near the island, which the enemy had allegedly left over a month earlier,[71] was hastily reported to the Aleutian Defense Command and Admiral Nimitz. In the early afternoon, six B-24s appeared over Kiska after a break of several days. However, due to bad weather conditions only one bomber dropped her bombs on the submarine base. Soon after, two B-26s tried to attack a transport ship anchored in the local harbour but did not score any hits.[72]

The presence of the Japanese on Attu was a big puzzle to the Americans.[73] They did not see precisely why the enemy decided to return to the island and what forces he had at his disposal. On 9 November, four P-38s guided by a single B-17 appeared over Attu and strafed six floatplane fighters and one reconnaissance seaplane moored in Holtz Bay. The crews later reported the destruction of all enemy aircraft, and partial confirmation of this fact is also found in the Japanese report.[74] Flying over the recently destroyed buildings, the Americans noticed tents and a group of 12 soldiers. One of the tents was set on fire, and then the planes withdrew to the base. On the same day, two B-26s and four P-38s struck the military installations and harbour on Kiska. The group decided to attack from a low altitude, and one of the fighters lost one of its engines due to the anti-aircraft fire. The pilot, however, managed to return safely to the base.[75]

On 11 November, the Alaska Defense Command received a cable from CINCPAC warning of a possible increase in enemy attacks intended to distract the US Navy from the planned *Nippon Kaigun* offensive off Guadalcanal. The intelligence predicted that the Japanese might use resources available at Paramushiru, Attu, and Kiska to launch an unspecified attack on Amchitka. Therefore, it was recommended to extend reconnaissance patrols over all enemy positions in the Aleutians soon and keep all naval and air forces alerted. If the Japanese decided to land on Amchitka, the Americans planned to counterattack by engaging their torpedo boats. Although a large-scale enemy offensive in the North Pacific seemed unlikely, that same afternoon, patrol planes located a transport ship escorted by a destroyer in Holtz Bay. This spotting ultimately confirmed the presumption that the Japanese had permanently returned to Attu.[76]

Due to terrible weather conditions for most of November, 11 AF was idle and conducted only reconnaissance missions over Kiska and Attu. Some bombers occasionally attempted to attack various ground targets, but the results were poor. On 17 November, following the previous announcement, *Indianapolis* and *Nashville* departed the North Pacific and were replaced by *Raleigh* and *Detroit*. The decisive victory in the naval battle of Guadalcanal lifted the spirits among the American officers who did not believe that the *Nippon Kaigun*

would quickly recover from this defeat. However, the relative peace in the Aleutian Islands was interrupted by a CINCPAC cable on 24 November. It reported that US Navy intelligence had intercepted enemy orders regarding a new amphibious operation. Admiral Nimitz's staff warned that a convoy comprising five transport ships screened by one destroyer and probably a Tama-class light cruiser had left Paramushiru in the morning. It was suspected that the Japanese aimed to capture the Semichi Islands. All American surface and air forces in the chain were suddenly ordered to maintain full combat readiness. The 11 AF aircraft and Fleet Air Wing 4 (Patrol Wing 4's name changed according to COMINCH order)[77] patrol boats were also instructed to fly additional reconnaissance missions in the following days to closely examine the enemy's moves.[78]

On 25 November, bomber crews who set off on reconnaissance flights before dawn did not confirm CINCPAC's earlier reports. While denying rumours about a Japanese amphibious operation in the Semichi Islands, the critical topic of building another air base in the western part of the Aleutians was raised. According to the initial proposal, it was supposed to be located on Amchitka. Unfortunately, bad weather prevented the analysis of local terrain conditions. In response to CINCPAC's inquiry, TF-8 Command also sent its estimates of Japanese forces in the Aleutian Islands—Rear Admiral Theobald's staff mentioned:

(1) 7,500 to 10,000 men of infantry, artillery, engineering and construction units on Kiska,
(2) 500 to 1,000 men from one battalion of the 82nd Infantry Regiment on Attu,
(3) probably 10-man reconnaissance or meteorological party on the Amchitka and the Semichi Islands.[79]

On 26 November, four B-26s and 4 P-38s scrambled from Adak against one transport ship spotted in Holtz Bay. Despite heavy anti-aircraft fire and two reconnaissance seaplanes defending the base,[80] the Americans claimed at least three direct hits and one near miss with 227kg high-explosive bombs.[81] The Japanese report confirms that the victim of this attack was the transport ship *Cheribon Maru*.

Martin B-26 *Marauder*. (NARA)

Table 5: Summary of American air operations against the Japanese, 20 October – 26 November 1942		
Date	Forces	Details/Targets
23 October	6 B-24s 6 P-38s 1 B-17	Kiska submarine base and military facilities
24 October	3 B-17s	Kiska submarine base and military facilities
25–27 October	-	-
28 October	6 B-24s	Kiska military facilities
29–30 October	-	-
31 October	2 P-39s 1 B-17	Kiska military facilities
1–2 November	-	-
3 November	? bombers	Kiska submarine base
4–6 November	-	-
7 November	6 B-24s 2 B-26s 1 B-17	Kiska harbour transport ship off Kiska Attu military facilities
8 November	6 B-24s 2 B-26s	Kiska submarine base and military facilities
9 November	4 P-38s 1 B-17 2 B-26s	seaplanes off Attu transport ship off Kiska
10–13 November	-	-
14 November	1 B-24	Attu military facilities
15 November	-	-
16 November	1 B-24	Attu military facilities
17–25 November	-	-
26 November	4 B-24s 4 P-38s	transport ship off Attu

A fire broke out on her board, soon becoming extremely difficult to extinguish. The skipper was forced to beach *Cheribon Maru* to prevent her from sinking in the anchorage.[82] This action ended the November raids of 11 AF on Japanese positions on Kiska and Attu, and their summary from 20 October is as shown in Table 5.[83]

Japanese Convoys to Attu and Kiska
アッツ島とキスカ島への日本の輸送
Attsu-tō to Kisuka-tō e no Nihon no Yūsō

During the preparations for reoccupying Attu, the Japanese adopted a plan to strengthen the garrisons in the western part of the Aleutians. Using Army and Navy transports for this purpose, they intended to transfer approximately 4,800 men (mainly from infantry, artillery and construction units), 36 anti-aircraft guns and four coastal guns (of unspecified calibre) to Attu and Kiska from the end of October to mid-December 1942. The envisaged convoys (later marked with letters from A to N), operating on the Kuriles–Aleutians route, were also to deliver ammunition, supplies, winter equipment and construction materials for the garrisons.[84]

The first November convoy, comprising the transport ships *Dover Maru* and *Dairin Maru*, screened by the ocean escort ship *Ishigaki*, departed Paramushiru on 6 November and arrived at Attu six days later. On 7 November, the second convoy, consisting of the destroyers

Wakaba, *Hatsushimo* and *Usugumo*, departed Paramushiru and arrived at Kiska four days later. In these two runs, the Japanese transported 545 men (mainly from the 35th Independent Anti-Aircraft Artillery Company) and 1,150 tons of food and fuel.[85]

On 9 November (Tokyo time), Vice Admiral Hosogaya ordered the commander of the 1st Torpedo Squadron to support the operation to reinforce the Attu and Kiska garrisons, and a day later, he also called to prepare for the capture of the Semichi Islands.[86] Thus, on 10 November, the naval forces began their concentration in Paramushiru and learned their upcoming tasks.

The Fifth Fleet intended to transfer troops and equipment to Attu in a few runs and then conduct a smaller 'jump' to the Semichi Islands to avoid an American air counterattack. First, a convoy consisting of the light cruisers *Abukuma*, *Kiso* and the destroyer *Wakaba* departed from Paramushiru late in the evening of 22 November. The 24th Independent Anti-aircraft Artillery Company arrived at Attu without any significant complications just after midnight on 25 November. Almost in parallel with this transport, on the evening of 22 November, a smaller Convoy B consisting of the transport *Cheribon Maru*, screened by *Ishigaki*, left Paramushiru. This group took weapons and winter equipment for the Attu garrison. It arrived on the island on the morning of 26 November and almost immediately became a target of American bombers raiding the base.[87]

In the early afternoon of 23 November, Convoy D, comprising two transport ships escorted by the light cruiser *Tama* and the destroyer *Hatsushimo*, left Kataoka Bay. It carried the bulk of the 303rd Independent Infantry Battalion, ordered to form the nucleus of the future Semichi Islands garrison. However, before the commencement of the landing operation, Convoy D was to join Convoy B off Attu and then set course for Shemya Island. These plans were thwarted by the American air raid on Attu on 26 November when *Cheribon Maru* was seriously damaged. Upon the arrival of the enemy's planes, the Japanese initially decided to postpone the operation to seize the Semichi Islands for two to three days. Yet, in the afternoon, Vice Admiral Hosogaya ordered Convoy D to return to Paramushiru for safety reasons. Soon, he also sent Operational Dispatch No. 19, informing the 51st Base Force and the Army detachment that all remaining convoy missions (except Convoy K) had been postponed indefinitely due to bad weather conditions and enemy aircraft activity. Two days later, the Fifth Fleet headquarters received a response from the 51st Base Force and the Army Forces, which criticised this decision and expressed the need to hastily reinforce the garrisons in the Aleutians. Nevertheless, on 29 November, Hosogaya confirmed his earlier instructions and explained that the convoys had only been temporarily postponed, and the forces intended for the landing on the Semichi Islands remained in combat readiness on Paramushiru. The Fifth Fleet commander also reaffirmed that Convoy K would soon be sent to Kiska, and the 303rd Independent Construction Company had been initially assigned to build an airfield on the island.[88]

As scheduled by the commander of the Fifth Fleet, Convoy K, consisting of the light cruisers *Abukuma* and *Kiso* and the destroyer *Wakaba*, departed from Paramushiru on the evening of 29 November. The ships boarded part of the 302nd Independent Infantry Battalion

(519 or 570 men).[89] The convoy arrived at Kiska after midnight on 3 December and, after hastily unloading troops and equipment in just 12 hours, immediately set course back to Paramushiru.[90] At the same time, *Abukuma* and *Kiso* took approximately 200 soldiers who had been on the island practically from the very beginning of the campaign and whose physical or mental condition required immediate evacuation.[91]

Of the convoys scheduled to Attu and Kiska up to mid-December, only one additional run was carried out by *Usugumo*, which took food and equipment necessary for the daily functioning of garrisons. The destroyer left Paramushiru on the evening of 5 December and arrived at Attu just after midnight on 9 December. The supply was unloaded without American intervention from the air, and the ship safely withdrew to the southwest.[92] Details of the Japanese convoys to Attu and Kiska in November–December 1942 are shown in Table 6.[93]

Table 6: Japanese convoys to Attu and Kiska in November–December 1942

Date	Route	Ships	Supplies
06–12 November	Paramushiru – Attu	Dover Maru, Dairin Maru, Ishigaki	35th Independent Anti-Aircraft Company (545 men) Food supplies and fuel (1150t)
07–10 November (Convoy No 6)	Paramushiru – Kiska	*Wakaba, Hatsushimo, Usugumo*	
22–25 November	Paramushiru – Attu	Abukuma, Kiso, Wakaba	24th Independent Anti-Aircraft Company
22–26 November (Convoy B)	Paramushiru – Attu	Cheribon Maru, Ishigaki	food and weapon supplies
23 November–X (Convoy D)	Paramushiru – Attu	Dover Maru, Dairin Maru, Tama, Hatsushimo	core of 303rd Independent Infantry Battalion Convoy turned back to Paramushiru on 26 November
29 November – 3 December (Convoy K)	Paramushiru – Kiska	Abukuma, Kiso, Wakaba	core of 302nd Independent Infantry Battalion (519–570 men)
5–9 December	Paramushiru – Attu	Usugumo	food and equipment supplies

The destroyer *Usugumo*. (NDL)

2
WINTER CHESS MATCH IN THE ALEUTIANS

アリューシャンにおける冬のチェスマッチ
Aryūshan ni okeru Fuyu no Chesu Macchi

By early December, the Americans had also significantly reinforced their garrisons in the North Pacific. Despite committing the bulk of the manpower and equipment to the South Pacific, 16,000 men and 547,000 tons of supplies had been sent to Alaska over the past three months. The Fifth Fleet and the Army detachment could only dream of such help, yet it did not change the fact that the enemy also had to face its problems. The most troublesome was the personal conflict between Rear Admiral Theobald and Major General Buckner. Already in early September General Marshall wrote to General Lieutenant DeWitt that 'relations between the Army and the Navy in Alaska have reached a point where there appears to be no other cure but a complete change.' King was to replace Theobald and the Army intended to replace Butler and Buckner but, as Marshall advised, in such a way as to avoid reflection on Buckner.[1] Since that time things had got even worse. The dispute affected the overall cooperation between the US Army and the US Navy in the Aleutian campaign to such an extent that Theobald himself submitted a request to be transferred to another position. The final straw was when Theobald quarrelled with Colonel Benjamin B. Talley, a distinguished US Army engineer, later called the 'father of military construction in Alaska', forcing CINCPAC to intervene firmly.[2] On 8 December, Admiral Nimitz dismissed Theobald as commander of TF-8. It was only a formal change at the time, as he would remain at his post until a new commander arrived in Alaska. Following this decision, the next day, Nimitz appointed Rear Admiral Charles McMorris as the new commander of TG-8.6, setting aside Rear Admiral Smith.[3]

On 8 December, Admiral King found on his desk Nimitz's report summarising the last six months of the struggle for the Aleutians. CINCPAC summarised the course of the campaign and presented

Rear Admiral Charles McMorris. (NARA)

the most critical current issues. Among them, he indicated the buildup of the Japanese garrisons on Attu and Kiska and predicted that the enemy would soon seize Shemya and probably Amchitka.[4] For this reason, Nimitz suggested that the US Army should forestall the Japanese and take control of the latter island as quickly as possible. Additionally, Kiska was within direct range of planes from Amchitka, so after establishing a new airfield, the Americans could harass the enemy garrison more effectively and rely on adequate air support during the envisaged amphibious operation. Still, Nimitz believed it was too early to plan a landing on Kiska. Based on photos taken during reconnaissance flights, the Japanese were estimated to have between 7,500 and 10,000 men on site and well-positioned anti-aircraft and coastal artillery positions. Such forces would certainly inflict heavy losses on the invasion force. Thus, CINCPAC recommended focusing on weakening the enemy's potential in the upcoming months and balancing the supply demands in the North and South Pacific.[5]

Weather conditions in the first week of December were so terrible that regular reconnaissance missions resulted in losing a B-25, B-26 and P-38, and a B-17 was seriously damaged during the landing on Umnak.[6] On 8 December, 11 AF attempted to bomb Kiska and Attu with six B-24s, six B-26s and eight P-38s, but due to a sudden weather breakdown, the planes were forced to turn back to Adak.[7] At the same time, all air bases in the Aleutian Islands were on high alert as the Alaska Defense Command received warnings of a possible enemy landing on the Semichi Islands.

After several unsuccessful attempts to strike Japanese positions in the Aleutians, three B-26s and four P-38s finally reached Kiska on 11 December. Liberators approached the enemy base from a low altitude and dropped eight bombs, claiming eight direct hits on a previously damaged transport anchored east of Trout Lagoon.[8] The *452nd Kaigun Kōkūkai* (formerly the *5th Kaigun Kōkūkai*) action report did not mention the 11 December raid,[9] but Japanese post-war publications confirm that seven fighters appeared over Kiska that day. In the afternoon, the commander of 11 AF presented Theobald with a proposal to deploy Patrol Wing 4 from Kodiak to Adak, where flying boats could be used to scout the entire western part of the Aleutian Islands.

By mid-December, the Americans felt so confident in Adak that larger surface vessels and submarines regularly circulated between the recently captured island and the remaining US Navy bases in the eastern part of the Aleutians. On 13 December, a B-26 escorted by two P-38s conducted a photographic mission over Kiska.[10] Despite poor visibility and rain squalls, the crews managed to spot two transport ships, one of which was identified as a previously damaged vessel that was later intentionally beached. In the early afternoon, a B-24 with Colonel Talley aboard conducted a photographic mission over Amchitka. He confirmed that there was no evidence of enemy

presence on the island. It meant that if the Americans wanted to make another leap towards Kiska, they had a unique chance to move forward without significant risk.[11]

On 14 December, the Americans temporarily sent TG-8.6 to Adak. After refuelling, it headed east to patrol local waters against Japanese submarines. The weather conditions did not favour the crews. Due to a violent storm, the anchor of the minesweeper *Annoy* broke off and the ship was pushed onto an underwater rock. She had a breach in the hull, but fortunately, the hole was small enough to prevent water from entering the compartments. A day later, the submarine *S-34* was ordered to reconnoitre the Semichi Islands and investigate whether the Japanese had captured them. The Americans were preparing for another move, as evidenced by the fact that in the afternoon Admiral Nimitz instructed Theobald to prepare for the landing on Amchitka at the earliest possible date. Based on intelligence data, attention was also drawn to the fact that the Japanese were building up their forces in the Aleutians, probably to destroy or even try to seize the American positions in Kuluk Bay.[12]

On 17 December, 11 AF observation planes confirmed that the Semichi Islands were still uncontrolled by the Japanese. Three hours later, four B-24s led by Captain Berry arrived over Kiska, and three of them dropped 35 bombs on three buildings north of the harbour and submarine base, claiming several direct hits. However, the Japanese sources mention only minor damage and one man killed.[13] The Americans attempted to strike again two hours later, but four B-26s, two B-25s, and eight P-38s were forced to turn back to Adak because of the bad weather. The 11 AF, in any case, achieved their primary goal as it diverted the enemy's attention from a small reconnaissance party commanded by Colonel Talley, which was transported to Amchitka by two Catalinas, covered by a B-24 and four P-38s.[14] After gathering all the information necessary to plan the landing operation and build a new airfield, on 19 December the soldiers were taken by flying boats back to Adak. Talley cabled that no enemy soldiers were met on the island, yet it was discovered that the Japanese had made several excavations in recent months. The scouting party also found used sauce bottles with Japanese labels. This led to the conclusion that the enemy had clearly tried to inspect

American mail transport to the Aleutians. (Dmitri Kessel/Life Pictures)

American personnel enjoying social life in a pub, Adak. (Dmitri Kessel/ Life Pictures)

the island and perhaps even maintained a small reconnaissance outpost for some time. Talley's men also reported that one twin-engine observation plane had appeared over Amchitka during the day, but they were sure the enemy did not see them due to bad weather.[15]

The first report from the inspection of Amchitka seemed very promising. According to the engineers, it would take two to three weeks to prepare a runway for fighters made from steel mats, while constructing a fully operational airfield (approximately 1,600 by 60 metres) would take three to four months. Talley also recommended the exact location for the runways – a tide pool at Constantine Bay after it had been drained and levelled.[16]

In the early afternoon of 20 December, five B-24s, four B-26s, and four B-25s, escorted by nine P-38s, raided the submarine base and military installations on Kiska. The crews recalled that they were welcomed by deadly anti-aircraft fire, but apart from one wounded fighter pilot, the group had no losses. The Japanese, in return, counted as many as 11 men killed that day and eight barrack buildings set afire by bombs.[17] The Americans maintained a combat patrol over Amchitka until dusk, consisting of a B-24 and two P-38s. In addition to taking detailed photographs of local terrain, they received the order to intercept an enemy reconnaissance plane if it tried to approach the island again.[18]

Preparations for celebrating the first Christmas since the beginning of the Aleutian campaign were marked by waiting for Admiral Nimitz's order regarding the occupation of Amchitka. Besides routine 11 AF patrol flights, between 21 and 31 December, the Americans focused on preparations for the amphibious operation and tried to use every opportunity to disorganise the Kiska garrison. On the afternoon of 21 December, the TF-8 command received a cable from the Joint Chiefs of Staff, tentatively scheduling the landing on Amchitka for 5 January, with minor possible changes.[19] As a result of this decision, *Indianapolis* left Pearl Harbor on 22 December and set course for the Aleutians.[20] She was returning to the North Pacific after more than a month of absence.[21]

At that time, all signs indicated that the Guadalcanal campaign would end in the US Navy's decisive victory. Although the Japanese still controlled part of the 'hell island', *Indianapolis* was considered unnecessary in the South Pacific and headed north to support the landing on Amchitka.

Due to winter storms and the extended wait for the arrival of *Indianapolis*, TG-8.6 had to delay the redeployment of its forces from Dutch Harbor to Adak. On Christmas Eve, it became clear that the ships would set sail on 28 December at the earliest. On Christmas Day, the Americans sent several reconnaissance planes over Attu, Agattu and Kiska to conduct a meteorological mission and find enemy surface vessels. Near the last island, the crews spotted five Japanese motorboats proceeding on a course of 45 degrees and unsuccessfully attempted to attack them with four bombs. Surprisingly, no seaplanes were detected. This was because the Rufes, which had arrived on Attu recently, had previously gone on a reconnaissance patrol.[22] The Adak ground personnel also witnessed two accidents on the same day when a P-38 and a B-24 crashed during landing. While the bomber's crew was fortunate because no one was seriously injured, the fighter crew had no chance to survive.[23]

On 26 December, six B-24s and nine P-38s took off from Adak and headed for Attu. No enemy aircraft were found in Holtz Bay, but before the crews decided to turn back to the base, P-38s bore in at low-level to strafe the Japanese military facilities. The fighters, however, were struck by the anti-aircraft defence, which shot down the fighter piloted by Captain D. Ralph Mattews. His plane erupted into flames and crashed into the water near the shore. Mattews did not manage to bail out. During the unfortunate pass the Japanese also managed to damage two other P-38s by knocking out one of their engines of each.[24] Lieutenant Arthur L. Kayser, who was piloting one of the crippled fighters, had to ditch in Tanaga Bay. Despite the icy water, he swam 150 yards to shore and was later picked up by a Catalina. Lieutenant Oliver Wayman also made it back to Adak although he was wounded in the attack.[25]

Social life in the barracks, Adak. (Dmitri Kessel/Life Pictures)

Meanwhile, six B-25s and four P-38s were sent over Kiska, but thick clouds made it impossible to identify ground targets and thus drop bombs. The additional survey of Amchitka once again confirmed no Japanese activity around the island. During the afternoon, 11 AF lost a P-40 on a routine patrol mission over Adak. The plane's engine unexpectedly burst into flames, and the pilot was forced to bail out on his parachute.[26]

On 27 December, the bad weather forced 11 AF to cancel a planned raid on Kiska. Despite numerous concerns about the treacherous waters of the North Pacific, *Indianapolis* arrived at Dutch Harbor without significant complications.[27] However, the Americans unexpectedly lost another ship near Unimak in the evening. Due to the storm, two depth charges were carried away from the deck of the minesweeper *Wasmuth*. They detonated right next to the stern and ruptured her keel, followed by the breaking-off of 70 feet of the stern. The engine room was immediately filled with water, and the flooding could not be controlled. The minesweeper broke in half and sank in less than 10 minutes, 35 miles south of Scotch Cap. No crew members were injured in the accident and they were rescued by the replenishment oiler *Ramapo,* which transported them to Dutch Harbor.[28]

On 28 and 29 December, strong winds and poor visibility prevented sending bombers against Kiska. Even planes which departed on photographic missions over Amchitka had to return to base. As the weather improved, on the morning of 30 December, three B-25s, escorted by 14 P-38s, scrambled from Adak and headed to Kiska to harass ground military facilities. Crews unexpectedly encountered two transport ships and three small submarines in the local bay. The most unpleasant surprise, however, came from the sky. The Americans were taken aback by nine floatplane fighters, which had not been seen in the Aleutians for almost two months and now appeared on the stage. The P-38s had to change their plans to strafe ground installations and turn against the enemy aircraft. After the dogfight, they reported shooting down one Rufe but lost two fighters in return, piloted by Lieutenant Kayser and Lieutenant John A. Leighton.[29]

While the Lightnings were engaged in combat with the Rufes, three B-25s rushed against the two largest ships in the anchorage. Two American bombers dropped six bombs but could not see the result of their attack. The third B-25, piloted by Lieutenant Julius Constantine, did not even manage to approach the target. He was directly hit by an anti-aircraft shell and was forced to ditch his bomber eight miles south of Little Kiska. The 11 AF sent Lieutenant Theodore T. Vasataka and his copilot, Lieutenant Baxter D. Thorton, in their OA-10 to recover the B-25 crew. They got the support of a P-38, which was supposed to escort them to the lost crew. However, the fighter was forced to return to base when the right engine began failing. The OA-10 soon disappeared, and the Adak signal team never heard back from them again. The wreck of the plane and the bodies were found on the side of Kiska Volcano after the island was occupied. The crew of the B-25 was also not found, as they probably sank with their aircraft.[30]

The report about the enemy transport ships off Kiska convinced 11 AF to scramble the second striking group from Adak, comprising five B-24s, four B-25s and four B-26s. They were to take off at approximately 1400 hours, just after the return of the first group. This time, the Americans also sent one Catalina with the bombers, whose task was to rescue pilots who had been shot down earlier. The group's primary target was the vessels in the harbour. They were attacked in three horizontal approaches by B-24s, B-26s and finally, B-25s. While the B-24s and B-26s managed to accomplish this task

Colonel Benjamin B. Talley. (Michael Livingston)

without significant obstacles, the last pair of B-25s bombers were chased by five floatplane fighters, which prevented one of them from approaching the target.[31] Still, the group's crews later claimed three direct hits on the large and one hit on the small transport ship. All bombers returned safely to Adak, and the only casualty was Corporal Donald O. Murphy, a tail gunner on one of the B-26s, killed by splinters from an anti-aircraft shell.[32]

In the afternoon, the Alaska Defense Command received a warning that the Japanese planned to send a large convoy from Paramushiru. The US Navy intelligence estimated that reinforcements for the garrisons in the Aleutians could be part of preparations for an offensive operation against Adak. TF-8 was therefore recommended to be in combat readiness and conduct additional reconnaissance patrols.

On the last day of 1942, six B-24s, escorted by nine P-38s, took off from Adak and headed against the Japanese transport ships off Kiska. The planes appeared over the island at about 1240 hours. According to the American testimonies, they were attacked by 12 Japanese planes, but only five Rufes rushed against them in reality. The bombers managed to drop 37 bombs on enemy vessels in the anchorage without confirming the results. In the dogfight, the crews claimed to have damaged one floatplane fighter and did not report any losses.[33] In parallel with the air campaign, early in the morning, the commander of TG-8.6 presented an idea to utilise his warships to intercept a Japanese convoy on its return route towards the Kuril Islands. Based on the quickly drafted plan, TG-8.6 was to hastily leave Adak on the morning of 31 December and take up a position about 100 miles southwest of Kiska to await enemy movements. However, before this idea was implemented, Rear Admiral McMorris was ordered to retreat. The Alaska Defense Command eventually chose to keep its forces combat-ready in case of a possible Japanese amphibious operation in the Semichi Islands, a much more critical target than intercepting the empty transport ships.[34]

Before the clock struck midnight, announcing the New Year, a plane carrying Vice Admiral Frank J. Fletcher, the 13th Naval District commander, landed on Adak. The veteran from the Coral Sea and Midway, having previously spent the entire day in Dutch Harbor, visited the westernmost American outpost in the Aleutian Islands as a part of his essential assignment. In addition to inspecting local military installations and garrisons, Fletcher was to draft a report on the actual personal situation between Theobald and Buckner.[35]

Vice Admiral Frank J. Fletcher. (NARA)

three times by the American bombers on 30 and 31 December, yet they still managed to unload the cargo. The Japanese paid the price for their sturdiness as *Urajio Maru* suffered from the aerial attacks. Her steering gear room No. 2 was flooded due to a near miss on the starboard side, causing the ship to lose power and the steering.[37] The vessel was initially left at anchorage for later repairs, but heavy snowfall and violent winds forced the Japanese to abandon her in the following days.[38]

Table 7: Summary of 11 AF operations against the Japanese, 1–31 December 1942		
Date	Forces	Details/Targets
1–10 December	-	-
11 December	3 B-26s 4 P-38s	vessels off Kiska
12–16 December	-	-
17 December	4 B-24s	Kiska submarine base and military facilities
18–19 December	-	-
20 December	5 B-24s 4 B-26s 4 B-25s 9 P-38s	Kiska submarine base and military facilities
21–24 December	-	-
25 December	? bombers	vessels off Kiska
26 December	6 B-24s 9 P-38s	Attu military facilities
27–29 December	-	-
30 December	7 B-25s 5 B-24s 4 B-26s 14 P-38s	vessels off Kiska
31 December	6 B-24s 9 P-38s	vessels off Kiska

As Nimitz's trusted man, he was supposed to help CINCPAC make staffing decisions, which will be discussed later.

The 31 December raid was the last American action in the Aleutian Islands in 1942. The activity of 11 AF throughout the month was as shown in Table 7.[36]

The presence of Japanese floatplane fighters and transport ships at Kiska and Attu in late December resulted from the Fifth Fleet's strategy of reinforcing garrisons in the Aleutian Islands under cover of poor weather conditions. On 25 December, *Kamikawa Maru* delivered the seven long-awaited Rufes to Attu, which had performed well in deterring American air raids. On 28 December, the transport ships *Kōan Maru* and *Yamayuri Maru* arrived at Attu, delivering winter equipment, ammunition for anti-aircraft guns, coal supplies and construction materials. Due to the raid by enemy bombers, the Japanese vessels hurriedly left the island in the evening after unloading most of the supplies (excluding coal). Meanwhile, unloading work was also underway at Kiska following the arrival of the transport ship *Nichiyū Maru*, screened by the destroyer *Usugumo*. On 30 December, *Urajio Maru* also dropped anchor off the island. In addition to the 303rd Independent Construction Company, the convoy transported food supplies and construction materials for the garrison. These two transport ships were attacked

3
LANDING ON AMCHITKA

アムチトカ島の上陸
Amuchitoka-tō no Jōriku
Both Americans and Japanese greeted the beginning of 1943 without much enthusiasm. It was challenging to find reasons to celebrate the New Year in a reality where the Aleutian Islands campaign, which turned into a complicated game of chess, had been going on for almost half a year. The Americans were gaining a gradual advantage, yet they could not turn it into an apparent success. The long-term strategy of approaching Kiska and harassing the enemy positions with bombing raids seemed rational for the Army and Navy. However, despite possessing limited resources, the Japanese started

to turn their bases in the Aleutians into strongholds – even Admiral Nimitz advised against a direct attack on Kiska, and he had a logical explanation for this. An ill-prepared landing operation without adequate air support could result in a bloodbath. For this reason, the next American goal was to secure Amchitka (code name Formula) and build another airfield while waiting for additional forces to be transferred to the North Pacific.

On 4 January, Rear Admiral Thomas C. Kinkaid officially replaced Rear Admiral Theobald as commander of TF-8.[1] This change allowed for the resolution of the personal conflict between the US Navy and US Army leaders in the North Pacific. Although

Rear Admiral Thomas C. Kinkaid. (NARA)

G.E. Wheeler, mentioned that Vice Admiral William Halsey appreciated his service in the South Pacific,[2] the new post also saved Kinkaid from the detailed investigation of commanding TF-61 at the key stage of Guadalcanal campaign, especially for the losses suffered during the battle of the Santa Cruz Islands. The reason why Kinkaid, the carrier task commander, was delegated to the area with no flattops remains unknown. Wheeler claimed that Admiral King, who personally approved flag officer assignments, wanted to send an experienced commander with the offensive mindset to clear the air with the Army and accommodate their expectations.[3]

The new commander of TF-8 received an order to establish a stable ground for cooperation between the Army and the Navy to prepare the plan to retake the western part of the Aleutian Islands. Developing cordial relations and reversing the mutual distrust required more personal contacts with Buckner, Butler and Lieutenant General DeWitt from Western Defense Command. Fortunately for the Americans, Kinkaid's relationships with Army officers, especially the moody and resolute Buckner, turned out to be very positive. For the first time, there was hope for CINCPAC to accelerate the path leading to a decisive victory in the North Pacific campaign. Additionally, to be in the centre of events and command during the landing on Amchitka and after some strong suggestions from Nimitz, Kinkaid moved his headquarters to Adak Island in mid-March, which became the most important American base in the chain in the next weeks.

On 5 January, a Catalina from Patrol Wing 4, which took off for a routine reconnaissance patrol, encountered a large armed Japanese transport ship off the Komandorski Islands. Soon after, three B-25s scrambled from Adak, found the enemy vessel and immediately sank it.[4] The Americans did not know they had thwarted a vital Japanese convoy headed for Kiska. The transport ship *Montreal Maru*, which set sail from Paramushiru on 29 December, transported part of the 303rd Independent Infantry Battalion, part of the 303rd Independent Construction Company, a medical detachment (831 men in all units) and construction materials necessary to build a new airfield on the island. Although *Montreal Maru* was equipped with several lifeboats, due to terrible weather conditions, no one survived this attack.[5]

Two hours later, a B-24 on a weather reconnaissance flight located another Japanese transport ship. The bomber found *Kotohira Maru*, which had set off from Paramushiru on the afternoon of 31

December with supplies of food, construction materials and fuel for the Attu garrison. Taking advantage of the snowstorm, the Liberator approached the vessel unnoticed and scored two direct hits. A fire broke out on ship, which soon became uncontrollable. High waves and poor visibility made it more challenging to reach the nearest land safely. On 7 January, a small life raft with three survivors unexpectedly arrived at Attu. Despite immediate medical assistance, two of them soon died due to sustained injuries as well as frostbite.[6]

Changes in the TF-8 command and extremely unfavourable weather forced Rear Admiral Kinkaid to postpone the landing on Amchitka. On 6 January, he asked Brigadier General Lloyd E. Jones, selected by Buckner to lead the operation on behalf of the Army, to set the new date and hour. Once he had discussed the plans and preparedness with the Navy commanders, Jones decided that the landing on Amchitka would take place on 11 January at 1030 hours. However, on 10 January, again because of the bad weather, Jones and Kinkaid agreed to postpone the operation for one day. But when on 11 January a storm was raging around the island, the Americans did not want to delay their plans any longer. As soon as the weather improved, before dawn on 12 January, the transport ships *Arthur Middleton*, *Delarof*, *Lakona* and *Vega*, which carried approximately 2,100 of Jones's men, were ordered to drop their anchors in Constantine Bay. These ships were directly screened by Captain Paul Perry's group, comprising the destroyers *Bancroft*, *Dewey*, *Worden*, *Gillespie* and *Kalk*. The ships could count on the support of Rear Admiral John Reeves Jr., who had one gunboat and four minesweepers under his command. The landing on Amchitka was also covered by TG-8.6 of Rear Admiral McMorris, consisting of the heavy cruiser *Indianapolis*, the light cruisers *Raleigh* and *Detroit*, and the destroyers *Bailey*, *Caldwell* and *Coghlan*.[7]

Although the Americans did not encounter enemy resistance, the landing operation was not easy, as it took place in a snowstorm with a strong wing. Based on Rear Admiral McMorris's order, *Worden* was the first ship to enter Constantine Bay to disembark a reconnaissance party. However, an unknown coastal current carried her onto a pinnacle of rock while retreating in the darkness. Water started to rapidly fill the engine room through the torn hull, causing a loss of power. The anchor was dropped to hold the bow and prevent the vessel going broadside into the main rock pile. At about 09400 hours, *Middleton* and *Deway* came along. The latter tried to take *Worden* in tow, but the rope snapped. The damaged destroyer, carried away by the current, finally ran aground on the rocky bottom near the island. After a few hours, her hull cracked in several places under the impact of subsequent waves and there was settling and listing to starboard. By about 1300 hours, all hands had been evacuated from the vessel, apart from 14 men who died or went missing during the accident.[8]

The next day, *Arthur Middleton* fell victim to the treacherous waters off Amchitka when she ran aground on the underwater rocks east of Constantine Bay, which tore her hull. The Americans attempted to continue unloading supplies from the damaged vessel for the rest of the day. However, the work was ultimately abandoned due to fears that *Arthur Middleton* would take on water and could not be set afloat.[9] Rear Kinkaid in his message to Admiral Nimitz described the views regarding the potential more serious landing operation:

> I am somewhat aghast at the amount and seriousness of storm damage to ships operating in this area. It is particularly serious in a small force like this with no replacements in sight. ... It is unusual, to say the least, to conduct our type of operations in

American landing on Amchitka. (NARA)

The loss of *Worden*. (NH&HC)

this area at this time of year. Our ships operate under vicious conditions and our personnel take it on the chin.[10]

In the days following the successful landing on Amchitka, a snowstorm raged across a vast area of the western Aleutian Islands.[11] Despite the extreme conditions, Colonel Louis H. Foote's 813th Engineer Aviation Battalion and the 896th Aviation Engineering Company worked intensively to prepare a new 1,000ft-long fighter strip and build other military facilities. As J. Cloe highlighted, a priority for a runway was essential. Once the Japanese on Kiska learned of the American presence on Amchitka, it would be only a matter of time before they would begin sending their aircraft against the American garrison.[12] Therefore, several patrols of P-38s were roaming over the island during the day, but the low-level clouds were the most excellent protection against enemy counterattacks.[13] On 19 January, Brigadier Jones reported that establishing the harbour for larger vessels would require additional equipment, and his engineers estimated that the construction would take at least three months.[14]

An article in *Air Force Magazine* described the Army aviation engineers' experience on Amchitka during the construction works:

Snow fell. The muck was up to [their] shoetops ... Getting heavy trucks, caterpillar tractors, trailers, scrapers and other machinery ashore through the surf was a real problem ... A mess truck made the rounds of workers in the field with hot food and drink. To keep the trucks and other machinery rolling, mechanics put "duck boards" down in the mud and lay on their backs [underneath the vehicles] to make repairs. The Japs attacked [by air] ... and several lives were lost in bombing raids.[15]

The Japanese learned about the American presence on Amchitka and the construction of a new airfield on 23 January from a Rufe pilot who took off from Kiska and went on a patrol westward.[16] In the following days, the Japanese regularly attacked the newly established enemy positions by sending several Rufes armed with bombs. Although these raids had limited effect, they were highly disruptive to American soldiers and were designed to create a feeling of complete isolation and helplessness. During this period, snowstorms over Adak prevented 11 AF from providing any cover. However, even if the weather allowed planes to scramble, the Americans usually did not wait for a signal from Amchitka asking for help. They took advantage of every opportunity to scramble raids against Kiska. Once the group was en route and received the cable informing of the intruders over Amchitka, it was complicated to redirect the aircraft to defend the base. The only solution for the Amchitka garrison was to wait patiently for the weather improvement or for the construction of the airstrip, which would allow for transferring some fighters to the island.

The nature of the Japanese sorties against the Amchitka garrison can be reflected by the transport ship *Vega* report from 24 January:

1. (omitted)
2. At 1013, January 24, 1943, General Quarters was sounded and Material Condition Abel was set when unidentified planes were first heard and then seen approaching from about 180° true by ship's signal officer and lookouts on port side of ship. The

planes were monoplanes, single float type and the first seen was observed to drop two bombs of estimated 100 pound size from an altitude of approximately 800 feet. The first bomb struck the water about 150 yards outboard of the ARTHUR MIDDLETON and the second bomb of same size struck about the same distance inboard of this ship. The plane was fired on by the ARTHUR MIDDLETON and the shore batteries, and the YP 400 and was last seen flying toward the Northwest. No damage was inflicted and there were no casualties. This plane glided into position with motor cut from out of the lower overcast.

The second plane was observed to be approaching this vessel from about 150° true at an altitude of approximately 1800 feet. At 1015 firing was commenced by the 3"/50 caliber anti-aircraft battery. Ship's 20mm guns, .50 caliber machine guns, Browning automatic rifles, and Springfield rifles fired as soon as range closed sufficiently. The barrage though short of the target was sufficient to cause the plane to veer from its course and bank to the left before dropping its bombs, It dropped two bombs of estimated 100 pound size in the direction of the S.S. DELAROF, Both bombs struck the water about 30 yards off the port wing of the bridge of the DELAROF with slight damage to the port life boats, There were no casualties.

The enemy was repelled at 1019 by the combined fire of the VEGA, ARTHUR MIDDLETON, DISCOVERER, DELAROF, NORTH COAST, YP 400, and shore batteries and was seen to circle the island out of range of gun fire towards the Northwest. Ammunition expended by this vessel was as follows: 19 rounds of 3"/50 caliber ammunition, 510 rounds of 20mm ammunition, 254 rounds of .50 caliber ammunition. Secure from General Quarters was given at 1115.

3. The control, gun crews, end damage control divisions functioned in a quick and efficient manner during the air attack. The gun firing was better than at any previous practice of engagement. The main defects noted were that the lookouts had to be constantly warned to maintain a lookout in their sectors and not watch the target. The guns which could no longer bear on the target did not return to their sectors promptly. All personnel functioned in very creditable manner and morale was excellent.[17]

The weather in the Aleutians became so dangerous that, after a series of accidents in the previous days, on 25 January, the commander of 11 AF, in consultation with Rear Admiral Kinkaid, ordered all routine bombing missions against Kiska to be suspended. The planes were to take off only after confirmation that the weather did not exclude any flight operations. The Japanese attuite was acting oppositely and continued their tactics of harassing the enemy despite the odds. In the late afternoon, two floatplane fighters returned over Amchitka and strafed the runways, killing one man. They also dropped seven bombs, two of which fell directly onto the steel mats.[18]

The air raids motivated the American engineers to make even greater efforts and complete the first stage of work. On the morning of 26 January, a patrol of four P-38s and one B-25 appeared over the island and was replaced by another group at about 1315 hours. However, less than half an hour later, the crews were forced to turn back to Adak due to a report of an approaching snowstorm. Bad weather also grounded the Japanese seaplanes, which did not attack Amchitka until the following afternoon. On that day, no major losses were caused to the defenders, and the crews reported about one damaged aircraft.[19]

On the morning of 28 January, 11 AF sent from Adak a patrol of four P-38s and one B-25 over Amchitka, which was replaced by a second patrol during the day. Once again, the weather forced the planes to return to Fireplace, but luckily, the Japanese floatplane fighters did not appear that day.[20]

Although the tactic of sending fighter patrols over Amchitka was troublesome for the American crews, it also had visible advantages. The Japanese stopped attacking the airfield under construction during the day and reduced the frequency of their sorties. According to a report from 29 January, the Amchitka garrison had grown to 3,820 men (two reinforced infantry battalions), with one battery of 75mm and 57mm guns each. The local anti-aircraft defence consisted of two batteries of four 37mm guns each and unknown number of 20mm guns.[21]

Once more workers and heavy equipment were brought to Amchitka, construction work began in full swing. Japanese floatplane fighters continued to disrupt the process, but apart from causing minor damage, they could only delay the inevitable. On 31 January, Kimikawa Maru delivered six additional Rufes and one Jake to Kiska, but it was too little too late. The Japanese could only rely on their limited resources and desperate actions. One of the daring actions took place on 1 February, when eight floatplane fighters and one reconnaissance seaplane dropped bombs on military facilities and attacked Dale and Long mooring at the anchorage. The crews thought they had managed to set the destroyers on fire, but none of the ships suffered.[22] The intruders lost two Rufes. Another major attack was launched on the evening of 14 February, when four floatplane fighters and three reconnaissance seaplanes dropped 20 bombs on ground targets and strafed the camp. The Americans, however, did not suffer any significant losses again. The next day, four Rufes and two Jakes appeared over Amchitka, but when the Japanese rushed to bomb the airstrip, they saw for themselves that they were practically ready for use.[23] The summary of the approximately three-week air offensive against the American garrison on Amchitka is shown in Table 8.[24]

Table 8: Japanese air offensive against the constructed airstrip on Amchitka, January–February 1943

Date	Forces	Details
24 January	2 Rufes	-
25 January	2 Rufes	-
26 January	-	-
27 January	2 Rufes	1 Rufe damaged
28–30 January	-	-
31 January	2 Rufes	7 new seaplanes arrived in Kiska
1 February	8 Rufes 1 Jake	2 seaplanes did not return
2–3 February	-	-
4 February	1 Jake	reconnaissance over Amchitka
5–13 February	-	-
14 February	4 Rufes 3 Jakes	-
15 February	4 Rufes 2 Jakes	-

Just before noon on 16 February, a P-40K piloted by Lieutenant Kenneth Saxhaug was the first to land at the new airport on Amchitka.[25] After the announcement that the runways were ready, seven additional P-40s were transferred there at 1430 hours and went

The seaplane tender *Kamikawa Maru*. (NDL)

Amchitka Army Airfield in January 1943. (NH&HC)

on their first patrol over the island in the evening.[26] The Americans then knew they had taken another important step, bringing them significantly closer to regaining control over Attu and Kiska.

First Bombardment of Attu and Sinking of a Japanese Ammunition Ship
第一次のアッツ島の砲撃及び日本の弾薬輸送船の撃沈
Dai Ichi Ji no Attsu-tō no Hōgeki oyobi Nihon no Danyaku Yusōsen no Gekichin

The beginning of 1943 brought a continuation of the Japanese strategy of building up the Attu and Kiska garrisons. The loss of two valuable transport ships and their entire cargo on 5 January was devastating, but it did not stop the Fifth Fleet from sending more reinforcements and supplies to both islands. After a temporary break caused by snowstorms, the convoys rushed again from the Kuriles to the Aleutian Islands. Japanese transports by the end of January were as shown in Table 9.[27]

The discovery of the American presence at Amchitka and the ongoing construction of the new airfield were a great shock to the Japanese.[28] The Fifth Fleet command barely had time to adjust its strategy concerning the enemy base on Adak, whose neutralisation was significantly beyond the capabilities of the *Nippon Kaigun* at that time. The solid American military presence in Amchitka, practically in the close neighbourhood of Kiska, meant that only bad weather could stop 11 AF from conducting regular raids on Japanese bases in the Aleutians. The discovery greatly overshadowed the momentary joy of several convoys reaching Attu and Kiska. The Japanese knew that although they had successfully returned to Attu and sent reinforcements and equipment, they had failed to capture the Semichi Islands or build their own fully operational airfield on Kiska.

When the information about the American capture of Amchitka reached Tokyo on 1 February, the Imperial Headquarters decided to issue an order regarding further cooperation of the Army and Navy in defending the North Pacific area. Firstly, taking advantage of the established positions on Attu and Kiska, the local garrisons,

Table 9: Japanese convoys to Attu and Kiska in early 1943			
Date	Route	Ships	Supplies
? – 5 January	Paramushiru – Kiska	*Nittei Maru, Numakaze*	construction materials for *Nippon Kaigun*
29 December –X (Convoy No 6)	Paramushiru – Kiska	*Montreal Maru, Ishigaki*	part of the 303rd Independent Infantry Battalion part of the 303rd Independent Construction Company medical detachment construction materials The convoy was destroyed on 5 January
30 December –X (Convoy No. 2)	Paramushiru – Attu	Kotohira Maru, Numakaze	food supplies, construction materials, fuel The convoy was destroyed on 5 January
11–16 January (Convoy No 7)	Paramushiru – Kiska	*Melbourne Maru, Fujikage Maru, Usugumo*	part of the 303rd Independent Infantry Battalion construction materials for *Nippon Kaigun*
26 January – X	Paramushiru – Kiska	*Kiso, Wakaba*	unspecified transport with infantry The convoy returned due to the storm
27–30 January (Convoy No. 10)	Paramushiru – Attu	*Sakito Maru, Kimikawa Maru, Kunashiri*	main part of the 303rd Independent Infantry Battalion (278 men) artillery detachment (290 men) 7 seaplanes
28 January – 2 February (Convoy No. 11)	Paramushiru – Kiska	*Akagane Maru, Numakaze*	food supplies, construction materials, fuel
30 January – 3 February (Convoy No. 12)	Paramushiru – Kiska	*Asaka Maru,* Wakaba	part of the 302nd and 303rd Independent Infantry Battalion

supported by *Nippon Kaigun*, were to keep their positions in the Aleutians at all costs. Full readiness to repel a possible American attack was to be achieved at the end of February. Secondly, the Imperial Headquarters confirmed the plans to build airfields and seaplane bases on Attu and Kiska. Details on the organisation of air bases were to be provided no later than the end of March.[29] In the meantime, Vice Admiral Hosogaya had only received the heavy cruiser *Maya* as a necessary reinforcement. She was formally attached to the Fifth Fleet on 30 January and was scheduled to set off for the North Pacific in the second half of February.

To understand the Imperial Headquarters' tardiness regarding the situation in the Aleutians, it should be noted that the Japanese Army

and Navy had much greater worries at that time. From mid-January to 7 February, the high command supervised the evacuation of the Seventeenth Army remnants from Guadalcanal, which required additional air and surface forces. The 'hell island' campaign, which lasted over half a year, ended in a tragic defeat. What was worse, it cost Japan significant resources and irreversibly handed the strategic initiative over to the enemy. Once the Americans had fully secured Guadalcanal, it seemed apparent they would continue their advance in the Solomon Islands.

Although the Japanese delayed starting construction of the airfields in the Aleutians, they never questioned the necessity of keeping Attu and Kiska. The end of the struggle for Guadalcanal meant the release of part of the US Navy forces, which could then be transferred to the North Pacific in preparation for a new offensive. Apart from the landing on Kiska, the Fifth Fleet saw the most profound threat in establishing close cooperation with the USSR, which could result in the encirclement of Japan on the northern flank. In early February, the Imperial Headquarters analysed a potential action against the Soviet Union, which was limited to estimating the Soviet forces in Siberia and a general survey of the garrisons in the Kamchatka Peninsula and North Sakhalin.[30]

To improve the organisation of Army and Navy forces in the North Pacific, on 5 February the Imperial Headquarters issued Army Order No. 747, which established the Northern Army (*Hoppōgun*) under the command of Lieutenant General Higuchi Ki'ichirō. On the same day, under Army Order No. 748, the North Sea Garrison Force was removed from the temporary operational control of the Fifth Fleet after more than three months and assigned to the Northern Army. The Army General Staff and the Navy General Staff also published a jointly signed instruction announcing close cooperation in the defence of the Aleutian Islands. As for the Navy, it committed to organising and securing the convoys, while the Army promised to lend its transports to transfer additional equipment and men to Attu and Kiska promptly. In the case of the latter island, the Navy was to implement a plan of assigning warships to convoys in response to the enemy's capture of Amchitka. Construction of the two new airfields, discussed later in this chapter, was to begin (even on a limited basis) as soon as possible and then accelerate once additional supplies and workers were delivered. On 13 February, the Imperial Headquarters also reorganised the North Sea Garrison Force, which was divided into Area No. 1 (Kiska) under the command of Colonel Satō Masao and Area No. 2 (Attu) under the command of Colonel Yamasaki Yasuyo. Despite the adopted principle that the Army and Navy must cooperate closely to establish two strong and independent fortresses in the Aleutian Islands, the Imperial Headquarters' decision to establish two parallel levels of command proved to be a great mistake in the future.[31]

On 15 February, after a conference with Lieutenant General Higuchi, Vice Admiral Hosogaya and Vice Admiral Kawase Shirō, commander of the Ōminato Naval Garrison, the Fifth Fleet decided to launch Operation A (*A-gō Sakusen*), which would consist of sending several convoys with troops and supplies to Attu and Kiska. However, the new American airfield on Amchitka was considered the greatest obstacle to executing this plan. Since late January, the

Lieutenant General Higuchi Ki'ichirō. (NDL)

Vice Admiral Kawase Shirō. (NDL)

enemy could conduct effective raids on ground facilities and directly threaten Japanese lines of communication in the Aleutian Islands. The Fifth Fleet and Northern Army staff clearly understood the defensive strategy of the North Pacific campaign and concentrated their efforts on halting the enemy advance towards the home islands.

American intelligence had failed to decipher the enemy dispatches fully, which caused some misinterpretation of their opponent's plans. After the floatplane fighters' offensive against the new airfield at Amchitka, it was expected that the Japanese would bring larger air forces to the Aleutian Islands to prepare for large-scale operations in the coming weeks. The TF-8 command also received a warning from CINCPAC about the planned enemy landing on the Semichi Islands, probably after the completion of the concentration on Attu. At the beginning of February, TF-8 finally decided to use its warships to shell the island to forestall the Fifth Fleet movements. Rear Admiral McMorris was tasked with bombarding the Attu harbour, as in comparison to Kiska, the Japanese had failed to hide most of their military facilities in underground bunkers. The Americans also estimated they might encounter enemy transport ships in Holtz Bay and Chichagof Bay, which started to avoid venturing to the Kiska area.

Upon learning of the final stage of construction work at the Amchitka, on the morning of 12 February, Rear Admiral McMorris's task force, consisting of the heavy cruiser *Indianapolis*, the light cruiser *Richmond*, and the destroyers *Bancroft*, *Caldwell*, *Coghlan*, and *Gillespie*, set off in two groups from Kuluk Bay and the Amchitka area. Both headed for a position east of Attu. Initially, McMorris intended to bombard the island just before sunrise on 21 February. However, in the following days, no enemy surface vessels were encountered en route, and the group was followed by a Japanese aircraft. Therefore, on 18 February, he decided to approach Attu and complete the mission before the schedule. The morning message from the submarine *S-22* also encouraged the Americans to change their plans, which indicated that there were probably three unspecified enemy vessels in Holtz Bay.[32]

After 1400 hours, McMorris' group began approaching Attu from the west, having catapulted their seaplanes moments earlier. They confirmed no presence of Japanese ships in Holtz Bay or Chichagof Bay. Initially, the American formation was led by *Richmond*, followed by *Indianapolis* and the destroyers, which took up positions on both sides of the cruisers. To provide more effective fire and remain in patrol positions when approaching the target, two destroyers moved to the front and two others to the rear of the formation. Soon after, one B-24 flew over the team and was mistakenly engaged by anti-aircraft artillery before the correct identification. At 1452 hours, having virtually perfect sea conditions and moderate wind from the north-west, the group made a simultaneous course change. At 1504 hours, American ships began bombarding enemy positions in Chichagof Bay from rages of 9,000–11,000m. After 10 minutes, McMorris ordered to cease fire and headed for Holtz Bay. At about 1625 hours, McMorris started shelling the local military facilities for 11 minutes from a distance of 8,000–10,000m, and then he changed the course to 40 degrees at a speed of 22 knots. The American reconnaissance planes did not notice any resistance from Rufes, and the garrison only opened anti-aircraft fire on the intruders over the island. By 1745 hours, McMorris' group recovered all the catapulted aircraft. Just before sunset, his ships were still being followed by one Japanese reconnaissance seaplane, which returned to base after an hour.[33]

The Americans were generally satisfied with the bombardment of Attu, although reality showed that they did not inflict significant losses on the enemy. At 1400 hours, during the approach towards Attu, McMorris' team was spotted by a Japanese reconnaissance seaplane, which remained in contact with him for the next four hours until he withdrew north. The crew warned the base of two cruisers and four destroyers 45 miles north-west of Attu and approaching the island. The garrison was able to evacuate the exposed positions in time. Fortunately for the Japanese, there were no transports in the local anchorage that day, and American shells proved largely inaccurate. Minor damage was reported only to a few buildings, and losses among soldiers remain unknown.[34]

Having ensured that no enemy reconnaissance aircraft lurked nearby, Rear Admiral McMorris set course west of Attu after sunset. He intended to mislead the enemy and faked his retreat to give his transports time to approach the island. To intercept enemy vessels more effectively during the route, the formation was divided into two smaller groups:

(1) the southern group under the command of Rear Admiral McMorris, comprising *Richmond*, *Bancroft* and *Caldwell*;
(2) the northern group under the command of Captain Nicholas Vytlacil, comprising *Indianapolis*, *Coghlan* and *Gillespie*.

After dark on 19 February, *Indianapolis* was approximately 120 miles southwest of Attu, proceeding 0 degrees at 17 knots. *Gillespie* provided direct cover for the cruiser, while *Coghlan* was less than six miles to the south. At 2037 hours, *Gillespie* received an order to take up a position six miles north of the flagship, which changed course to 162 degrees about an hour later. At 1020 hours, *Coghlan*'s SC radar displayed two contacts at a distance of 9.6 miles. The crew cabled this discovery urgently through TBS to *Indianapolis,* and Captain Vytlacil ordered the destroyers to close to the flagship. Five minutes later, the cruiser's observers noticed a smoke trail on the starboard side. At the same time, the SG radar screen made contact with a vessel bearing 204 degrees, at a distance of about 23km. *Indianapolis* abruptly changed course to 220 degrees and then to 210 degrees. Within 20 minutes, *Coghlan* took the position forward of the cruiser, and Gillespie placed herself astern.

By 2312 hours, Indianapolis and the destroyers were close enough to the enemy ship for the crews to see it for themselves. She was an approximately 150m-long freighter with a displacement of 5,000 tons, apparently loaded with explosives and other stores.[35] As

Captain Nicolas Vytlacil. (Alfred J. Sedivi Collection via US NIP)

the ship did not respond appropriately to the recognition signal, the Americans opened fire at 2316 hours. After a while, *Indianapolis* scored the first direct hit from the third main artillery salvo. The enemy vessel burst into flames. She instantly illuminated the entire area and became a convenient target for destroyers. The Japanese replied with three or four salvos from a small-calibre gun and a long burst from machine guns, but the outcome was miserable. The ship soon ceased fire, which meant she was unable to continue fighting.

Probably due to extensive damage in the engine room, the Japanese ship stopped at 2325 hours, and a minute later, the *Indianapolis* scored another hit. The explosion caused a massive fire on board, leading to several minor explosions of stored fuel and ammunition. Seeing the burning ship silhouette, the Americans ceased fire. However, she did not sink instantly. Her burning wreck, still floating in the water, brightly illuminated the area. Since this could enable the American group to be spotted from submarines or aircraft, Captain Vytlacil ordered his destroyers to finish off the enemy with torpedoes.

One minute before midnight on 20 February, *Coghlan* fired a single torpedo from 2,700m. Although its path seemed correct, it passed under the Japanese ship and did not explode. At 0010 hours, the destroyer fired a second torpedo, which exploded approximately 450m before the target, probably as a result of hitting an underwater wreck. Bad luck did not leave the Americans that night since the third torpedo, fired from 1,800m, passed a few metres from the stern of the victim.

In response to *Coghlan*'s problems with sinking the defenceless and immobilised ship, *Gillespie* fired her first torpedo, but it missed the target by a small margin. The destroyer's commander decided to fire the second and last torpedo. Yet, immediately after leaving the tube, it started jumping and passed behind the vessel's stern.

The annoyed Americans decided to use their proven artillery. Soon after, *Coghlan* fired four salvos from the main guns, scoring several hits below the waterline. Despite subsequent explosions and a furious fire on the deck, the victim did not want to go down. *Coghlan* tried to finish her with a torpedo, but the warhead exploded 45m before the target. Finally, at 0124 hours, the destroyer fired two salvos, and the ship sank by the stern. The Americans decided to close the distance and look for survivors, but they did not find anyone alive. They could only see Army life jackets and one empty bamboo life raft floating in the water.[36] After the action, the northern

The escort ship *Hachijō*. (NDL)

group continued patrolling the waters around Attu to intercept more Japanese convoys to the Aleutians. On 21 February, Captain Vytlacil reported not encountering any other enemy vessels in Chichagof Bay. Despite the planned reconnaissance of Kiska for 24 February, the following day in the morning, McMorris returned with all his ships to Adak.[37]

The vessel sunk by the Americans near Attu was *Akagane Maru*. On 13 February, she departed Paramushiru as part of Convoy No. 16, screened by the escort ship *Hachijō*. *Akagane Maru* carried food supplies and ammunition for the Attu garrison. When Captain Vytlacil's group spotted the convoy, both Japanese ships maintained a distance, so the Americans could not find *Hachijō* despite initial

radar contact. After sinking the *Akagane Maru*, the escort ship retreated safely towards the Kuril Islands.[38]

The destruction of *Akagane Maru* was a painful loss for the Japanese, but it was certainly not the most critical convoy trying to reach the Aleutian Islands at the time. In parallel with the decisions of the Imperial Headquarters and the adopted principle of close cooperation between the Army and Navy, most of February was marked with the Fifth Fleet's serious commitment to reinforcing the Attu and Kiska garrisons by transferring equipment and construction materials necessary for the airfield construction on both islands. A summary of Japanese convoys is shown in Table 10.[39]

Table 10: Japanese convoys to Attu and Kiska in February–March 1942			
Date	**Route**	**Ships**	**Supplies**
7–11 February (Convoy No. 13)	Paramushiru – Attu	*Yamayuri Maru, Ishigaki*	weapons for infantry airfield construction materials
12 February – X (Convoy No. 14)	Paramushiru – Kiska	*Sakito Maru, Shunkō Maru, Kiso, Wakaba, Hatsuharu*	one company from the 303rd Independent Infantry Battalion Convoy returned to base upon the report of the enemy presence near Kiska
17–21 February (Convoy No. 15)	Paramushiru – Kiska	*Kurita Maru, Abukuma, Inazuma*	32nd Independent Anti-Aircraft Unit 30th Construction Unit (Specialist) airfield construction materials
13 February – X (Convoy No. 16)	Paramushiru – Attu	*Akagane Maru, Hachijō*	food and ammunition supply The convoy was destroyed on 19 February
X (Convoy No. 17)	Paramushiru – Kiska	*Fushimi Maru, Fujikage Maru, Kiso,* 21st Destroyer Division (minus *Hatsuharu*)	anti-aircraft guns construction materials The convoy did not set off
19 February – X (Convoy No. 18/1)	Paramushiru – Attu	*Dover Maru, Kunashiri,*	The convoy returned due to the engine damage of the transport ship
X (Convoy No. 18/2)	Paramushiru – Attu	*Yamayuri Maru*	The convoy did not set off
6–9 March (Convoy No. 21 "I")	Paramushiru – Attu	*Kimikawa Maru, Kurita Maru, Sakito Maru,* Main part of the Fifth Fleet	6 Rufes 2 Jakes construction materials food supply specialist personnel (342 men)

A vital convoy for the Fifth Fleet, described as No. 21 "I", was organised to deliver seaplanes to Attu, construction materials and specialised personnel necessary to accelerate building the airfields in the Aleutians. The group comprising transport ships *Kurita Maru*, *Sakito Maru* and the seaplane tender *Kimikawa Maru*, which was screened by the core of the Fifth Fleet (heavy cruisers *Nachi* and *Maya*, light cruisers *Kiso*, *Abukuma* and *Tama*, destroyers *Wakaba*, *Hatsushimo*, *Ikazuchi*, *Inazuma* and *Usugumo*, and escort ships *Kunashiri* and *Hachijō*), set off from Paramushiru on 6 March. Assigning such a strong escort to the convoy directly resulted from the sinking of *Akagane Maru* and the Fifth Fleet order issued on 22 February, which recommended increased preventive measures in subsequent runs to Attu and Kiska.[40] Convoy No. 21 "I" was thus sufficiently secured by the Japanese warships if the enemy naval or air forces tried to intercept it. Despite serious concerns about the convoy's safety, it encountered no obstacles and reached its destination on 9 March. After hastily unloading equipment and troops, the transport ships and their escorts set off for Paramushiru, arriving there safely three days later.[41]

Apart from providing a sufficient escort for the convoys heading Attu and Kiska, the Japanese were still struggling with the insoluble issue of American bombing raids. Since June 1942, the air campaign in the Aleutians went through three phases: (1) limited attacks by bombers or by flying boats from bases in the eastern part of the Aleutians; (2) more frequent sorties of bombers with fighter escort from the Adak airbase established in September 1942; (3) regular sorties of bombers and fighters from the Amchitka airbase. For most of the winter, the highly unfavourable weather in the Aleutian Islands had been the ally of the Japanese. However, with the inevitable arrival of spring and the construction of a new American airfield just off Kiska, 11 AF was well on its way to reducing the weather factor. Having achieved air superiority, the Americans could raid both garrisons and engage Rear Admiral McMorris' task force to bombard the Japanese positions. Finally, they could commence the long-term preparations to retake both islands from the enemy hands. In the first months of 1943, however, an air war of attrition remained the primary strategy, aimed at preventing the build-up of Attu and Kiska and forcing the Fifth Fleet to leave the Aleutians due to fear of losing valuable warships and transports. The American documents also evidence that there were plans to further encircle the enemy by seizing Agattu and building another runway for fighters. The analysis performed at the beginning of March included four proposals for the location of the future airfield on the island. Whichever one was chosen, it was a mortal threat to the Attu garrison, which would be within operational range of American fighters. The situation of the Kiska garrison would look even more grave as it could be effectively encircled and cut off from supplies.[42] A summary of 11 AF activities from January 1943 to the battle of the Komandorski Islands is shown in Table 11.[43]

In addition to the improving weather conditions, 11 AF intensified air strikes against Kiska since its reconnaissance plane had discovered unmistakable traces of the airfield under construction on the island. The airstrip for fighters was located southwest of Salmon Lagoon, near the main base garrison. The next day, it was confirmed that one transport ship was moored in the local bay. A more detailed observation of the indicated areas allowed the scouting planes to estimate that the runway was approximately completed at 50 percent.[44] This time, the Americans, previously convinced that the enemy had abandoned the fight for air domination, had to clash with reality and the construction works just before their eyes. Although they were wrong about the advancement level, the

Ordinary life in the Aleutian bases in 1943. (Dmitri Kessel/Life Pictures)

Japanese started building new airbases after receiving orders from the Imperial Headquarters in the first days of February. According to the instructions, the runway for fighters at Kiska would be just over 1,000m long, allowing for its quick construction and easy maintenance. The rocky terrain and gusty winds caused great difficulties for the Japanese, but the biggest obstacle was the lack of skilled workers. It was not until the arrival of Convoy No. 15 with the 30th Construction Unit and prefabricated housing modules that 250 men were regularly present at the construction site since 24 February.

When it seemed that the situation was finally getting better, in early March, the commander of the Kiska garrison decided to withdraw most of the workers to the main camp as he feared an enemy landing. The airfield construction was less critical than the Imperial Headquarters order, which called for defending the island at all costs, using all available means, including armed workers. Less than a hundred men remained on the construction site. They soon became a target for American bombers from Adak and Amchitka. Consequently, only 55 percent of the runways had been constructed by the end of March.[45] It was insufficient to provide air cover for the convoys heading to the Aleutian Islands, scheduled for March and early April. Finally, the original plans were revised, and the airstrip was to be 20 percent shorter and narrower. The Japanese construction units worked without any breaks, and at the end of April, the Kiska garrison announced that it had its operational airfield.

The progress of construction works on the new airfield at Attu (1,100m x 200m) initially looked much better than on the neighbouring Kiska. It directly resulted from selecting an exceptionally convenient place – a narrow sandy peninsula in the eastern part of Massacre Bay. It quickly turned out to be a perfect spot for the Japanese workers, who began marking out the airstrip and levelling the ground on 24 February. However, the Attu garrison still struggled with a lack of soldiers to defend the island in the event of an enemy landing. At the beginning of March, the Japanese made a difficult decision to move some of the workers to the main camp. This resulted in only 50 percent of the airfield being completed by the end of the month. Since further convoys to the Aleutian Islands were suspended after the battle of the Komandorski Islands, the successful completion of the new Attu airfield became implausible. Despite hard-headed calculations, the Japanese intended to achieve their goal by the end of May. Ambitious plans were thwarted by preparations to repel the American invasion, eventually ruining the chances of opening the Attu airfield.[46]

Table 11: Summary of American air operations against the Japanese in the Aleutians, 1 January to 27 March 1943.

Date	Forces	Target/Details
5 January	1 B-24 3 B-25s	enemy transport ships
6 January	5 B-24s 12 P-38s 6 B-25s	Kiska submarine base and military facilities
7 January	4 B-24s	Kiska military facilities
8–17 January	-	-
18 January	1 B-24	Kiska anchorage
19 January – 3 February	-	-
4 February	3 B-17s 3 B-24s 5 B-25s 4 P-38s 8 P-40s	Kiska anchorage
5–7 February	-	-
8 February	5 B-24s 5 B-25s	Kiska anchorage
9 February	-	-
10 February	4 B-24s 2 B-17s 8 B-25s 8 P-38s	Kiska anchorage
11–12 February	-	-
13 February	5 B-24s 6 B-25s 10 P-38s	Kiska anchorage
14–19 February	-	-
20 February	5 B-24s 6 B-25s 8 P-38s	Kiska anchorage
19–22 February	-	-
23 February	6 B-24s 10 B-25s 8 P-38s	Kiska anchorage
24 February	-	-
25 February	6 B-24s 5 B-25s	Kiska anchorage
26 February	-	-
27 February	6 B-24s 6 B-25s 4 P-38s	Kiska anchorage
28 February	6 B-24s 6 B-25s	Kiska anchorage
1–6 March	-	-
7 March	4 P-38s 10 B-25s 7 B-24s	Kiska anchorage
8 March	-	-
9 March	6 B-24s 10 B-25s 12 P-38s 1 F-5-A 4 P-40s	Kiska anchorage
10 March	10 B-25s 12 P-38s 6 B-24s 1 F-5-A 4 P-40s	Kiska anchorage
11–12 March	-	-
13 March	20 P-40s 8 P-38s	seaplanes at Kiska, Kiska anchorage
14 March	-	-
15 March	28 P-38 8 B-24s 17 B-25s 1 F-5-A 4 P-40s	Kiska military facilities
16 March	12 B-24s 12 B-25s 8 P-38s	seaplanes at Kiska, Kiska military facilities
17 March	-	-
18 March	6 B-24s 6 B-25s 20 P-38s	seaplanes at Kiska, Kiska military facilities
19–20 March	-	-
21 March	12 B-24s 6 B-25s 46 P-38s 4 F-5-As	seaplanes at Kiska, Kiska military facilities
22–23 March	-	-
24 March	4 B-24s 8 B-25s 12 P-38s	seaplanes at Kiska, Kiska military facilities
25 March	11 B-24s 3 B-25s 12 P-38s	seaplanes at Kiska, Kiska military facilities
26 March	-	-
27 March	13 B-24s 11 B-25s 8 P-38s	enemy transport ships and warships Attu military facilities

The degree of Japanese preparations for the defence of Kiska and Attu against a potential but still unlikely American landing is to some extent reflected in the comparison of the actual and planned number of troops of the North Sea Garrison in March–April 1943. According to February's Northern Army order, the *Nippon Rikugun* (Imperial Japanese Army) intended to gather approximately 11,400 men on Kiska and Attu with artillery and engineering detachments. After completing the winter convoys (deducting losses resulting from the loss of some vessels), 2,500 men were transferred to the Aleutian Islands, while another 5,700 men were waiting for transport at the earliest possible date.[47] Considering the Army and Navy personnel from the 51st Base Force who were already stationed on Kiska and Attu, it can be roughly estimated that the Japanese gathered only 65 percent of the forces (approximately 7,500 men from the Army and the Navy, 4,700 of whom were gathered on Kiska), which they intended to deploy to hold the Aleutian Islands as long as possible.[48]

Taking a bath on Amchitka. (Dmitri Kessel/Life Pictures)

4

CONVOY NO. 21 "RO"

第二十一「ロ」船団
Dai 21 "Ro" Sendan

Once Convoy No. 21 "I" returned safely to Paramushiru on 13 March, the Japanese began preparations to organise another, even larger transport to the Aleutian Islands. Once the heavy cruiser *Maya* arrived in the North Pacific in late February, on 14 March, the Fifth Fleet finally sent the light cruiser *Kiso* to Maizuru for long-planned repairs and modernisation. The transport ship *Kurita Maru* also headed towards the home islands, which was replaced by the refrigerated cargo ship *Asaka Maru* on 17 March.

The Japanese intelligence estimations on the American bomber wing in the Aleutians were as shown in Table 12.[1]

Table 12: Japanese intelligence estimations of the American bomber wing in the Aleutians, mid-March 1943

	Army bombers	Navy bombers
Kodiak	1	0
Fort Glenn	14	10
Fort Randall	0	-
Anchorage	0	-
Adak	55 (two squadrons)	31
Amchitka	1	1
Dutch Harbor	-	4

On 19 March, the commander of the Fifth Fleet issued Secret Operational Order No. 4, which called for a second run of Convoy No 21, this time described as "RO". The exact content of Vice Admiral Hosogaya's order remains unknown, but it can be presumed that the convoy was instructed to deliver to Attu by 26 March approximately 550 Army soldiers, anti-aircraft and mountain guns, a field hospital unit and supplies.[2] The ships also boarded the staff officers and field hospital detachment for the Kiska garrison and parts for the constructed harbour. The high importance of this undertaking was evidenced by the fact that *Sankō Maru*, the so-called 'slow army freighter', was loaded with significant food and ammunition supplies, as well as materials for the airfield construction. The core of the Fifth Fleet screened the convoy, which was also supposed to destroy the enemy task force if it wanted to interrupt the run. The organisation of Convoy No. 21 "RO" was as shown in Table 13.[3]

Detailed guidelines of the convoy mission were attached to the *Secret Operational Order of the Screening Force No. 2* of 20 March. It recommended taking special precautions against submarines and mines (especially when approaching Attu) and suggested that *Asaka Maru* and *Sakito Maru* separate before unloading troops and supplies. Both transport ships were to be screened by Rear Admiral Mori Tomokazu's 1st Torpedo Squadron. The slower *Sankō Maru* and destroyer *Usugumo* were to join the rest of the group just before reaching Attu. After that, *Sankō Maru* would drop anchor off *Sakito Maru*, and *Usugumo* would remain at the spot to patrol the nearby waters. The Main Force, commanded personally by Vice Admiral Hosogaya, was supposed to watch over the proper execution of the entire operation. He could join the action anytime with his three cruisers and two destroyers. The commander of the Fifth Fleet knew that the Americans had an advantage in virtually every possible area of the Aleutian campaign except one – surface forces. Thus, if the Japanese had any chance to capitalise on their strengths, the Fifth Fleet should press for the naval artillery engagement by using its superiority in numbers and experience compared to TF-8.

Table 13: Organisation of Convoy No. 21 "RO"			
Unit	Commander	Forces	Tasks
Main Force	Commander of the Fifth Fleet, Vice Admiral Hosogaya	21st Cruiser Squadron heavy cruisers *Nachi* (F), *Maya* light cruiser *Tama* 21st Destroyer Division destroyers *Wakaba*, *Hatsushimo*	1. Supporting the convoy 2. Destroying the encountered enemy task force
1st Escort Unit	Commander of the 1st Torpedo Squadron, Rear Admiral Mori	1st Torpedo Squadron light cruiser *Abukuma* 6th Destroyer Division destroyers *Ikazuchi*, *Inazuma* transport ships *Asaka Maru*, *Sakito Maru*	1. Direct support for the Convoy "RO" (*Asaka Maru*, *Sakito Maru*) 2. Indirect support for *Sankō Maru* 3. Helping the Main Force during the engagement
2nd Escort Unit	Commander of *Usugumo*	destroyer *Usugumo* transport ship *Sankō Maru*	1. Direct support for *Sankō Maru*

The transport ship *Sakito Maru*. (NDL)

An essential part of the convoy for the Attu garrison was providing preliminary reconnaissance of the route on its various sections. The Fifth Fleet assigned the submarines *I-31*, *I-168*, *I-169* and *I-171*, which operated from Paramushiru. Reconnaissance seaplanes from the *452nd Kaigun Kōkūtai* were also engaged in reconnaissance patrols, as they flew alone or in pairs around Attu and Kiska since 15 March. On 21 March, one of the aircraft spotted an enemy surface team 140 miles southeast of Attu. According to the report, it comprised one cruiser and two destroyers, proceeding on a course of 145 degrees at 18 knots. In the following days, the Japanese could not find those ships again, and they presumed that the enemy had probably returned to their base.[4]

Although the Fifth Fleet was unsure of the enemy's intentions, it decided to send Convoy "RO" based on the initial arrangements. At 1500 hours on 22 March, *Sankō Maru* and *Usugumo* were the first to leave Paramushiru. The next day at 1000 hours, the 6th Destroyer Division set off, followed at noon by *Abukuma*, *Asaka Maru* and *Sakito Maru*. At about 1700 hours, after sunset, the Main Force headed towards Attu.[5] The convoy proceeded in four groups to confuse the Americans, primarily their submarines and reconnaissance aircraft. It was not earlier than a day before the planned arrival at Attu that they intended to form one strong formation that would be able to repel a potential American counterattack.

However, before the Japanese could move far away from Paramushiru, their plans became complicated due to the sudden weather deterioration. Meteorological data indicated a drastic drop in atmospheric pressure to only 734 mmHg in the eastern part of the Kuril Islands. In the early morning of 24 March, the convoy entered the storm area and experienced 20m/s wind with three-metre-high waves. It became apparent to Hosogaya that maintaining the current speed of advance towards the Aleutians could end in disaster. Therefore, despite the initial belief in overcoming the difficulties, he decided to save the boilers and fuel on his ships, and the next day, he postponed reaching Attu by one day, namely from 26 to 27 March.[6]

In the afternoon of 25 March, the weather improved temporarily, but the Japanese could not make up for the lost time and focused on completing the mission following the new guidelines. Due to the gradual approach to the concentration point before the last section of the route to Attu, on the morning of 26 March, all ships were put on high alert in case they encountered American reconnaissance planes, submarines or any Soviet merchant ships. At 1400 hours, the Main Force and the 1st Escort Unit joined approximately 180km south of the Komandorski Islands. However, Vice Admiral Hosogaya was still waiting for *Sankō Maru* and *Usugumo*, which had a much longer delay than the rest of the convoy due to stormy weather in the last few hours. After 1500 hours, he ordered an eastern course and, just over three hours later, instructed the Main Force and the 1st Escort Unit to proceed northward temporarily. Before midnight on 27 March, they were supposed to turn south to link up with *Sankō Maru* and *Usugumo* between 0700–0800 hours. At the same time, both late vessels were to proceed at 12 knots to the concentration point indicated in the orders. Finally, after regrouping with the convoy, they were to take up positions at its rear.

At 2250 hours, Hosogaya's force changed the course to the south after reaching the Komandorski Islands. As precious hours passed, he still did not know when or even if the 2nd Escort Unit could join the convoy and arrive at Attu as planned by the evening of 27 March. Meanwhile, before dawn, at about 0400 hours, upon learning that the 2nd Escort Unit would ultimately not be able to arrive on time, he ordered *Usugumo* to join the rest of the convoy on her own.[7] Hosogaya left *Sankō Maru* without any escort, which seemed to him the lesser evil since the fate of the entire convoy and the accompanying warships were much more critical than one transport ship.[8]

American Strategic Planning and Intercepting the Convoy to Attu
アメリカの戦略計画及びアッツ島への船団を迎撃する
Amerika no Senryaku Keikaku oyobi Attsu-tō e no Sendan o Geigeki Suru

Upon the victory in the Guadalcanal campaign, the idea of reconquering the Aleutian Islands from the enemy in the following months became an important topic for the American planners. US Navy intelligence knew that the Fifth Fleet implemented the plan to strengthen the Attu and Kiska garrisons significantly. Thus, it was essential to intensify air strikes against Japanese ground targets and use TF-8 more actively to intercept convoys heading for both islands. However, Admiral Nimitz was aware that Rear Admiral Kinkaid could not simply wait for the enemy to appear. With Adak and Amchitka's air support, Nimitz hoped that the enemy's numerical advantage in warships would be eliminated, and quick sorties against the shipping lines could be highly effective in the long term. Regardless of any assessments, TF-8 desperately needed reinforcements. On 11 March, CINCPAC eventually decided to deploy the heavy cruiser *Salt Lake City* to the North Pacific, the veteran from the Guadalcanal campaign. She was damaged during the battle of Cape Esperance in October 1942 and spent the next four months in the shipyard in Pearl Harbor. After the repairs, her crew was hastily replenished. Therefore, half of the new members were to take part in combat for the first time (about 70 percent of the fire control teams were rookies), and she could seem unfit for combat, especially in such a demanding theatre of war.[9] The Americans attempted to make up these deficiencies by accelerated weekly training after returning to service on 1 March since there was not enough time to keep the ship in temporary reserve. Despite all shortcomings, the mere presence of *South Lake City* in the North Pacific was considered a great support for TF-8. The heavy cruiser could be used to put pressure on the enemy or screen the friendly convoys heading towards the Aleutian Islands from the West Coast.

The capture of Amchitka and the airfield construction on the island gave the Americans more room for strategic planning in the Aleutians. On 3 March, Rear Admiral Kinkaid sent a cable to CINCPAC with a suggestion of seizing Attu and the Semichi Islands. He intended to bypass Kiska, constantly bombarded by 11 AF, as the Japanese had fortified the island. The TF-8 command believed that Attu, whose garrison had no more than 3,000 men, no fortified positions, or well-positioned artillery, would be an easier target. At the same time, Kinkaid envisaged building on the Semichi Islands, specifically on Shemya, another airbase, which could be used to neutralise the emerging Japanese airfield on Attu. The airfield on Shemya would also pose a severe threat to the Kiska garrison as it could cut off the shipping lines with the Kuril Islands.[10]

The Joint Chiefs of Staff tentatively approved his idea and issued a communiqué on 11 March with the recommendation for its implementation after careful preparations and training. General Marshall supported the landing on Attu but needed to carefully consider the plans for transportation, as in early March the only method of supplying forces along the Aleutians was by air transport due to losses of coastwise shipping. The new garrison at Amchitka had to be supplied by air as well for some time.[11] On 15 March, TF-8 was renamed TF-16. Rear Admiral Kinkaid was officially responsible for planning and executing the Attu invasion operation. In the meanwhile, 11 AF was redesignated TG-16.1. Its command moved from Kodiak to Adak to closely monitor air strikes against Japanese positions in the Aleutian Islands.[12] On 22 March, the Joint Chiefs of Staff, after examining all options, finally gave the green light for the invasion of Attu. The amphibious operation was supposed to be launched as soon as possible and was codenamed Landcrab.[13] A day later, Lieutenant General DeWitt received confirmation in a telephone conversation with Washington that the US Army could use as many as three infantry regiments in the North Pacific to proceed with the landing.[14] Thus, the 70th Regiment of the 17th Infantry Division was to occupy Attu, while the 4th Combined Regiment was to occupy Shemya, and the 32nd Regiment was to remain in active reserve. The following week, CINCPAC and the Western Defense Command published more detailed guidelines, which set the invasion date as 7 May.[15]

Returning to the current issues, in early March, TF-8 intended to resume regular patrol missions west of Attu to harass the enemy supply line connecting the Aleutian Islands with the Kuril Islands.

Lookouts in Dutch Harbor. (Dmitri Kessel/Life Pictures)

After making the necessary repairs to the destroyers in Dutch Harbor and carrying out additional training for the anti-aircraft artillery and torpedo crews, on the evening of 15 March, Rear Admiral McMorris departed Unalaska with the light cruiser *Richmond* and the destroyers *Bailey* and *Coghlan*. Passing through Adak on the way to replenish fuel supplies, TG-16.6[16] under his command headed southwest of Kiska, hoping to encounter a Japanese convoy or any lonely transport ships. These three American vessels were spotted on 21 March by a Japanese reconnaissance seaplane.[17] That same afternoon, Rear Admiral McMorris was ordered to link up with *Salt Lake City* and the destroyers *Dale* and *Monaghan* at 0900 hours the next day at coordinates 50°38'N, 174°E.[18] Although the heavy cruiser never cooperated with him or *Richmond*, S.E. Morison aptly commented that *Salt Lake City* would soon unexpectedly become the 'sword, shield and buckler' for the entire team.[19]

Table 14: Organisation of TG-16.6 during the battle of the Komandorski Islands, 27 March 1943

Task Group 16.6 ("Mike"), commander: Rear Admiral Charles McMorris
heavy cruiser *Salt Lake City*
light cruiser *Richmond* (flagship)
14. Destroyer Division, Captain Ralph Riggs
destroyers *Coghlan, Bailey, Dale, Monaghan*

As planned, at 0945 hours on 22 March, *Salt Lake City* and her escorts joined Rear Admiral McMorris' group on patrol southwest of Attu. On 23 March, Rear Admiral Kinkaid moved his headquarters to Adak to better oversee naval operations in the western Aleutian Islands. By 25 March, TG-16.6 still had no detailed information about the enemy convoy, but in the afternoon, it established radar contact with one unidentified aircraft at 22 miles. After five minutes, contact with the machine was lost, which disappeared on a course of 290 degrees. On this day, however, Rear Admiral McMorris had more severe concerns as while heading west, his task force faced a storm that damaged *Salt Lake City*'s catapult and carried away starboard life rafts. The high waves of the frosty North Pacific were not only dangerous for the vessels. They also posed a deadly threat

to crew members who performed their duties despite adversities. This is how George O'Connell described his experiences:

> I put on long-handled underwear, jungle-cloth clothing, an aviation arctic suit [which consisted] of a zippered, fur-lined jacket, a pair of high-suspendered, fur-lined leather trousers which zippered up the sides, a pair of fur-lined leather flight boots, and a fur-lined leather helmet. Over all this, I wore a waterproofed, canvas foul weather parka suit. Heaven help anyone so clothed who might lose his footing, because he would probably require someone else to help him get back on his feet.[20]

The waters of the North Pacific were so rough that day that some of the crew members who had been serving on *Salt Lake City* for several years recalled that they did not remember a more dangerous storm. Some of them confessed that they had already accepted their fate. The Americans, however, avoided tragedy and the following day greeted them with an exceptionally calm sea, allowing the task force to replenish fuel supplies on *Bailey* and *Coghlan* partially. In addition, *Salt Lake City* provided additional rations and supplies to the destroyers: bread, sugar, eggs, sweets, cigarettes and, ironically, containers of ice cream. The refuelling of *Dale* and *Monaghan* was initially scheduled for 29 March, but its execution was questioned. Late in the afternoon, Rear Admiral McMorris received a cable from CINCPAC warning him that the Japanese convoy comprising six ships was approaching Attu. For over two hours, TG-16.6 had been on a south-westerly course with an average speed of 15 knots and thus, contact with the enemy could be expected in less than 24 hours. The American group proceeded in a line formation with six miles between individual vessels. The order of the ships was as follows: *Coghlan, Richmond, Bailey, Dale, Salt Lake City* and *Monaghan*. Just before midnight on 27 March, Rear Admiral McMorris ordered to execute the plan to intercept an enemy convoy west of Attu. Calm sea, moderate wind and expected visibility of up to 12 miles promised excellent conditions for a naval artillery engagement.[21]

5
COMPARISON OF THE JAPANESE CONVOY AND US NAVY TASK FORCES

米海軍任務部隊と日本海軍の船団の比較
Beikaigun Ninmu Butai to Nippon Kaigun no Sendan no Hikaku

This chapter contains a brief technical description of the Japanese and American warships that participated in the battle of the Komandorski Islands. Besides presenting commanders, this part of the book focuses on comparing the combat potential of both task forces.

Nippon Kaigun warships
Nachi (那智)

One of the four Myōkō-class heavy cruisers approved in the 1923 Naval Expansion Plan following the ratification of the Washington Treaty by the Empire of Japan. She was named after Mount Nachi located in Wakayama Prefecture. The ship was laid down at the naval shipyard in Kure on 26 November 1924. After being launched on 15 June 1927, she was armed and commissioned on 26 November 1928. The construction cost was 21.9 million yen. The ship underwent last modernisation before the battle of the Komandorski Islands in February 1943. Her skipper was Captain Sone Akira.

The heavy cruiser *Nachi*. (NDL)

Operational History of *Nachi*

At the time of the attack on Pearl Harbor, the cruiser was the flagship of the 5th Cruiser Squadron, the Third Fleet. The squadron commander, Rear Admiral Takagi Takeo, was ordered to set off from Palau and screen the invasion forces taking part in the Philippines campaign. On 11 December, after the successful landing at Legazpi, *Nachi* and *Myōkō* returned to Palau, where Rear Admiral Tanaka Raizō took over command of the cruisers and transferred his flag to *Myōkō*. On 19 and 24 December, both vessels screened the invasion forces of Davao and the Jolo Islands. On 4 January 1942, American bombers raided Davao and damaged *Myōkō*, causing Tanaka to transfer the flag to *Nachi*. Until the end of January and early February, the cruiser took part in the landings on Sulawesi and Ambon. On 27 February, she participated in the victorious battle of the Java Sea. The seaplane from *Nachi* located the Allied task force and helped Japanese gunners to hit targets. Two days later, cooperating with other Japanese ships, she intercepted the escaping British cruiser *Exeter*, accompanied by destroyers *Encounter* and *Pope*.

On 17 March, *Nachi* arrived in Sasebo. She was temporarily detached from the 5th Cruiser Squadron and modernised to prepare the vessel for operations in the Bering Sea. She was on patrol duty in the waters surrounding the Kuril Islands for most of April and May. On 26 May, she became the flagship of the Northern Forces under Vice Admiral Hosogaya and set off for the Aleutian Islands invasion operation. After completing the landing, the cruiser remained at Attu. She additionally performed patrol duties against American submarines. At the end of June, *Nachi* returned to Japan and was modernised at the naval shipyard in Yokosuka in the second half of July. At that time, she was assigned to the 21st Cruiser Squadron, the Fifth Fleet, along with *Kiso* and *Tama*. From August 1942 until March 1943, *Nachi* moved between various bases in Northern Japan and the Kuriles, except for two weeks in February, when routine maintenance and modernisation work was carried out at Sasebo.

Table 15: Technical specification of *Nachi*	
Displacement	13,300 long tons
Length and beam	203.76/20.73 metres (after the modernisation in 1940)
Armour	main belt – 100mm upper deck – 37mm turrets – 25mm barbettes – 75mm
Propulsion and power	4 × geared steam turbines 12 × boilers 4 × shafts 130,000shp
Max speed and range	33.3 knots/9,000 miles at 14 knots
Armament	5 x 2 20cm (203mm)/50 Type 3 No. 2 (turret Mod. "D") guns 4 x 2 127mm/40 Type 89 guns 4 x 2 25mm/60 Type 96 anti-aircraft guns 4 x 4 610mm Type 92 Mod. 1 (24 torpedoes Type 93 Mod. 1) torpedo tubes
Aircraft carried and aerial equipment	3 seaplanes 2 catapults Type Kure Nr 2 Mod. 5 mounted on the upper deck, on the starboard and port sides, above the torpedo magazine 1 x crane
Radars	none – before the battle, a stand for the future radar equipment was installed on the cruiser
Complement	920

Maya (摩耶)

One of the four Takao-class heavy cruisers approved in the 1927 Naval Expansion Plan. It was named after Mount Maya, located in Hyōgō Prefecture. She was laid down at the Kawasaki Naval Shipyard in Kobe on 4 December 1928. After being launched on 8 November 1930, she was armed and commissioned on 30 June 1932. The construction cost was 21.9 million yen. The ship underwent last modernisation before the battle of the Komandorski Islands from 12 to 16 February 1943. Her skipper was Captain Takeshi Matsumoto.

Operational History of *Maya*

At the time of the attack on Pearl Harbor, Maya was part of the 4th Cruiser Squadron stationed at the Pescadores. Initially in reserve, on 8 December, she set off to support the landings in Vigan and Lingayen Gulf, together with *Ashigara* and *Kuma*. At the end of the year, the cruiser was assigned to cover the capture of the Natuna Islands and then to screen the *Kidō Butai* during the raid on Darwin. The end of the month was marked with the Combined Fleet order to pursue and sink Allied vessels trying to escape from the Dutch East Indies. Operating from Staring Bay, on 4 March, *Maya*, *Atago* and *Takao*, destroyed a convoy set out from Tjilatjap. After returning to Japan on 18 March, the ship was sent to the naval shipyard in Yokosuka, where her anti-aircraft armament was modernised. The surprise Doolittle Raid on Tokyo forced the Combined Fleet to assign the cruiser to pursue the enemy carriers, but she was soon withdrawn to the home islands.

In early June, *Maya* and *Takao* participated in Operation AL, supporting the landings on Attu and Kiska. During reconnaissance flights over the Aleutian Islands, *Maya* lost one seaplane and the other was seriously damaged. On 24 June, the ship returned to Japan, and the Combined Fleet ordered her to join the Guadalcanal campaign less than two months later. Since *Maya* departed from Truk on 11 August, she did not make it in time to witness the battle of the Eastern Solomons. On 15 October, with *Myōkō* and *Isuzu*, she took part in the bombardment of Henderson Field and then, at the end of the month, in the battle of the Santa Cruz Islands. On 14 November, again as a part of the bombardment force, she shelled Henderson Field. During the return route, the cruiser was narrowly missed by torpedoes fired by the American submarine *Flying Fish*. On the same day, *Maya* was attacked by dive bombers from *Enterprise*, which scored one near miss close to the stern. One of the American planes also snagged its wing on the main mast and then crashed into the ship's port side, setting some of the shells on fire and killing 37 men. The crew was forced to jettison the torpedoes, but *Maya* eventually returned safely to Shortland. On 8 December, it was decided in Kavieng to withdraw her to Japan. On 5 January 1943, she docked at Yokosuka and remained in repairs for the next two weeks. On 30 January, the cruiser was assigned to the Fifth Fleet and left Yokosuka on 20 February. After a short stay in Ōminato, Maya set course for Paramushiru.

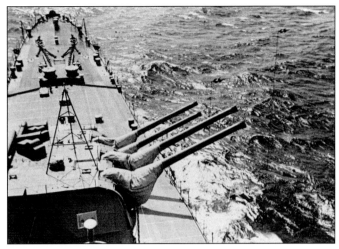

The heavy cruiser *Maya*. (NDL)

Table 16: Technical specification of *Maya*	
Displacement	9,690 long tons
Length and beam	203.76/19 metres
Armour	main belt – 102mm sides of ammunition magazine – 127mm upper deck – 25–35mm turrets – 25mm barbettes – 75mm
Propulsion and power	12 × boilers 4 × shafts 130,000shp
Max speed and range	35.5 knots/8,000 miles at 14 knots
Armament	5 x 2 20cm (203mm)/50 Type 3 No. 2 (turret Mod. "E_1") guns 4 x 1 120mm/45 Type 10 anti-aircraft guns 2 x 2 25mm/60 Type 96 anti-aircraft guns 2 x 4 13mm Type 93 machine guns 4 x 2 610mm Type 90 torpedo tubes (24 torpedoes Type 93 Mod. 1)
Aircraft carried and aerial equipment	3 seaplanes (none during the battle) 2 catapults Type Kure No. 2 Mod. 5, mounted on the upper deck, on the starboard and port sides, between main mast and turret No 4 1 x crane
Complement	996 (planned)

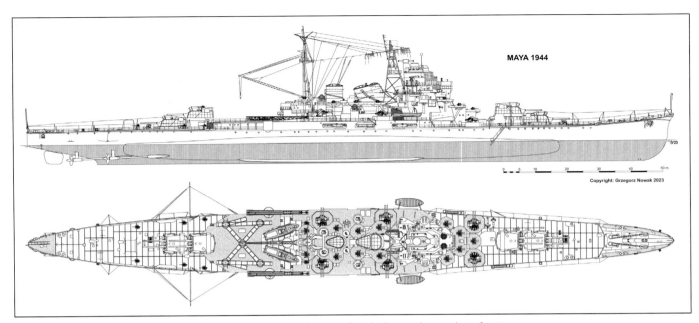

A line drawing of the Japanese heavy cruiser *Maya* as it appeared in 1944, by which time the number of anti-aircraft guns had been significantly increased. (Drawing by Grzegorz Nowak)

Tama (多摩)

One of five Kuma-class light cruisers approved in the '8-4' Fleet Expansion Plan from 1917. She was named after the Tama River, which flows through the Kantō Plain and the capital city of Tokyo. Tama was laid down at the Mitsubishi Naval Shipyard in Nagasaki on 10 August 1918. After launching on 10 February 1920, she was armed and commissioned on 29 January 1921. The ship underwent last modernisation before the battle of the Komandorski Islands from 9 January to 6 February 1943. Her skipper was Captain Kanome Zensuke.

The light cruiser *Tama*. (NDL)

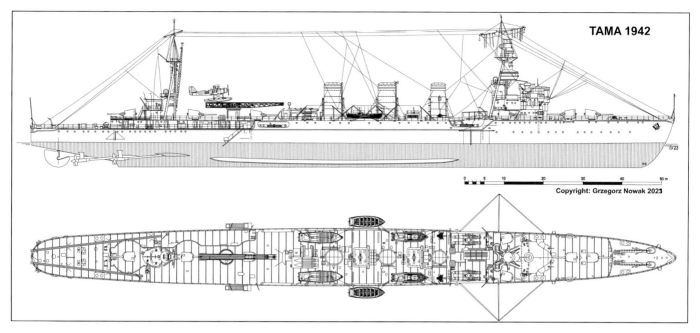

The light cruiser *Tama* as it appeared in 1942. (Drawing by Grzegorz Nowak)

Table 17: Technical specification of *Tama*	
Displacement	5,100 long tons
Length and beam	162.15/14.17 metres
Armour	main belt – up to 64mm upper deck– up to 29mm
Propulsion and power	12 × boilers 4 × steam turbines (Gihon) 4 x shafts 91,377shp
Max speed and range	35.5 knots/5,300 miles at 14 knots
Armament	7 x 1 14cm (140mm)/50 Type 3 guns 2 x 2 25mm/60 Type 96 anti-aircraft guns 4 x 2 533mm Type 6 torpedo tubes (16 torpedoes Type 6) 48 x naval mines
Aircraft carried and aerial equipment	1 seaplane (none during the battle) 1 catapult Type Kure No. 2 Mod. 3, mounted on the upper deck, between turrets No 5 and 6 1 x crane
Complement	450

Table 18: Technical specification of *Abukuma*	
Displacement	5,570 long tons
Length and beam	162.15/14.17 metres
Armour	main belt – up to 63mm upper deck– up to 29mm
Propulsion and power	12 × boilers 4 × steam turbines (Gihon) 4 x shafts 90,000shp
Max speed and range	36 knots/6,000 miles at 14 knots
Armament	6 x 1 14cm (140mm)/50 Type 3 guns 2 x 3 25mm/60 Type 96 anti-aircraft guns 1 x 2 13.2mm/76 machine guns 2 x 4 610mm Type 92 Mod. 1 torpedo tubes (16 torpedoes Type 93 Mod. 1) 48 x naval mines
Aircraft carried and aerial equipment	1 seaplane (none during the battle) 1 catapult Type Kure No. 2 Mod. 3, mounted on the upper deck, near turret No 6 1 x crane
Complement	438

Abukuma (阿武隈)

One of six Nagara-class light cruisers approved in the 1918 '8-6' Fleet Expansion Plan. She was named after the Abukuma River, which flows through the Tōhoku region. *Abukuma* was laid down at the Uraga Naval Shipyard in Yokosuka on 8 December 1921. After being launched on 16 March 1923, she was armed and commissioned on 26 May 1925. On 12 December 1942, the cruiser entered the dry dock at the Sasebo Naval Shipyard to undergo modernisation of main and anti-aircraft artillery. By January 1943, *Abukuma* returned to the patrols in the Northern Pacific, cooperating with other vessels from the Fifth Fleet in the defence of Attu and Kiska. *Her* skipper was Captain Shibuya Shirō.

The light cruiser *Abukuma*. (NDL)

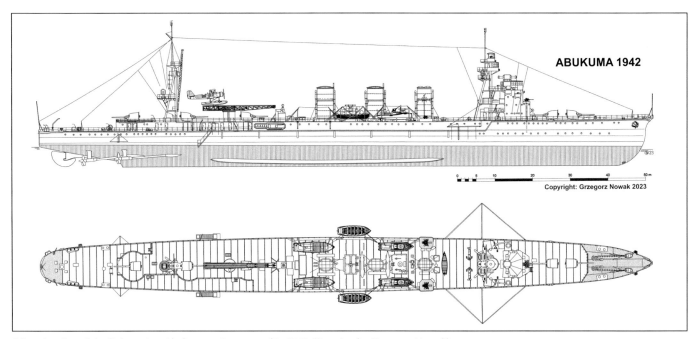

A line drawing of the light cruiser *Abukuma* as it appeared in 1942. (Drawing by Grzegorz Nowak)

Wakaba (若葉)

One of six Hatsuharu-class destroyers approved in the 'Maru 1' Fleet Expansion Plan from 1931. Its name in Japanese means 'young green leaf'. The ship was laid down at the naval shipyard in Sasebo on 12 December 1931. After being launched on 18 March 1934, she was armed and commissioned on 31 October 1934. The ship underwent last modernisation before the battle of the Komandorski Islands at the end of 1942. Her skipper was Commander Iritomo Atsuo.

Hatsushimo (初霜)

Next of six Hatsuharu-class destroyers. Its name in Japanese means 'first frost'. The ship was laid down at the Uraga Naval Shipyard in Yokosuka on 31 January 1933. After being launched on 4 November 1933, she was armed and commissioned on 27 June 1934. The ship underwent last modernisation before the battle of the Komandorski Islands at the end of 1942. Her skipper was Commander Kuroki Masakichi.

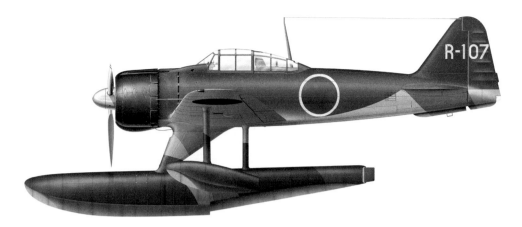

Based on the A6M-2 Type 0 Model 11 and referred to as the *Suisen 2* (Hydro Fighter Type 2), the Nakajima A6M2-N, known by the Allied codename Rufe, was a float-equipped variant of the famous Zero fighter. Six examples of this, the most important Japanese aircraft type during the Aleutians campaign, were delivered to Kiska by the seaplane tender *Chiyoda* and were involved in the campaign from 5 July 1942. Exactly as envisaged, it was primarily tasked with supporting amphibious operations and the air defence of remote bases. In the Aleutians, these aircraft provided air defence to the Attu and Kiska garrisons against American bomber attacks. (Artwork by Jean-Marie Guillou)

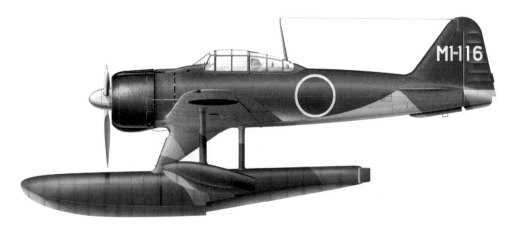

The first unit operating *Suisen 2*s in the Aleutians was the *5th Kōkūtai*. The first six Rufes to reach the Aleutians in July 1942 were painted in *Amee-Iro* (grey-green) overall and wore black and red codes on the fin, prefixed with the letter R. In August 1942, the unit was brought to its full strength through the addition of six Rufes. While retaining codes prefixed with R (as shown in the first artwork) these were the first to be painted in a dark green camouflage colour on upper surfaces in sides. In November 1942, the *5th Kōkūtai* was reorganised as the *452nd Kōkūtai* and reinforced with six additional Rufes. Painted in dark green on upper surfaces and sides, these received codes prefixed with M1, as shown here. (Artwork by Jean-Marie Guillou)

In addition to *Suisen 2*s, the *5th Kōkūtai* also operated Aichi E13A Jake reconnaissance seaplanes during the Aleutian campaign. While their primary task was reconnaissance, they also flew air strikes on US positions. Although these had very limited effects, the Imperial Japanese Navy continued reinforcing the *5th Kōkūtai* with additional Jakes through August (when the aircraft illustrated here arrived at Kiska) and also in November, when the unit was reorganised into the *452nd Kōkūtai*. (Artwork by Jean-Marie Guillou)

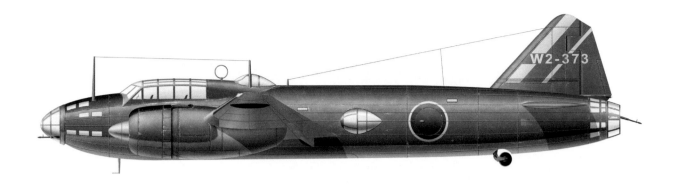

The Mitsubishi G4M, also known by the Allied codename Betty, was the primary Japanese land-based Navy bomber. The Japanese Navy command considered allocating one bomber unit to the Aleutians to harass the American positions in Adak and Amchitka. Obviously, the use of bombers depended on the availability of suitable airfields, and with none available at Kiska and Attu in May 1943 it fell to G4M1s of the *752nd Kōkūtai*, based at Kurabu on Paramushir (Paramushiru-tō) in the northern Kuril islands, to try attacking US Navy warships in the Aleutians. Both such attempts were, however, frustrated by bad weather. (Artwork by Jean-Marie Guillou)

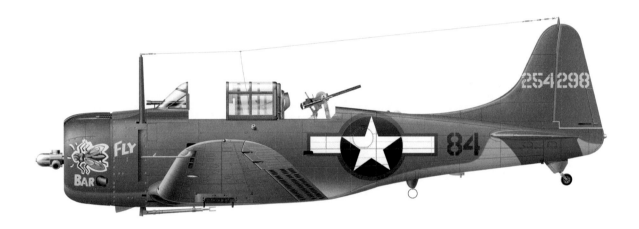

In summer 1943, the USAAF deployed Douglas A-24B Banshees – the Army-operated version of the famous Douglas SBD Dauntless – of the 407th Bombardment Group to the island of Amchitka. Gauging by available photographs, none of these was equipped with radar but, for operations from the slippery Aleutian airstrips, all had block-tread tires. While it is not entirely certain that this specific aircraft was deployed to Amchitka, the aircraft with serial number 42-54298 of the 407th Group is known to have been nicknamed the 'Bar Fly'. (Artwork by Jean-Marie Guillou)

The Consolidated B-24 Liberator, one of the Second World War's most famous American heavy bombers, was brand new to service in 1941 and proved a good, longer-ranged alternative to the Boeing B-17 Flying Fortress. Radar-equipped B-24Ds of the 21st Bombardment Squadron were deployed to Adak from late 1942 and flew regular air strikes against Kiska and Attu. Like most USAAF aircraft of 1942–43, it was painted in olive drab on upper surfaces and sides, and neutral grey on undersurfaces, usually with sharp delineation between the two colours. In addition to national markings, all aircraft wore the service title 'U. S. Army' on the bottom surfaces of the wing. (Artwork by Jean-Marie Guillou)

The North American B-25 Mitchell was one of the most famous medium bombers of the US Army Air Force in the Second World War. This radar-equipped B-25C or B-25D (note the Yagi-antenna installed low on the nose) was operated by the 77th Bombardment Group from Adak in autumn 1942. As far as weather permitted, they regularly harassed the Japanese positions on Kiska and Attu. (Artwork by Jean-Marie Guillou)

By mid-1943, the 77th Bombardment Group was partially re-equipped with B-25Gs (shown here is serial number 42-64754, coded 54). This variant featured improved armour for the cockpit, bigger internal fuel capacity and had a 75mm M4 cannon installed low on the left side of the nose (the muzzle is visible recessed a little below the position of the nose-mounted machine guns); one of the largest weapons ever fitted into an aircraft. The breach of this weapon was installed in the new navigator's position, moved from the nose (covered by glass on earlier variants) to behind the pilot: the weapon was manually operated by the navigator, who had to signal to the pilot whenever the weapon was ready. The pilot fired using a button on his control wheel. (Artwork by Jean-Marie Guillou)

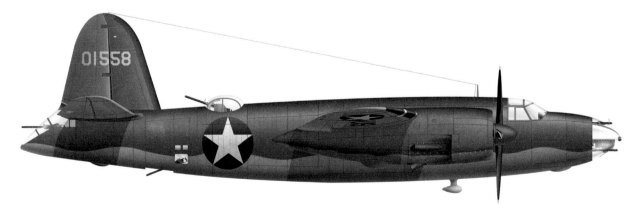

Introduced to service in 1941, the Martin B-26 Marauder earned itself a dubious reputation as a 'widow maker' due to its early accident rate. By 1942 it was improved enough to be deployed in combat by the 73rd Bombardment Squadron, 28th Bombardment Group during the Aleutians campaign. Operating from Cold Bay, on 4 June 1942, one of the squadron's aircraft is known to have narrowly missed the aircraft carrier *Ryujo*: released at much too high speed, a bomb ricocheted from the sea surface, flashed over the deck and crashed into the ocean on the other side without exploding. The example illustrated here had the serial number 40-1558. (Artwork by Jean-Marie Guillou)

The Lockheed P-38 Lightning was one of the first fighters of the US Army Air Force to see combat during the Aleutian campaign. Equipped with P-38Es and F-5-As (the photoreconnaissance version), the 54th Fighter Squadron was deployed at Adak (September 1942 – February 1943), Amchitka (March – October 1943), and Attu (Alexai Point, November 1943 – March 1946). Other than the F-5-As, 54th Squadron's Lightnings were marked by a yellow nose, and wore two-digit codes applied in white or yellow, in the 60–90s range. Several had nicknames painted in yellow, low on the side of the nose section. As of May 1943, the aircraft depicted here, serial number 41-2252, nicknamed 'Lorna D', was flown by Lieutenant Colonel John K Geddes. (Artwork by Jean-Marie Guillou)

The most numerous USAAF fighter of 1942 was the Bell P-39 Airacobra. In the Aleutians in that year, they were operated by the 54th Fighter Group from an airfield bulldozed at Kukuk Bay on the barren island of Adak. P-39Fs like this example (serial number 41-7241) began attacking Japanese invasion forces on Attu and Kiska immediately upon their arrival in June 1942. However, Airacobras were troubled by their inability to fly high, their relatively short range and – even more so – by poor weather. Low clouds, mist, fog, driving rain, snow, and high winds made flying extremely dangerous and caused more losses than the enemy forces. The 54th remained in Alaska until November 1942, when it was returned to the USA. (Artwork by Jean-Marie Guillou)

Curtiss P-40E Warhawk fighters of the 11th Fighter Squadron (343rd Fighter Group) were probably the most decorated US fighters of the Second World War, and earned the unit the nickname 'Aleutian Tigers'. This example – probably serial 40-610, coded 20 and presumably nicknamed 'Julia' – was operated from Otter Point in summer 1943. In addition to white identification stripes applied prior to arrival in the Aleutians, in July 1942 11th Squadron's aircraft present at Umak had tiger head artworks and spinners painted in yellow. (Artwork by Jean-Marie Guillou)

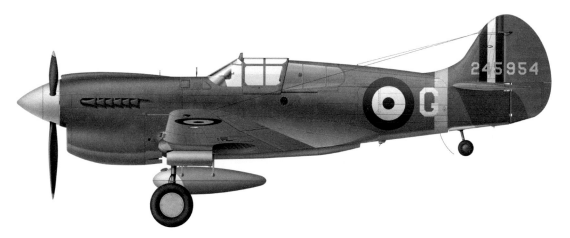

In September 1942, No. 111 Squadron Royal Canadian Air Force was deployed at Adak Island for forward operations through the winter and summer of 1943. The unit was equipped with ex-USAAF P-40Es and P-40Ks (the other RCAF unit involved in the Aleutians campaign, No. 14 Squadron, flew ex-USAAF P-40Ks only). Unlike USAAF-operated examples, they were painted in 'Commonwealth camo', consisting of Dupont dark earth and medium green on upper surfaces and sides, and wore large single-letter codes usually applied in white or grey. This was the P-40K serial number 42-45951/A, operated by No. 111 Squadron from Amchitka as of April 1943. (Artwork by Jean-Marie Guillou)

By spring 1943, 18th Fighter Squadron (343rd Fighter Group) at Amchitka included several P-40Ks wearing the Commonwealth camouflage – in addition to white stripes down and across the fin. Notable on this example is the application of red superimposed on the national insignia. The measure proved not particularly successful and was eventually abandoned: the red was overpainted in dark blue, resulting in the typical US national 'Star and Bars' national insignia in use ever since. (Artwork by Jean-Marie Guillou)

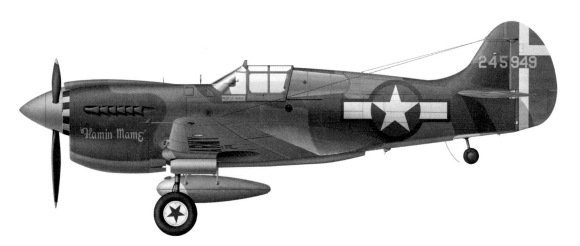

As of autumn 1943, the Amchitka-based 18th Fighter Squadron (343rd Fighter Group) was still flying P-40Ks wearing the Commonwealth camouflage – although many aircraft also had replacement panels in 'fresh' olive drab, and/or medium green patches, or entire (replacement) rudders in olive drab with blotches in medium green (as common on USAAF aircraft of 1942-43). The aircraft with serial number 42-45949 and the nickname 'Flaming Mame', shown here, wears the final version of the 'Star and Bars' national insignia. (Artwork by Jean-Marie Guillou)

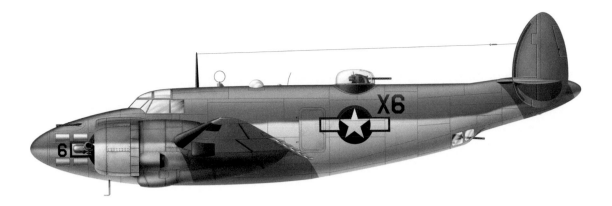

The Lockheed PV-1 Ventura medium bomber entered service with the US Navy in 1941, and the first unit equipped with them – VB-136 - reached the Aleutians in April of the same year. The aircraft coded X6 is known to have continued serving from Adak island well into 1943, when it was assigned to Lieutenant R. R. Lawson. (Artwork by Jean-Marie Guillou)

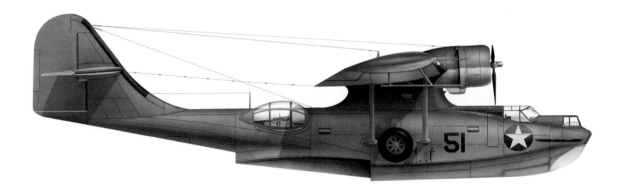

Radar-equipped Consolidated PBY-5A Catalina reconnaissance amphibians and patrol bombers of Patrol Wing 4 were transferred to the Aleutians by seaplane tenders like USS *Casco* (AVP-12) and USS *Teal* (AVP-5). Forward deployed on different islands, they were frequently paired with destroyers of the US Navy to find and attack Japanese submarines resupplying Attu and Kiska. This aircraft is shown wearing the national insignia as applied between May 1942 and June 1943. (Artwork by Jean-Marie Guillou)

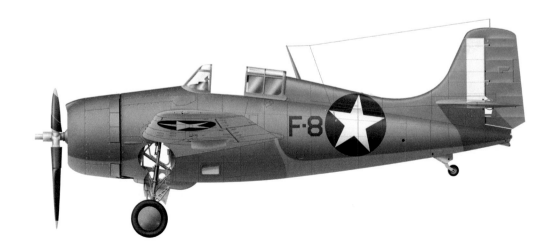

VMO-155 was originally a Marine Observation Squadron, flying Curtiss SBC Helldiver biplane dive bombers and Grumman J2F-5 Duck amphibious biplanes. In December 1942, the majority of the unit was sent to Guadalcanal where it was assigned as replacements: a cadre of six officers and 15 enlisted men was retained to create a new unit at Camp Kearny in San Diego. In early 1943, they began training on Grumman F4F-3P Wildcat fighters designed for photographic reconnaissance but as soon as the unit was ready it embarked the USS *Nassau* (CVE-16) for participation in the counter-invasion of Attu, conducted from 11-20 May 1943. This made the unit the first Marine squadron to operate from an aircraft carrier in the Second World War, and the only Marine unit involved in the Aleutians campaign. (Artwork by Jean-Marie Guillou)

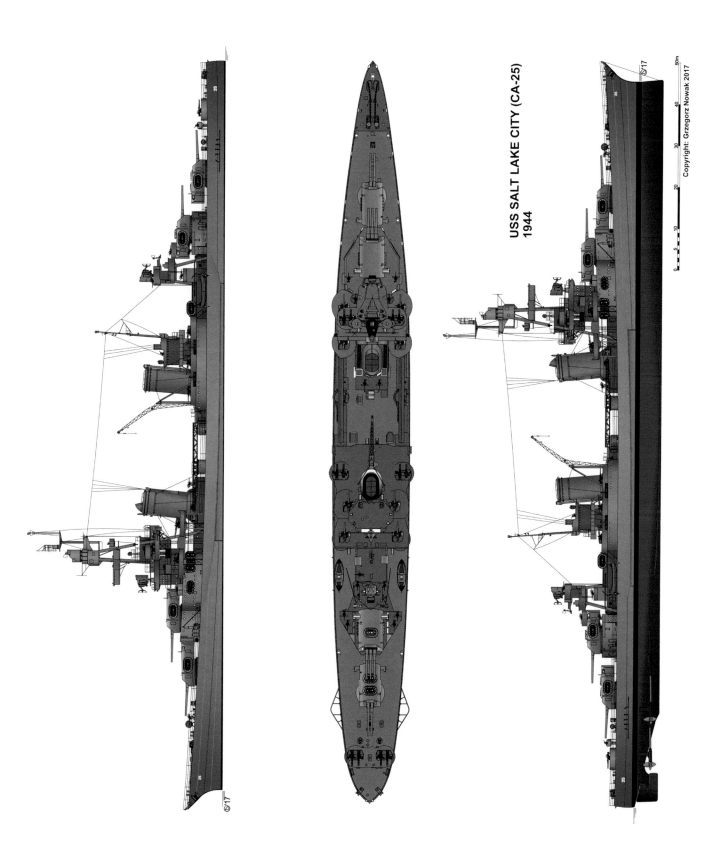

USS SALT LAKE CITY (CA-25)
1944

Copyright: Grzegorz Nowak 2017

USS *Salt Lake City* (CL/CA-25) was a heavy cruiser of the Pensacola-class, launched on 23 January 1929 at the Philadelphia Navy Yard, and commissioned on 11 December of the same year. Assigned to the Pacific Fleet, she was with the aircraft carrier USS *Enterprise* (CV-6) during the Japanese attack against Pearl Harbour on 7 December 1941. The cruiser continued serving with that carrier throughout the Doolittle Raid on Japan and the Battle of Midway, but then escorted USS *Wasp* (CV-7) during the campaign to seize Guadalcanal. After being lightly damaged during the Battle of Cape Esperance, USS *Salt Lake City* spent four months undergoing repairs at Pearl Harbour, before departing for the Aleutians, where it became involved in the Battle of the Komandorski Islands on 26 March 1943. Badly damaged and left dead in the water, the ship was saved by a dense smoke screen and vigorous support from escorting destroyers. Following repairs, USS *Salt Lake City* covered the liberation of Attu and Kiska before continuing her distinguished service for the rest of the Pacific Campaign. The ship was deactivated in October 1945 and used as a target hull for atomic bomb tests in 1948. (Artworks by Grzegorz Nowak)

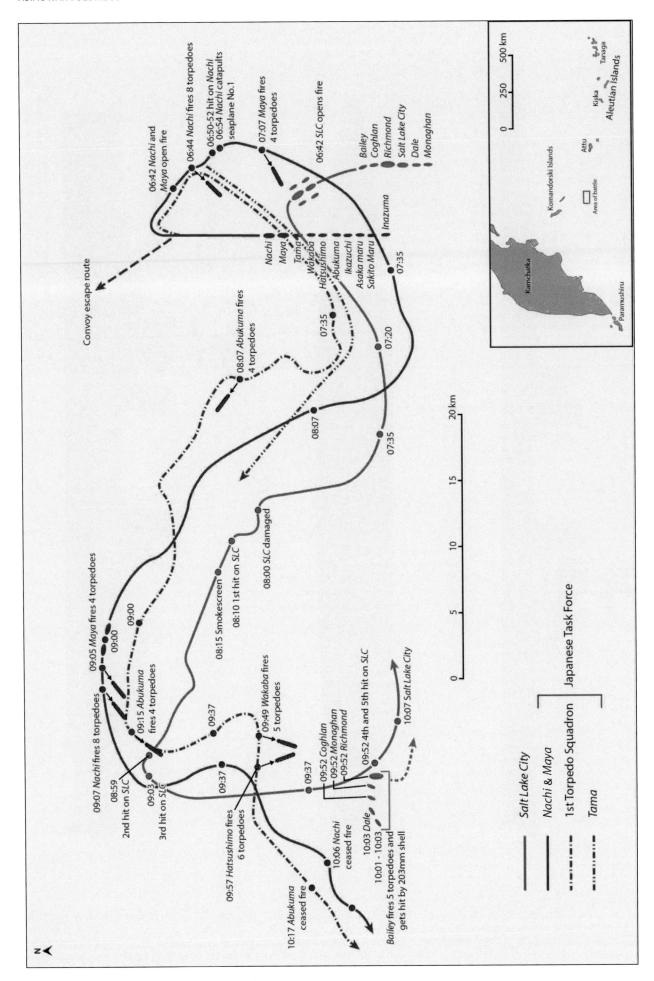

Battle of the Komandorski Islands, 27 March 1943
(Map drawn by George Anderson)

The destroyer *Wakaba*. (NDL)

Table 19: Technical specification of *Wakaba* and *Hatsushimo*	
Displacement	1,802 long tons
Length and beam	109.5/10 metres
Propulsion and power	3 x boilers 2 x shaft geared turbines (Kampon) 2 x turbines 42,000shp
Max speed and range	33.3 knots/4,000 miles at 14 knots
Armament	2 x 1 and 1 x 1 127mm/50 Type 3 guns 2 x 2 25mm/60 Type 96 anti-aircraft guns 3 x 3 610mm Type 90 torpedo tubes 2 x depth charge launchers (36 bombs)
Complement	205

Table 20: Technical specification of *Usugumo*	
Displacement	1,750 long tons
Length and beam	118/10.36 metres
Propulsion and power	4 × boilers (Kampon) 2 × Type Ro geared turbines (Kampon) 2 × shafts 50,000shp
Max speed and range	34 knots/5,000 miles at 14 knots
Armament	3 x 2 127mm/50 Type 3 guns 2 x 2 25mm/60 Type 96 anti-aircraft guns 3 x 3 610mm Type 90 torpedo tubes 4 x depth charge launchers (36 bombs and 18 min naval mines)
Complement	219

Usugumo (薄雲)

One of 24 Fubuki-class destroyers, approved in the Fleet Expansion Plan from 1923 (first five vessels), extended in subsequent years. Its name in Japanese means 'slightly cloudy'. The ship was laid down at the Fujinagata Naval Shipyard in Osaka on 7 March 1930. After being launched on 25 February 1932, she was armed and commissioned on 15 November 1932. The ship underwent last modernisation before the battle of the Komandorski Islands in February 1943. Her skipper was Lieutenant Commander Ikeda Shunsaku.

Ikazuchi (雷)

The next Fubuki-class destroyer, belonging to the *Akatsuki* subclass. Its name means 'thunderbolt' in Japanese. The ship was laid down at the Uraga Naval Shipyard in Yokosuka on 7 March 1930. After being launched on 22 October 1931, she was armed and commissioned on 15 August 1932. The ship underwent last modernisation before the battle of the Komandorski Islands in January–February 1943. Her skipper was Lieutenant Commander Maeda Saneho.

Inazuma (電)

Another Fubuki-class destroyer, belonging to the Akatsuki subclass. Its name means 'lightning' in Japanese. The ship was laid down at the Fujinagata Naval Shipyard in Osaka on 7 March 1930. After launching on 25 February 1932, she was armed and commissioned on 15 November 1932. The ship underwent last modernisation before the battle of the Komandorski Islands in January 1943. Her skipper was Lieutenant Commander Terauchi Masamichi.

The destroyer *Inazuma*. (NDL)

Table 21: Technical specification of *Ikazuchi* and *Inazuma*	
Displacement	1,750 long tons
Length and beam	108/10.36 metres
Propulsion and power	4 × boilers (Kampon)
	2 × Type Ro geared turbines (Kampon)
	2 × shafts
	50,000shp
Max speed and range	34 knots/5,000 miles at 14 knots
Armament	3 x 2 127mm/50 Type 3 guns
	1 x 2 25mm/60 Type 96 anti-aircraft guns
	3 x 3 610mm Type 90 torpedo tubes
	4 x depth charge launchers (36 bombs and 18 naval mines)
Complement	219

Asaka Maru (浅香丸)

A 7,399-ton refrigerated cargo ship ordered by Nippon Yūsen, which was laid down on 18 February 1937 at the Mitsubishi Naval Shipyard in Nagasaki. After being launched on 7 July 1937, she was commissioned on 30 November 1937. Her length was 147.75m and beam 19m. The ship's maximum speed was 19.2 knots, and she could reach up to 36,000 miles at an economic speed of 15 knots. The complement was 61 sailors and officers. Her load capacity was 2,500 tons.

On 10 April 1940, *Asaka Maru* was requisitioned by the *Nippon Kaigun* and was soon reclassified as an auxiliary cruiser, stationed at Yokosuka Naval Base. On 6 July, the ship was returned to the owner, but on 24 December it was again requisitioned by the Navy. Two days later, the reconstruction work began. On 15 January 1941, she returned to service as an auxiliary cruiser/army transport armed with two 120mm Type 11 guns and two twin 13mm Type 93 machine guns.

Sakito Maru (崎戸丸)

7,126-ton passenger ship/freighter ordered by Nippon Yūsen, which was laid down on 16 April 1938 at the Mitsubishi Naval Shipyard in Nagasaki. After being launched on 27 October 1938, she was commissioned on 29 January 1939. Her initial role was to operate on the route to New York. The length was 145 metres and beam 19 metres. The ship's maximum speed was 19.7 knots, and she could reach up to 37,000 miles at an economic speed of 16 knots. Her load capacity was 2,950 tons. On 3 December 1941, *Sakito Maru* was requisitioned by the Army and was soon reclassified as Army Transport No. 992. She participated in Malaya and Guadalcanal campaign. In early 1943, she was deployed to the North Pacific.

Sanko Maru (三興丸)

A 4,958-ton passenger ship/freighter, which was laid down in 1936 at the Osaka Ironworks Naval Shipyard in Hiroshima. After being launched on 29 May 1937, she was commissioned on 15 August 1937. On 27 October, *Sanko Maru* was requisitioned by the Army and reclassified as Army Transport No. 394. On 10 January 1939, the ship was returned to the owner, but on 14 October 1941, she was requisitioned by the Army again. During the first stage of the Pacific War, she transported about 350 prisoners of war from Manila to Palawan. Since *Sanko Maru* had engine of insufficient power, she was designated as a 'slow auxiliary transport'.

US Navy Warships
Salt Lake City (CA-25)

One of two Pensacola-class heavy cruisers that were supposed to meet the requirements of the Washington Treaty. It was named after the capital of the state of Utah. The ship was laid down at the New York Shipbuilding Corporation shipyard in New Jersey on 9 June 1927. After being launched on 23 January 1929, she was armed and commissioned on 11 December 1929. The ship underwent last modernisation before the battle of the Komandorski Islands in January–March 1943. Her skipper was Captain Bertram J. Rodgers.

The heavy cruiser *Salt Lake City*. (Source: NARA)

Table 22: Technical specification of *Salt Lake City*	
Displacement	9,100 long tons
Length and beam	178.46/19.89 metres
Armour	main belt – up to 102mm conning tower – 32mm turrets – 19–64mm barbettes – 19mm upper deck– 25–44mm
Propulsion and power	12 × White-Forster boilers 4 × Parsons reduction steam turbines 4 × screws 107,000shp
Max speed and range	32.7 knots/10,000 miles at 15 knots
Armament	2 x 3 and 2 x 2 8-inch (203mm/55) guns 8 x 5-inch (127mm/25) anti-aircraft guns 6 x 4 40mm Bofors anti-aircraft guns 20 x 20mm Oerlikon anti-aircraft guns
Aircraft carried and aerial equipment	4 x Vought OS2U Kingfisher seaplanes (2 x during the battle) 2 x amidship catapults 1 x crane
Radars	FC radar SG radar
Complement	1,250

Operational History of *Salt Lake City*

At the time of the attack on Pearl Harbor, *Salt Lake City* was with Vice Admiral Halsey's TF-8 on the way back from Wake. During the first week of the war, the cruiser conducted patrol missions against Japanese submarines off Hawaii and prepared to support the defenders of Wake. These plans were eventually abandoned on 23 December, and *Salt Lake City* was assigned to screen convoys to Midway and Samoa. In early February, she took part in the raid against the Marshall Islands, where she was attacked by two enemy bombers, which were shot down. Due to this successful sortie, subsequent air operations against the Japanese positions on Marcus Island were carried out in March. The following month, the cruiser participated in the Doolittle Raid. She was then deployed to the South Pacific to support the aircraft carriers *Yorktown* and *Lexington*. The ship did not make it in time to join Rear Admiral Frank Fletcher in the battle of the Coral Sea and was thus ordered to return to Pearl Harbor. *Salt Lake City* was on patrol duty in the Midway area in June, anticipating a major battle near the atoll. In August, the cruiser was assigned to escort the aircraft carrier *Wasp* during the landing on Guadalcanal. On 15 September, after the I-19's successful torpedo attack on *Wasp*, she assisted in rescuing the carrier's crew members. The moment of glory came on the night of 11–12 October, when *Salt Lake City*, as part of Rear Admiral Norman Scott's TF-64, intercepted the Tokyo Express in the battle of Cape Esperance. During the engagement, however, the cruiser received three direct hits. The damaged vessel was withdrawn to Espiritu Santo and then proceeded to Pearl Harbor for necessary repairs. In March 1943, the cruiser returned to service and was assigned to TF-8 to prevent the Japanese from delivering reinforcements and supplies to the Attu and Kiska garrisons.

Richmond (CL-9)

One of 10 Omaha-class light cruisers approved for the Fleet Expansion Plan during the First World War. She was named after the city of Richmond, Virginia. The ship was laid down at the William Cramp & Sons Naval Shipyard in Philadelphia on 16 February 1920. After being launched on 29 September 1921, she was armed and commissioned on 2 July 1923. *Richmond* underwent last modernisation before the battle of the Komandorski Islands in 1940. Her skipper was Captain Theodore Waldschmidt.

Coghlan (DD-606)

One of 30 Benson-class destroyers approved in the Fleet Expansion Plan from 1938. She was named after Joseph Coghlan, a US Navy Admiral, who lived at the turn of the nineteenth and twentieth centuries. The ship was laid down at the Bethlehem Shipbuilding Corporation Naval Shipyard in San Francisco on 28 March 1941. After being launched on 12 February 1942, she was armed and commissioned on 10 1942. Her skipper was Commander Benjamin Tompkins.

Table 23: Technical specification of *Richmond*	
Displacement	7,050 long tons
Length and beam	169.32/17 metres
Armour	main belt– up to 76mm upper deck – 38mm conning tower – up to 38mm bulkheads – 38–203 mm
Propulsion and power	12 × White-Forster boilers 4 × Parsons reduction steam turbines 4 × screws 90,000shp
Max speed and range	33.7 knots/10,000 miles at 15 knots
Armament	2 x 2 and 6 x 6-inch (150mm/53) guns 8 x 3-inch (76mm/50) anti-aircraft guns 4 x 40mm Bofors anti-aircraft guns 2 x 3 533mm torpedo tubes
Aircraft carried and aerial equipment	2 x Vought OS2U Kingfisher seaplanes 2 x amidship catapults 1 x crane
Radars	FC radar SG radar
Complement	823

The light cruiser *Richmond*. (NARA)

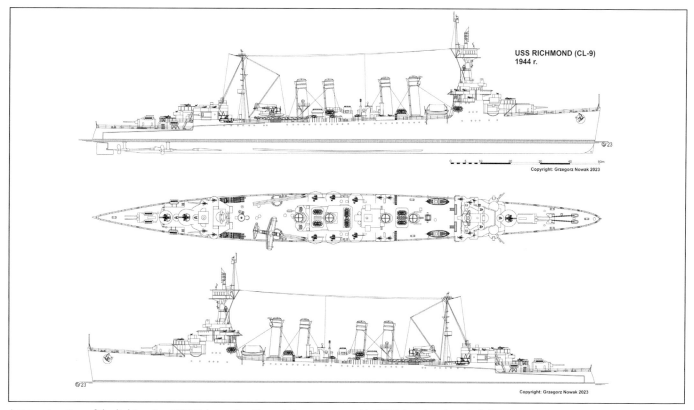

USS RICHMOND (CL-9)
1944 r.

Copyright: Grzegorz Nowak 2023

Copyright: Grzegorz Nowak 2023

A reconstruction of the light cruiser USS *Richmond*, as it would have appeared in 1944, by when her air defences were significantly bolstered through additional 20mm anti-aircraft guns. (Drawing by Grzegorz Nowak)

Bailey (DD-492)

The next Benson-class destroyer. She was named after Theodorus Bailey, a US Navy Admiral, who lived in the nineteenth century. The ship was laid down at the Bethlehem Mariners Harbor Naval Shipyard in New York on 29 January 1941. After being launched on 19 December 1941, she was armed and commissioned on 11 May 1942. Her skipper was Lieutenant Commander John Atkeson.

Table 24: Technical specification of *Coghlan* and *Bailey*	
Displacement	1,620 long tons
Length and beam	106.12/11 metres
Propulsion and power	4 x boilers (Babcock & Wilcox) 2 x steam geared turbines Bethlehem Steel (*Coghlan*)/ Westinghouse (*Bailey*) 50,000shp
Max speed and range	37.5 knots/5,000 miles at 15 knots (*Coghlan*) 37 knots/5,000 miles at 15 knots (*Bailey*)
Armament	4 x 5-inch Mark 12 (127mm/38) guns 2 x 2 40mm Bofors anti-aircraft guns 5 x 20mm Oerlikon anti-aircraft guns 5 x 533mm torpedo tubes 2 x depth charges launchers
Radars	FC radar SG radar
Complement	262 (*Coghlan*) 276 (*Bailey*)

Dale (DD-353)

One of eight Farragut-class destroyers approved in the Fleet Expansion Plan from 1918, which was then implemented in the following years. She was named after a US Navy officer, Richard Dale, who lived at the turn of the eighteenth and nineteenth centuries. The ship was laid down at the Brooklyn Navy Yard in New York on 10 February 1934. After being launched on 23 January 1935, she was armed and commission on 17 June 1935. Her skipper was Commander Anthony Rorschach.

Monaghan (DD-354)

The next Farragut-class destroyer, name after US Navy officer John R. Monaghan, who lived the nineteenth century. She was laid down at the Naval Shipyard in Boston on 21 November 1933. After being launched on 9 January 1935, she was armed and commissioned on 16 April 1935. Her skipper was Lieutenant Commander Peter Horn.

Table 25: Technical specification of *Dale* and *Monaghan*	
Displacement	1,500 long tons
Length and beam	104.01/10.44 metres
Propulsion and power	4 x boilers (Yarrow) 2 x steam geared turbines (Parsons) 42,800shp
Max speed and range	37 knots/5,000 miles at 15 knots
Armament	5 x 5-inch Mark 12 (127mm/38) guns 2 x 2 40mm Bofors anti-aircraft guns 5 x 20mm Oerlikon anti-aircraft guns 2 x 4 533mm torpedo tubes 2 x depth charge launchers
Radars	FC radar SG radar
Complement	160

The destroyer *Bailey*. (NARA)

The destroyer *Dale*. (NARA)

Commanders
Hosogaya Boshirō (細萓戊子郎)

Born on 24 June 1888 in Sakurai village (now the city of Saku) in Nagano Prefecture. On 21 October 1908, he graduated from the Imperial Japanese Naval Academy (*Kaigun Heigakkō*) sixteenth among 190 graduates of the thirty-sixth class. In 1910, he was promoted to lieutenant. In 1914, after graduating from the Torpedo School at the Imperial Japanese Naval Academy (*Kaigun Suirai Gakkō*), he served on the destroyer *Kaba*, and then became a staff officer of the so-called 'Special Task First Fleet' (*Dai 1 Tokumu Kantai*) and then adjutant at the Sasebo Naval District. In 1920, he graduated from the Officer Academy at the Naval War College (*Kaigun Daigakkō*) as one of 29 graduates of the eighteenth class. Within a short time, he was appointed a staff officer at the Naval General Staff and as a jury at the military court for the Kantō region. In 1924, he was promoted to the rank of Lieutenant Commander. In 1927, he was sent overseas to the United States and Europe for one year. He served as an Executive Officer on the light cruiser *Yūbari* and the battleship *Hyūga*. After being promoted to the rank of Commander, he became a skipper of the heavy cruiser *Chōkai* and, in 1934, the battleship *Mutsu*. On 15 November 1935, he was promoted to the rank of Rear Admiral, and then served as commander of the 5th Destroyer Squadron, Head of the Communications and Torpedo School, commander of the 4th Torpedo Squadron and the 1st Carrier Squadron. On 15 November 1939, he was promoted to the rank of Vice Admiral and took over as commander of the Ryojun Naval District. On 15 November 1940, he was appointed commander of the First China Area Expeditionary Fleet, and then, in connection with preparations for the Pacific War, became a commander of the Fifth Fleet based in Ōminato.

Hosogaya's task was to defend the so-called 'North Pacific Area' – waters around Hokkaido, Sakhalin and the Kuril Islands. In June 1942, he was responsible for executing Operation AL, which ended with the successful occupation of Attu and Kiska. Until March 1943, the remained in command of the Fifth Fleet, ordered to defend advanced positions in the Aleutian Islands at all costs. Due to obvious mistakes made during the battle of the Komandorski Islands, he was transferred to the reserve. Later, he held administrative functions, i.e. Governor of the South Pacific Mandate. He died on 8 February 1964.

Mori Tomokazu (森友一)

Born on 28 February 1893 in Ishikawa Prefecture, the son of the principal of a third-grade school and one of the high schools in Kyoto. On 19 November 1914, he graduated from the Imperial Japanese Naval Academy sixty-second among 117 graduates from the forty-second class. He completed an additional course at the Torpedo School, and then, after being promoted to the rank of Lieutenant, he subsequently was appointed a skipper of the destroyers *Ariake* and *Ashi*. He held staff positions in the 5th Cruiser Squadron and the Yokosuka Naval District for a short period. As a torpedo specialist, he became a torpedo officer on the battleship *Nagato* and then a lecturer at the Communications, Artillery and Torpedo Schools at the Imperial Naval Academy. Associated with various squadrons, in 1939, he was appointed a skipper of the seaplane tender *Kamoi*. After a few months, he was transferred to the light cruiser *Tama* and, after a year, to the heavy cruiser *Aoba*. At the outbreak of the Pacific War, he held the rank of Captain and was a skipper of the heavy cruiser *Haguro*. He participated in the battle of the Java Sea, where his good decisions contributed to the sinking of the British heavy cruiser *Exeter* and the Dutch destroyer *Kortenaer*. In the

following months, he took part in the battles of the Coral Sea and Midway. In November, he advanced in rank to Rear Admiral. At the same time, Mori took command of the 1st Torpedo Squadron to help provide supplies to the Attu and Kiska garrisons. During the battle of the Komandorski Islands he probably suffered from an intracranial bleed. In June 1943, after a sudden deterioration of his health, he was transferred to the Yokosuka Naval Shipyard as director of the experimental department of naval mines. Until the end of the war, he worked as a commander of a training unit at the Kure Naval District. He died on 23 January 1959.

Charles Horatio McMorris

Born on 31 August 1890 in Wetumpka, Alabama. After graduating high school on 26 June 1908, he entered the United States Naval Academy. He was classified fifth in his class, and on 8 June 1912, he received the rank of Ensign. He served on the battleships *Delaware*, *Montana* and *New Hampshire*. In 1914, he took part in the occupation of Veracruz as part of the American intervention in Mexico. Until 1918, he served on the destroyers *Shaw* and *Meredith*. In the last year of the First World War he was promoted to Lieutenant and he took command of his first ship, the destroyer *Walke*, a year later. In the interwar period, he advanced in rank to Lieutenant Commander in 1922 and Commander in 1931. In the meantime, McMorris held various positions until he graduated from the Naval War College in 1938. Shortly thereafter, he was promoted to Captain. From 1939 to 1941, he was an operations officer at the Honolulu Naval Base. In February 1941, he was assigned War Plans Officer on the staff of the Commander-in-Chief Pacific Fleet and soon earned the Legion of Merit for 'his special contribution to the development of the operational plan against the Empire of Japan.' From May to November 1942, he was a skipper of the heavy cruiser *San Francisco*. He screened the landing on Guadalcanal and participated in the battle of the Eastern Solomons and the battle of Cape Esperance. For his exceptional heroism in the night action against the Tokyo Express, McMorris received the Navy Cross. On 14 November, he was promoted to the rank of Rear Admiral, and a month later, he took command of TG-8.6. On 22 March 1943, he received a cable to intercept the Japanese convoy that set off from Paramushiru. This order led to the battle of the Komandorski Islands a few days later. In June, he assumed the position of Chief of Staff of the Pacific Fleet and, thus, became a personal aide to Admiral Chester Nimitz. McMorris held this position until the war's end and earned the Gold Star in lieu of a second Distinguished Service Medal. He remained in active service until 1948, first as commander of the Fourth Fleet, then as president of the General Board at the Navy Department, and finally, as commander of the Fourteenth Naval District at Pearl Harbor. After retiring, he settled in Marietta, Pennsylvania, where he died on 11 February 1954.

Summary

On the eve of the upcoming battle of the Komandorski Islands, the Japanese had an almost double numerical superiority over TG-16.6. Vice Admiral Hosogaya's impact potential relied on the heavy cruisers *Nachi* and *Maya*. Although these were ships built and commissioned in the 1920s, under the restrictions of the Washington Treaty, their main artillery (203mm/50 Type 3) aroused justified respect, especially after the South Pacific campaign. Their maximum range was 29km, which meant that Japanese heavy cruisers could keep the entire enemy team at a distance.[1] Rear Admiral McMorris could counter *Nachi* and *Maya*'s 20 high-calibre guns with only *Salt Lake City*'s 10 guns. Additionally, the American 8-inch (203mm/55)

Type 93 torpedo, also known as 'Long Lance'. (Wikimedia Commons)

gun was designed from the same period, but its muzzle velocity and range were slightly inferior to those of its Japanese counterparts.[2]

The situation was equally unfavourable for the Americans in the number of light cruisers, as Hosogaya also had a two-fold numerical superiority. It should be noted, however, that the combat potential of both Japanese vessels was only slightly more significant, as they had a total of 13 140mm/50 Type 3 guns, while *Richmond* had 10 6-inch (150mm/53) guns. In addition, unlike the main artillery of heavy cruisers, American shells on light cruisers had greater range and muzzle velocity than their Japanese counterparts.

As for the destroyers, the Americans were slightly outnumbered on paper, although it should be considered that the Fifth Fleet detached *Usugumo* to screen the convoy, and thus, she did not directly participate in the battle. Comparing the number of secondary armament guns, the Japanese had 34 120mm or 127mm guns, while the Americans had 26 127mm guns. Although the standard shells of the Japanese destroyers had greater range and muzzle velocity, the American 5-inch (127mm/38 Mk 5) gun was a newer design, resulting in a better fire rate and armour penetration capability.

Apart from the artillery, the Japanese had a straightforward numerical and qualitative superiority in torpedo armament. Following the doctrine of the decisive battle (*kantai kessen*) established in the interwar period, virtually all heavy cruisers, light cruisers and destroyers had 610mm torpedo tubes. Massive torpedo attacks were the *Nippon Kaigun*'s specialty. Their exceptional effectiveness resulted from the training of the crews and the quality of the weapons themselves. At the beginning of 1943, the primary torpedo fired from surface vessels was the Type 90 torpedo (from some destroyers) or the Type 93 Mod. 1 (most cruisers and the

rest of the destroyers). The latter was called the 'Long Lance' by the Allies, as it was 9m long. The Japanese called it an 'oxygen torpedo' (*sanso gyorai*), because the propellant consisted of kerosene or similar oxidised with oxygen-enriched air. The total weight was 2,700kg, with the warhead being about 490kg. The torpedo could go as fast as up to 50 knots, and at a speed of 33 knots it was able to cover a distance of over 40km, although the official specification stated that the maximum range was 11km. The Long Lance had showed its usefulness already in the first stage of the Pacific War, but it achieved the greatest successes during the Guadalcanal and the Solomon Islands campaign. The deadly toll it took on Allied ships can be explained by its high speed with an objectively large weight of explosive charge, the ability to not leave a visible wake, relative reliability, and the denial of its performance by the Americans.[3]

Vice Admiral Hosogaya's group (minus *Usugumo*) had 76 torpedo tubes at its disposal – 68 were 610mm and eight 533mm. TG-16.6 McMorris had 32 533mm torpedo tubes, which gave the Japanese more than twice the numerical superiority, considering the above qualitative advantages.

The equipment of both groups included seaplanes, which were intended to provide the most up-to-date and precise information on the movements of surface vessels, submarines, and the situation in the enemy's bases. Japanese commanders were equally eager to use seaplanes to observe weather conditions in the area, especially if it was an area that was difficult to access and had poor communications. Both sides catapulted seaplanes from the decks of the cruisers, and after the reconnaissance mission, they were retrieved using a ship's crane. The entire procedure was carried out provided that the sea conditions allowed the recovery and that there was no risk that the group would be surprised by an enemy submarine.

Each American cruiser had two Curtiss SOC-1 Seagull seaplanes. Theoretically, all Japanese cruisers should also be equipped with seaplanes; *Nachi* and *Maya* three each, and *Tama* and *Abukuma* one each. However, *Maya* and the two light cruisers had not embarked their seaplanes before the battle of the Komandorski Islands, leaving only *Nachi* to conduct air operations. Vice Admiral Hosogaya's flagship was equipped with two Petes and one Jake at the time.[4]

Regardless of the number of seaplanes and their technical specifications, the aerial reconnaissance capabilities of both groups were very similar. The Americans and Japanese usually kept one to three planes in the air. Selecting the correct observation sector, correctly identifying enemy surface vessels and establishing effective radio communication with the team determined the success or failure of the reconnaissance flight and, often, the entire operation.

A key factor giving the Americans an advantage in reading enemy intentions was that all their ships were equipped with radars. Apart from the destroyers *Bailey* and *Coghlan*, which had only older SC radars, all other ships had the improved 50kW SG radar. It worked at 775, 800 or 825Hz frequencies and could detect bombers at altitudes above 150m, destroyers from 15 miles and battleships from 22 miles. Its additional advantage was that it helped in navigation by distinguishing enemy ships from geographical objects, giving a complete vision of the waters and surrounding islands.[5]

In terms of development of radar technology, the Japanese lagged far behind the Allies from the very beginning of the Pacific War. The first, still partially experimental Type 2 Mod. 2 radar (commonly called No. 21) was installed on the aircraft carrier *Shōkaku* no sooner than in August 1942, while it became part of the equipment of some cruisers and destroyers but since the spring of 1943. This was far too late to reverse the unfavourable position of the *Nippon Kaigun* in the war with the US Navy.

In comparing the combat potential of both groups, the Japanese had a clear advantage in terms of firepower and experience. The Fifth Fleet's most prominent need on the eve of the naval engagement with TG-16.6 was to implement strategic plans that involved providing an escort for a convoy comprising three transports. Japanese warships had to protect them from interception and keep in mind the safety of slower ships carrying supplies and reinforcements for the Attu garrison. Transporters significantly limited the manoeuvring capabilities and prevented Hosogaya from taking risks that might have been justified in other circumstances. On the contrary, the freedom to operate in the waters of the North Pacific and a simple plan to destroy an enemy convoy were the main chances for Rear Admiral McMorris to use them for his advantage in a naval battle against a stronger opponent.

6
BATTLE OF THE KOMANDORSKI ISLANDS

アッツ島沖海戦
Attsu-tō oki Kaisen

The prolonged wait for the arrival of *Sankō Maru* and *Usugumo* was a severe issue for Vice Admiral Hosogaya, who wanted to reach Attu with the convoy as soon as possible. Barely an hour had passed since he ordered *Usugumo* to join his group on her own, and there were still a few minutes left before the planned turn northwards. The Japanese warships were on a southerly course in line formation, starting with *Nachi* (flagship), followed by *Maya*, *Tama*, *Wakaba*, *Hatsushimo*, *Abukuma*, *Ikazuchi*, *Asaka Maru*, *Sakito Maru* and *Inazuma*. Slow and fragile transport ships were placed between the 1st Torpedo Squadron destroyers, making a surprise attack more difficult for enemy submarines.

According to the plan, at 0500 hours, *Nachi* turned north, followed every few minutes by subsequent Japanese warships. Suddenly, at 0508 hours, *Inazuma*, placed at the rear of the formation, sent a cable to the entire group: 'Enemy spotted!' *Abukuma*, which also saw the blurred silhouettes of two ships on the horizon, did not confirm this information. After a while, however, she transmitted her message: '*Sankō Maru* and *Usugumo* sighted!' In Japanese documents, this contact was indicated at the coordinates 53°25'N, 168°40'E, less than 100km southeast of Copper Island.[1] Initially, the Japanese were confused because they could not determine whether their own or enemy vessels were in their way. The following minutes of close observation could have given time to analyse the situation with a calm mind, but the formation was in the middle of the turn, so the Japanese chose to believe that it was only *Usugumo* and *Sankō Maru*.[2]

The Japanese could not have known it then, but before dawn on 27 March, the two opposing task forces had spotted each other. Rear

Admiral McMorris's crews had just finished eating breakfast when, at 0530 hours, the forwardmost *Coghlan* made radar contact with three vessels at just over 13km, bearing 10 degrees. The destroyer sent this information to the rest of the group via TBS, and at almost the same time, *Richmond* confirmed another radar contact at a distance of 25km, bearing 7 degrees. 'Concentrate on me,' McMorris passed his word and, a minute later, also ordered boiler condition one to gain enough speed to manoeuvre with the entire group.[3] Within the next five minutes, *Coghlan* reported radar contact with five enemy vessels, while *Richmond*'s radar showed only three. The crew on the destroyer's deck could already see several blurred silhouettes of Japanese ships, and after a while, the light cruiser's men also saw them.[4]

The opponent appeared confused by the presence of TG-16.6 west of Attu, as American sailors noted attempts to communicate via reconnaissance signals, which were utterly ignored. Based on *Coghlan*'s radar contacts, Rear Admiral McMorris had his first guess on the composition of the enemy force. He interpreted five vessels in one group as two transport ships screened by one or two destroyers and one light cruiser.[5] If he had come across a typical convoy, he would have been correct, as the Japanese assigned two or three warships to a single transport mission. This time, however, he met the main part of the Fifth Fleet in front of him. The blissfully unaware TG-16.6 was informed at 0540 hours that the enemy was within a bearing of 10 degrees, a distance of approximately 20km, proceeding on a course of 80 degrees at a speed of 13 knots. The group received an order via TBS to follow parallel to the enemy formation to maintain contact, but without reducing the distance for now, until all ships are gathered, and further information is obtained.[6]

The Japanese *Senshi Sōsho* indicates that Vice Admiral Hosogaya's group should have first realised that it had encountered an enemy team at 0537 hours.[7] However, *Abukuma* soon sent a radiogram to all ships with the following content: 'I confirm, one destroyer and the silhouette of one probable transport heading west, bearing 200 degrees.'[8] Such a cable could definitely be interpreted as spotting *Sankō Maru* and *Usugumo*, especially since both vessels were expected to appear nearby. The Japanese calmed down and started thinking about how to merge both groups smoothly. Although they were looking through binoculars towards the two ships, their silhouettes did not cause much concern to the observers. Worse, they were sure that these were the 2nd Escort Unit. After a while, visual contact with the supposedly friendly group was lost. Vice Admiral Hosogaya continued his advance north as planned and prepared to reach the rendezvous point indicated in earlier orders as quickly as possible.

At 0600 hours, the Americans maintained a distance of approximately 25km from the enemy, slowly tightening their formation and preparing to attack. The rising sun gradually lit up the area, although clear identification of the enemy team was still tricky due to the morning fog and smoke coming from the stacks of the Japanese ships. Many pairs of American binoculars were trained on the masts in the distance. At 0611 hours, observers in *Richmond* reported to Rear Admiral McMorris that they only saw one destroyer, one larger and three smaller transports. Although another destroyer was sighted four minutes later, and it was noted that the two transports might be heavy cruisers, this warning was ignored entirely. The Americans were over the moon since they falsely believed in their superiority over the Japanese. The early assessment that 'a Roman holiday was in prospect' was a terrible

mistake. As the commander of TG-16.6 admitted later, he did not know that he had decided to walk straight into the lion's den.[9]

The planned continuation of the convoy mission to Attu was interrupted by a message from *Asaka Maru's* observers, who noticed something disturbing at 0610 hours. They counted more than two masts.[10] 'Masts detected, bearing 165 degrees!' – the news spread quickly to all ships. From the deck of *Abukuma*, they began to count them frantically again and assess the class of vessels based on their height and the degree of 'branching'. Three minutes later, the light cruiser issued the first warning to the rest of the team, indicating that they had encountered not a friendly but an enemy group. 'Enemy detected: one Omaha-class light cruiser and two destroyers!', but the Japanese sailors were still not at their battle stations, and the officers were waiting for more details. At 0626 hours, the initial radiogram was supplemented with information about three more ships: one Pensacola-class heavy cruiser and two destroyers. In just a few minutes, the Japanese learned they were facing an enemy team of six warships, including two cruisers.[11]

At *Nachi's* bridge, the officers quickly met to assess the situation and decide on the next moves. They unanimously agreed that the group should use its numerical superiority to destroy the enemy task force. The action plan envisaged sending two transports north to await the battle's outcome. The rest of the team, following *Nachi* directly, was to change course to starboard and maintain a speed of 32–33 knots to close the distance and then prepare a torpedo attack from the starboard tubes. The Japanese intended to cut off the Americans' escape route to the east and cross the T (*T-ji Sempō*). They also wanted to put their guns into the wind so the enemy team approaching from the south would be in an unfavourable position when opening the artillery fire.[12]

Painting by I.R. Lloyd presenting the Battle of the Komandorski Islands. (NH&HC)

The 8-inch guns of the *Salt Lake City*. (NH&HC)

American officers aboard the *Salt Lake City* planning the action against the Japanese, 26 March 1943. They definitely did not plan to go straight into the trap! (NH&HC)

Once the Japanese correctly identified all ships in TG-16.6, the situation of the Americans started to change to their disadvantage by the second. After the initial joy of encountering several defenceless enemy vessels, the bitter truth about the actual composition of the enemy convoy began to emerge at about 0620 hours. Observers on *Richmond* recognised the silhouette of the first heavy cruiser and then a second one. They were described as the Nachi-class and Atago-class, meaning both were armed with deadly 203mm guns.[13] Four minutes later, the American flagship's radar made contact with another four vessels. More detailed surveillance through binoculars must have been a pulse-pounding experience for the Americans. 'Two heavy cruisers, one or two light cruisers and six destroyers at a distance of 36,500m, high speed!': the cable reached *Salt Lake City*, and everyone knew this was not an ordinary convoy to Attu.[14] Moments later, it became clear that two of the six destroyers, mistakenly described as the Hubuki-class, were large transport ships. However, it was only partial good news. TG-16.6 was still facing enemy forces practically twice their number. Even though crew members could be heard running around the deck, and someone was constantly contacting the observation post by telephone, a deafening silence on *Richmond*'s bridge expressed great consternation.

Theoretically, the Americans could have tried their best and attacked immediately, but Rear Admiral McMorris still had not gathered his formation. What is worse is that the Japanese understood the situation and took the first decisive steps. Their transports separated from the main formation, which suddenly changed course to the southeast. The distance between the two groups began to shrink rapidly. The Americans had to decide immediately: accept the battle, flee, or maintain contact from a safe distance. If to withdraw, where? East towards Adak and their base, but directly under enemy guns? Or to the seemingly safer western direction, at the risk of entering the range of Japanese bombers from the Kuril Islands? The joining of 11 AF to the battle within the next hour, on the other hand, seemed unlikely. Therefore, Rear Admiral McMorris had to escape the death trap alone. He was responsible for the lives of almost 3,000 sailors, and at the same time, he was still bound by the order to prevent the Japanese convoy from reaching Attu.[15]

At 0630 hours, the crews welcomed long-awaited sunrise. The sea seemed exceptionally calm. The temperature was around 0°C, with light south-easterly wind and decent visibility. The commander of TG-16.6 made his decision. The enemy's transport ships remained

his most important target. Analysing the situation, his staff officers calculated that if the group started to approach them, there was still a chance of destroying them at the limits of the main artillery range before the Japanese warships entered the action. The Americans also concluded that he was more likely to make mistakes if they forced the opponent to fight near the convoy. Once committing to a long-range engagement, at 0633 hours, Rear Admiral McMorris ordered a course change to 330 degrees. By this time, *Dale* had managed to get close to *Monaghan*, which was on *Salt Lake City*'s side. However, the distance between all three ships and the more advanced group centred around *Richmond* was still approximately 4,500m. *Salt Lake City* and *Richmond* were instructed to catapult seaplanes to provide reconnaissance and support for the gunners. For unexplained reasons, the first cruiser received this cable, but did not send her only available aircraft into the air. The flagship's command, on the contrary, argued and convinced McMorris that their seaplane could become an asset in the later phase of the battle.[16]

The memoirs of one of the Fifth Fleet's staff artillery officers, Lieutenant Commander Kinoshita Hajime, give a good overview of the Japanese opinions on the Americans' manoeuvres:

From detecting the enemy to changing [our] course, the forward guns were set at an angle of approximately 40 degrees, and the after guns were initially completely lowered and gradually increased their angle of elevation. I wasn't concerned that the enemy was heading towards the convoy due to our change of course. We had a clear advantage, and I thought destroying the opposing task force first would be a good idea.[17]

Another Japanese account is also worth mentioning. The staff aviation officer, Lieutenant Commander Miura Kintarō, slightly clarified Vice Admiral Hosogaya's battle plans:

When we encountered the enemy, staff officers explained that a plan envisaged cutting off the retreat route. Furthermore, I do not believe the formation was intentionally positioned against the wind; it was more like a lucky coincidence. Due to the change in our course, the torpedo tubes on the side from which we intended to attack were not yet ready.[18]

Despite a clearly defined objective and a relatively well-executed change of course, it must be stated that on the morning of 27 March, the Japanese were utterly unprepared to engage the enemy. The

1st Torpedo Squadron experienced the most significant problems, and its commander tried to keep up with Hosogaya's orders. The situation in the 21st Cruiser Squadron was not much better since the crews had not yet had time to take up battle stations and prepare all the guns and the torpedo tubes. Japanese historians indicated the following circumstances as the reasons for the Fifth Fleet's insufficient preparation:

1. The encounter with Rear Admiral McMorris' task force occurred in an area much further west than initially expected.
2. The Japanese ships' crews were tired and relaxed simultaneously. After several days of exhausting struggles with rough seas and strong winds, the sailors felt relief due to significantly better weather. Thus, they were exhausted and used free time to take a break.
3. When the enemy was detected, a sudden increase in speed was ordered. However, before that, the Fifth Fleet's command instructed crews to save the fuel as much as possible. Additionally, barrels were delivered to the boiler room too slowly. When *Abukuma* gave a clear signal to accelerate, her group did not have time to adapt to the new orders.
4. Routine exercises were carried out at battle stations early in the morning. After that, the crew members were dismissed. Moments later, the order calling for a return to the battle stations was a necessary but chaotic step.
5. Due to previous storms, the seaplane on *Nachi* was heavily tied up, and the aircrew were not at their stations. Thus, the after guns could not turn towards the enemy formation and were not ready for combat.
6. Some sailors and officers were still confused due to the lack of clear identification of the encountered team – many contradictory rumours about spotting *Sankō Maru* with her screening destroyer or the enemy warships were circulating on board.

The Japanese could not wait forever for their crews to take battle stations. At 0642 hours, *Nachi* and *Maya* opened fire with their main batteries. Their target was 'a large cruiser, probably the Omaha-class.' In reality, it was *Richmond* at a distance of 19,300m.[19] *Maya*'s crew recalled that 'in the morning twilight, they saw six silhouettes similar to black sesame seeds floating on the water and fired at the largest of them.'[20] However, they did not know then that the target was not the largest vessel in the group. Although the Japanese correctly estimated the course of the light cruiser, their first shells fell too short, less than 900m in front of her starboard side. The second, slightly corrected salvo also missed the target and flew behind her, spraying the water pillar several metres away. However, the blast was so great that it shook *Richmond*'s crew, thinking for a moment that they had been hit directly. For now, it was only a demonstration of the destructive power of the Japanese 203mm guns, which aroused justified respect among Allied sailors.

However, the opening fire in a situation where the Japanese cruisers were not fully ready to fight had its painful price. The main artillery's recoil irreversibly damaged two seaplanes on *Nachi*, which had previously been securely tied to the catapult. Moreover, due to human error, the power supply was switched too quickly from the forward to the stern power generator at too low steam pressure in the boilers, which resulted in the main artillery turrets and their equipment (rammers, turret rotation mechanisms and gun lifters) losing power just as their gunners were on their way to scoring the first hits on the target. The guns suddenly jammed in one

position, and all corrections had to be done manually for the next few minutes.[21]

Soon after 0642 hours, *Salt Lake City* and *Richmond* also opened fire. A few dozen seconds later, when the first shells straddled the Japanese warships, a smoking seaplane on *Nachi* was spotted through binoculars. *Salt Lake City*'s crew mistakenly took it as evidence of direct hits by the third and fourth salvos. After a while, *Bailey* and *Coghlan* joined the cannonade, trying to help their cruisers from a distance of 15km. At 0645 hours, TG-16.6 was ordered to increase speed to 25 knots and change course 40 degrees to port to maintain distance from the enemy formation. A large water pillar rose near the American ships every moment, yet no direct hits had been received. Three minutes later, the Americans increased their speed to 28 knots, and the Japanese transports heading north-west slowly disappeared from their line of sight.[22]

Between 0644 and 0646 hours, *Nachi* fired eight torpedoes at the American ships leading the formation. The result of this attack would not be apparent for about a dozen or so minutes, but with such a long distance to the enemy, each course change could end up in the fiasco of an entire salvo. Having failed to prepare her starboard tubes, *Maya* had to wait patiently for her turn to unleash the 'fish'. Instead, her main artillery left *Richmond* alone and moved its interest to *Salt Lake City*.[23] For now, the 1st Torpedo Squadron did not participate in the fight, as it still had trouble keeping up with the 21st Cruiser Squadron. Ultimately, Rear Admiral Mori decided to separate from the main formation and set a course of 200 degrees. In the longer term, the Japanese intended to use this manoeuvre to outflank the enemy task force, placing it between two groups of their ships. At 0647 hours, *Tama* also followed the 1st Torpedo Squadron's steps. Thus, only the two heavy cruisers continued their advance on a south-easterly course, drawing the full attention of TG-16.6. Three minutes later, *Nachi* received two direct hits from 203mm shells from *Salt Lake City*'s third salvo.[24] The first hit was scored on the navigation platform, where signalmen were located. As a result of the explosion, 11 crew members were killed and 21 were injured, including the torpedo commander. Although his legs were covered in blood, he continued in command for the rest of the morning after receiving medical help on the upper part of the bridge. Just a few seconds apart, the second shell from *Salt Lake City* hit the mast, but this time it did not cause significant damage.[25]

Undoubtedly, the most important effect of the first hit on *Nachi* was the breaking of power circuits supplying the main artillery turrets. This led to the failure of the calculator and her gun sights jammed in the firing position at a distance of 10,000m for about 30 minutes.[26] The Japanese later admitted that this particular damage influenced the limited effectiveness of the heavy cruiser in the first phase of the battle and also had an overall impact on its final result.[27]

Apart from those two hits, the following salvos from *Salt Lake City* and *Richmond*, clearly distinguished by the Japanese who saw blue and red/orange colour markers, generally fell 100 to 400m short of the target. However, some of them were clearly more accurate, and at 0652 hours, *Salt Lake City* scored a third hit on *Nachi* with its fourth salvo, crashing into the torpedo room. The damage was not significant but included two killed and five wounded men. The crew of the heavy cruiser had greater worries at that time as the failure of the main artillery calculator turned out to be more severe than initially expected, and the skipper was forced to pass the word to cease fire.

Taking advantage of a respite on board, at 0654 hours, *Nachi* catapulted seaplane No. 1, whose task was to reconnoitre the rear of the enemy formation and direct artillery fire. Seaplanes No. 2 and

3, damaged in the first minutes of the battle, were unfit for service. Although they were immediately extinguished after an accidental fire, the skipper decided to jettison them so as not to tempt a major fire on board. The Japanese damage control units, working hard and under great pressure, were unable to fully fix the calculator. Still, at 0656 hours, *Nachi* changed course to the south (and then southwest to the south) to open fire from approximately 20,000m on the heavy cruiser, described as the Chicago-class. Two minutes later, *Maya*, concentrating her fire on the same ship, reported the first direct hit. None of these shells were accurate.[28] After more than half an hour of struggling to deliver the fuel barrels to the boiler room, the commander of the 1st Torpedo Squadron was finally able to order his group to pursue the enemy at maximum speed (32.3 knots) to join the battle from the left flank of the American formation.[29]

At 0651 hours, Rear Admiral McMorris sent Rear Admiral Kinkaid an initial report on the encounter with the enemy task group comprising two heavy cruisers, two light cruisers, four destroyers and two transport ships. Shortly after that, the commander of TG-16.6 saw from *Richmond*'s deck an enemy seaplane being catapulted. He ordered a course change to 230 degrees, which was corrected to 250 degrees after three minutes to allow all ships in the group to come within range. At this point, the Japanese knew that the torpedoes fired by *Nachi* were unlikely to hit the targets. Still, they were spotted by *Richmond*'s skipper, although after a moment of reflection, he incorrectly concluded that they were only a school of small fish.[30] At 0657 hours, observers from *Salt Lake City* confirmed that the fourth salvo had hit the enemy heavy cruiser at the head of the formation.[31] This success, however, did not reverse the Americans' chances. Vice Admiral Hosogaya, who had already sorted out most of the issues in the first phase of the battle, was about to launch a furious counterattack.

The Japanese Counterattack
日本の反撃
Nihon no Hangeki

After the first claimed hit on *Salt Lake City*, the Japanese felt that it was the right time to push for settling the battle, and thus, they increased the speed and launched a dramatic pursuit of the enemy. The 21st Cruiser Squadron, with the damaged *Nachi*, almost single-handedly swung against the TG-16.6, hoping that the gunners would soon prove the *Nippon Kaigun*'s favourable reputation, and the famous Long Lances would help get the job done. At 0707 hours, *Maya* fired four torpedoes, but as in the case of *Nachi*, minor course corrections ordered by Rear Admiral McMorris made the probability of hitting the target slim.[32] The catapulted seaplane from *Nachi* slowly began to take its toll on the Americans. The destroyers and *Richmond*, however, successfully chased it away with their anti-aircraft artillery. McMorris hoped to maintain his distance at all costs and gather his warships to fire more effectively at the enemy. At 0710 hours, he instructed *Dale* and *Monaghan* to move off the starboard side of *Salt Lake City* and join *Richmond*. The destroyer crews were delighted to do so as the cannonade of the Japanese ships, more and more accurate with each salvo, was concentrated on the American heavy cruiser. Staying in the line of fire seemed like suicide. *Salty Lake City*'s skipper, Captain Rodgers, had been skilfully evading the enemy shells, which repeatedly landed exactly in the place where the ship would have been several seconds later if the course had not been changed. However, at 0710 hours, the heavy cruiser narrowly avoided a 203mm shell from *Maya*, which landed just off the port side, shaking the entire ship. Ten minutes later, the

The *Salt Lake City*'s skipper, Captain Bertram J. Rodgers. (NARA)

crew perceived another near miss as a direct hit, but fortunately, no damage was reported.[33]

The time between 0707 and 0751 hours contains little information in Japanese documents and research pieces. To reconstruct the engagement from the Japanese perspective, it is necessary to use the map included with *Senshi Sōsho*. The diagram shows that after confirming two hits on *Salt Lake City*, *Maya* ceased fire at 0730 hours. Five minutes later, the 1st Torpedo Squadron finally managed to catch up with the rest of the group and made visual contact with the 21st Cruiser Squadron at a distance of 11,000m, bearing 145 degrees, but on the other side of the American formation.[34] The damage control party on *Nachi* still had not resolved the failure with the calculator, but they reported to the skipper that they had at least repaired the broken electrical circuits. Both Japanese heavy cruisers tried to chase TG-16.6, but zigzagging to avoid enemy shells eliminated their slight speed advantage. Meanwhile, a catapulted seaplane tried its luck once again and approached *Salt Lake City* but it was again chased off by anti-aircraft artillery.[35] At 0743 hours, the skipper of *Nachi* ordered to hold fire and focus on catching up with the Americans.[36]

A negative effect of the 1st Torpedo Squadron's pursuit of the rest of the team was attracting TG-16.6's attention. At 0743 hours, the Americans, who were already firing sporadically at Rear Admiral Mori's group, established that the light cruiser at the head of his formation had become an excellent target. They changed the course to 320 degrees to close the distance to *Abukuma* while keeping the speed of retreat from *Nachi* and *Maya*. At 0750 hours, the course was corrected to 330 degrees. *Abukuma* noted the first shells falling short of her bow just a minute later. Captain Mori instantly ordered his squadron to slow down to 28 knots and proceed north-west to north. He also informed Hosogaya about the circumstances of his decision.[37] The emotions associated with being under fire were described by the light cruiser's Executive Officer, Lieutenant Commander Y. Saitō:

Close, far, close… when I thought another [shell] would probably hit us, we somehow dodged it. A moment later, we changed our course, again and one more time in quick succession to outmanoeuvre the enemy. I felt our speed suddenly dropped because we were [likely to be] hit at one point.[38]

At 0753 hours, Rear Admiral McMorris ordered to head north in a last attempt to close to the Japanese transport ships. After five minutes, however, he changed the course to 25 degrees and slowed to 28 knots, as breaking through to the convoy seemed extremely difficult. For now, he decided to use the temporary advantage over the 1st Torpedo Squadron. After a while, *Nachi* and *Maya* resumed firing on *Salt Lake City*, profiting from the cables from a seaplane circling over *Richmond*. The Americans saw the smoke on one of the Japanese cruisers and thought they had scored another hit. The reality was somewhat different. *Nachi* had mostly overcome the technical problems on Vice Admiral Hosogaya's group would soon launch a decisive advance. At 0800 hours, *Salt Lake City*'s rudder was temporarily jammed, probably due to the constant zigzagging, and prevented the ship from correcting its course to the starboard side. Fortunately for the crew, the enemy did not manage to score any hits during this critical time. After a quick inspection and finding the cause of the failure, the course was changed to 330 degrees at 0805 hours. Once shifting the steering control settings to aft, she got a 10-degree play on each side.[39]

In response to McMorris' cable, who in the morning shared with TF-16 a plan to follow a 300-degree course and continue the naval engagement at the limit of his guns' range, just after 0800 hours, Rear Admiral Kinkaid suggested he withdraw from the action and wait for air support to arrive. Although the suggestion to disengage from the fight with the enemy seemed sensible, the bombers from Adak or Amchitka would not appear earlier than 1230 hours. Even if some flying boats could have reached the battlefield a little earlier, Kinkaid's advice was maliciously commented upon as leaving the task group to continue fighting independently.[40]

The gradual approach of TG-16.6 towards the north worried Vice Admiral Hosogaya so much that he decided to cut off the enemy's intention of closing on the convoy. Based on Lieutenant Commander Kinoshita's testimony, it is known that the Japanese were constantly reacting to the American manoeuvres and adjusting their battle plan – 'Once we grasped the enemy's plan to head north, we were instantly dedicated to chase him down westbound.'[41]

Just before 0800 hours, the 21st Cruiser Squadron crossed the current track of the enemy formation and was on its starboard side, the same side as the 1st Torpedo Squadron. The commander of the Fifth Fleet did not want to allow the Americans to break through to the north, as evidenced by his order issued at 0802 hours. 'The entire group, advance!', an explicit instruction to pursue the enemy reached the communication posts of all Japanese ships.[42] Based on this cable, at 0807 hours, *Abukuma* fired four torpedoes in the direction of the enemy formation, which gradually changed the course to the north-west (95 degrees, distance of 13,500m). It soon turned out that all 'fish' were inaccurate.[43]

At 0810 hours, after more than an hour and a half of 'chasing Japanese salvos', *Salt Lake City* received the first hit from *Maya*'s 203mm projectiles. It struck the main deck between frames 8 and 9, went through the chain locker and finally tore a hole in the starboard side below the waterline. Fortunately for the ship, this shell did not explode, which is probably why, except for a few men in the forwardmost stations, the crew did not feel the hit much. As J. Lorelli described, 'Damage control personnel were quickly at the scene and as a precautionary measure, shored bulkhead Number 10. Flooding was limited to five small compartments, and although the ship was thereafter a little down by the head, her speed was unimpaired.'[44]

At 0812 hours, McMorris ordered the destroyers *Bailey* and *Coghlan* to prepare to lay a smokescreen off *Salt Lake City*. As

The American destroyers laying the smokescreen off *Salt Lake City*. (NH&HC)

planned, the course was changed to 300 degrees so the enemy could not see the American ships heading west. Three minutes later, *Bailey* and *Coghlan* began belching thick black clouds of smoke with their stacks and chemical smoke generators on the fantail. After camouflaging the retreat, the Americans regretted that they had not decided to catapult at least one seaplane earlier, which would have provided great support for the TG-16.6 gunners in poor visibility.[45] At the same time, the unfortunate absentee from the battle so far, the light cruiser *Tama*, did her best to join the fight. At 0815 hours, she finally opened fire after a long period of lonely pursuit. However, seeing that the enemy had put an effective smokescreen, the cruiser ceased fire after only three minutes.[46]

Trying to use their clear advantage, *Nachi* and *Maya* continued their cannonade, aiming to destroy *Salt Lake City*. At 0819 hours, observers on the first Japanese cruiser noted scoring a direct hit on the enemy ship, although they were seeing things.[47] Despite this wrong assessment, seeing thick smoke ahead, Hosogaya ordered to cease firing and decided to regroup his group at 0825 hours. The Americans were constantly escaping west: they changed course to 240 degrees and hid behind a smoke screen. Thus, a moment later, the Japanese also headed further west. *Nachi* and *Maya* separated for a while to change their order in the formation and give priority to the vessel that had previously performed better in the artillery fire. Still, the flagship of the Fifth Fleet fired several salvos between 0829 and 0831 hours, trying to stab the enemy through small holes in the smokescreen. At the same time, the observers on *Nachi* also confirmed that the 1st Torpedo Squadron was only 5,000m away, bearing 222 degrees.[48]

After the overtaking manoeuvre was completed, *Maya* led the formation of the 21st Cruiser Squadron at 0837 hours. Fire from the main artillery was opened again, and as the next step, Vice Admiral Hosogaya ordered the 1st Torpedo Squadron to move to the front line. Thus, at about 0840 hours, the Japanese heavy cruisers increased the distance to TG-16.6, and the destroyers led by *Abukuma* were to become more active in pursuing the enemy, becoming Hosogaya's trump card.[49]

The regrouping of the Japanese vessels coincided with *Dale* and *Monaghan* putting up an additional smokescreen. At 0840 hours, the Americans spotted an enemy light cruiser bearing west at a distance of approximately 12,500m. She started firing on *Bailey* but was soon successfully deterred by *Richmond* and the other destroyers. *Maya* and *Nachi*, alternately ceasing fire and shooting at *Salt Lake City*, continued their advance on a north-westerly course. This time, however, they both had greater freedom of manoeuvre while remaining within the effective firing range of their guns. At 0852 hours, *Tama* reported that she had become a prime target for American destroyers and saw a large number of projectiles falling abeam.[50]

Salt Lake City's luck ended at 0859 hours, when she received a second, much more severe hit. A 203mm projectile from *Maya* struck the starboard catapult and set the seaplane on fire, showering part of the deck with deadly shrapnel that killed two and wounded another two men. The Americans had many painful memories with planes burning like torches on board their ships, and immediately after extinguishing the fire, they jettisoned the SOC Seagull. *Salt Lake City*, however, unfazed by this blow, maintained 28 knots and sought to respond to the enemy with her main artillery.[51]

The second hit looked much worse from the deck of the *Richmond*, where Rear Admiral McMorris made an important decision regarding the further battle plan. TG-16.6 could no longer flee westwards as it was getting closer to Paramushiru by each minute. Instead of receiving support from Adak or Amchitka, he could expect enemy bombers to appear overhead. Therefore, McMorris decided that laying the smokescreen was the right time to change course to the south – *Monaghan* also reported some problems with her engine room. At 0902 hours, TG-16.6 corrected the course to 210 degrees and increased its speed to 30 knots, hoping to break away from the enemy group.[52]

Despite the American decision to set up the smokescreen and to withdraw south, the Japanese gunners on the heavy cruisers finally matched the perfect angle and distance. At 0903 hours, *Salt Lake City* was hit for the third time by a 203mm projectile from *Maya*. According to the crew, this one shook the entire ship so much that, unlike the previous two hits, no one had any doubts that a massive blow had just been received. Sea2c Mike Van Kessel, one of the new crew members, recalled those moments in the following words:

> We were sitting on the laundry hatch cover and a shell exploded right below us. The compartment flooded with water which I could hear coming in. I said to the Chief, "Water is coming in". With that, he took off forward before I could get the words out of my mouth. This scared me and I went the other way. I soon realized there was no problem in the mess hall so I sat back down. Several shells hit the side [sic] very close to us under water. It sounds like thousands of pinging sounds hitting metal.[53]

Although no one was hurt as a result of this hit, it was very dangerous for *Salt Lake City*. The projectile, coming from an angle of 45 degrees, struck the port quarter between frames 102 and 103, below the waterline. The precise description was provided by the heavy cruiser's damage report:

[previous points omitted]
9. The principal damage suffered by SALT LAKE CITY was caused by the 8-inch projectile (hit No. 2) which penetrated the port shell between frames 102 and 103 just below the first platform (photo 6 -plate III). This projectile was falling at an angle of about 45 degrees when it struck the water off the port quarter of SALT LAKE CITY. It did not detonate or ricochet but passed downward and pierced the hull underwater (photo 7). It passed through fuel oil tank D-4-F (100% full of fuel oil) (photo 8) and then traveled downward, forward and inboard. In following this

course it passed through swash bulkhead 100 (photo 10), the outboard bulkhead of No. 4 shaft alley and was deflected inboard by No. 4 shaft. Continuing on, it passed through the inboard bulkhead of No. 4 shaft alley between frames 98 and 99 (photo 11) and into the forward part of fuel oil tank D-2-F where it detonated, rupturing the inboard and outboard boundaries of this tank. D-2-F was 80% full at the time. This projectile traveled approximately 28 feet within the ship to the point of detonation.
10. The immediate effects of this hit were to flood No. 3 and No. 4 shaft alleys with a mixture of oil and salt water and contaminate fuel oil tanks D-4-F and D-2-F. The after gyro room D-501-E flooded to the overhead through three fragment holes in the port bulkhead. Five-inch AA handling room D-401-M flooded to the overhead from the gyro room through a hatch which was not watertight, (presumably designed as a watertight hatch, but not fully effective) and 5-inch AA magazine D-402-M flooded completely from D-401-M through two doors left partially undogged by personnel evacuating these spaces. The laundry was flooded to the waterline (about 3-1/2 feet above the first platform) with a mixture of water and oil which came up through ruptured first platform deck plating and a damaged manhole cover to D-4-F. The athwartship passage at frame 98 on this level likewise flooded to the waterline through the doorway leading from the laundry which was open. Ice machine room D-301-E flooded slowly to a depth of about one foot through a door which was improperly dogged and through an unblanked small cable hole in the inboard bulkhead of this compartment just aft of bulkhead 97. The after engine room flooded to a depth of about five feet as a result of leakage through the bulkhead stuffing boxes on No. 3 and No. 4 shafts, a fragment hole and damaged fuel oil manifold connections on bulkhead 97. This combined flooding resulted in a 4-degree list to port.
11. As an immediate damage control measure, flooded compartments were covered with CO_2 to prevent the possibility of fires. The 4-degree port list was removed by pumping overboard the salt water ballast in the port boiler room wing tanks using the fire and bilge pumps. Attempts to stop flooding of the after engine room by plugging the fragment hole and other leaks in bulkhead 97 proved unsuccessful. In order to control the inflow of oil and water into the engine room, two fire and bilge pumps and the main circulating pump were used - about 10 minutes were required to pump down to a safe level. Intermittent pumping was then required every 15 or 20 minutes. Throughout this whole period No. 3 and No. 4 shafts remained in operation although they were submerged in fuel oil and were fouled by damaged plating.
12. The detonation of the projectile in D-2-F caused rupture and deflection of the inboard longitudinal bulkhead bounding No. 3 shaft alley. The lower strake of the bulkhead plating between frames 98 and 99 was blown into the shaft alley and around No. 3 shaft (photo 12). Fuel oil suction lines passing through D-2-F were severed and torn loose at the bulkhead connection (photo 11). This caused contamination of the after fuel oil tanks. Contamination of these tanks was not a factor because no service tanks were involved.[54]
[note that he photographs referred to are not reproduced here]

When the damage control team had done everything they could to protect *Salt Lake City* from tragedy, at 0908 hours, Rear Admiral McMorris ordered TG-16.6 to change course to 180 degrees. To the

Famous photo of *Salt Lake City* during the Battle of the Komandorski Islands. (NH&HC)

surprise of the entire crew of the heavy cruiser, she did not slow down for the time being, and the entire formation began a retreat south.[55]

Before scoring a critical hit on *Salt Lake City*, slightly irritated but still believing in the final victory, Vice Admiral Hosogaya issued his next order at 0900 hours. 'All ships, charge!'[56] This could mean only one thing – focusing on destroying the enemy with torpedoes. Noticing the change in the course of the American formation from the deck of his flagship, the commander of the Fifth Fleet knew that he needed to make appropriate calculations and, just in case, check the track of the 1st Torpedo Squadron. At 0905 hours, *Maya* fired four torpedoes, targeting the leading ship in the enemy team heading southwest. Still, for unknown reasons, *Nachi* fired eight torpedoes in a completely wrong direction two minutes later, having no chance to hit the target.[57] Both Japanese heavy cruisers, like *Abukuma* and her destroyers, maintained a stable southwest towards a west course, opening and ceasing artillery fire occasionally. After more than two and a half hours, *Tama* finally returned to the rear of the formation of the 21st Cruiser Squadron. She could have been a valuable reinforcement in the final stage of the battle.[58]

Collected accounts of Japanese officers participating in the battle of the Komandorski Islands clearly show that after Hosogaya's order to charge on the fleeing enemy, the Japanese felt that a favourable opportunity to destroy the American task force in the first stage of the battle had been forfeited.[59] However, it was not over yet, and after *Abukuma* fired four torpedoes at 0915 hours (they also missed the target), the commander of the Fifth Fleet instructed his task force to regroup one more time. His goal was to continue the artillery

engagement to the starboard of the Japanese formation and bring the 21st Cruiser Squadron back to the front positions. *Abukuma* made a tighter turn south at 0920 hours, followed by *Maya*, *Nachi* and *Tama* in a slightly larger arc in the same direction. After a few minutes, all Japanese ships crossed the TG-16.6 track and began preparations for the final charge on the enemy.[60]

Salt Lake City's Troubles
ソルトレイクシティの悩み
Saruto Reiku Shiti no Nayami

At 0922 hours, Rear Admiral McMorris ordered a change of course to 160 degrees and slowly prepared to withdraw from the battlefield towards the east. The American and Japanese cruisers were firing at each other, and the situation was looking increasingly worse for *Salt Lake City*, which avoided increasingly precise enemy salvos. At 0930 hours, she slowed down to 20 knots due to the flooding of the aft engine room to a depth of approximately 150cm. Since the leaks could not be sealed, the damage control team focused on pumping out the water to maintain a safe level. After failed communications with *Dale*, *Monaghan* assisted the damaged cruiser while the remaining three destroyers prepared to fire torpedoes. Their approach attracted the attention of the Japanese and drew most of the enemy's fire on them.[61] This bold move, however, gave *Salt Lake City* a moment of respite. Her crew managed to partially repair the engine room in just a few minutes, thanks to which the speed was increased to 26 knots. The retreat was smoothly continued to the southeast towards the east. Since there was no longer a need to halt the rushing enemy warships, the torpedo attack of three destroyers was called off at 0938 hours. Instead, they were to return to the main formation and lay an additional smokescreen.[62]

The Americans knew the Japanese ships were following them southward through black smoke. *Salt Lake City*'s damage led to gradually diminishing the distance between both teams, which at one point decreased to only 13,000m.[63] According to Lieutenant Commander Kinoshita's memoires, it can be stated that at 0932 hours, *Nachi* noted a direct hit on the American heavy cruiser, which started to leak oil. Vice Admiral Hosogaya tried to contact the seaplane to find out more details about the technical condition of the enemy vessel, but subsequent transmissions yielded no result. He suspected that the American flagship, as he wrongly described *Salt Lake City*, was probably critically damaged. In the meantime, the Japanese also spotted four destroyers in the rear of TG-16.6, which were laying the smokescreen. The rapidly shrinking distance between the two opposing formations was also a huge unknown to the commander of the Fifth Fleet since he feared that the Americans were preparing for a torpedo counterattack. Additionally, and this factor remains crucial when considering the reasons for abandoning the pursuit, Hosogaya received erroneous information about the stock of ammunition in *Nachi*'s forward magazines. He learned that his flagship was about to expend all ammunition for the 203mm guns. Based on this report, at 0938 hours, Hosogaya decided to change course again and position himself on the left flank of the American formation to prepare for the return to Paramushiru while maintaining partial contact with the enemy.[64] *Salt Lake City* continued her salvos against at the 21st Cruiser Squadron and the 1st Torpedo Squadron, which proved that the outcome of the battle was not certain, and both sides could still fight for a victory. At 0940 hours, Hosogaya ordered the cruisers in his group to change course to 240 degrees, and five minutes later, *Abukuma* and her destroyers were on a course of 260 degrees. The 1st Torpedo Squadron was now in an excellent position to deliver a *coup de grâce* to the enemy, who was clearly fleeing southeast, trying to save his most valuable warship from destruction.[65]

At 0947 hours, TG-16.6 changed course to 170 degrees and, after two minutes, to 150 degrees. Rear Admiral McMorris cabled to Rear Admiral Kinkaid about the circumstances of the naval battle: actual position, struggle to disengage from the enemy, and the critical condition of his heavy cruiser. The message may have sounded ominous, but the situation of TG-16.6 seemed mostly under control except for the fact that *Salt Lake City*'s after guns were slowly running out of ammunition. To prevent the ship from being completely put out of action, the Americans decided to manually deliver the shells from the forward magazines. This task was hastily completed by the crew and thus, the cruiser could contribute to the American effort in the battle until the very end. It was probably when she scored her fourth hit on *Nachi*, which struck the side part of turret No. 1. The projectile did not explode but temporarily blocked the turret's rotation mechanism and killed two men.[66]

Below the deck, *Salt Lake City*'s damage control team managed to extinguish the fire and pump out most of the water. After this, the men were forced to put aside the pump due to low suction pressure. When additional compartments were opened and more water flowed in, pumping was resumed to get rid of the list on the port side. Probably due to confusion or misunderstanding of the orders, one of the crew members made a fatal mistake at 0950 hours. The ballasted wing tanks were connected to the fuel oil suction line, which began to suck in fuel contaminated with salt water. This ultimately resulted in extinguishing the fires in the boilers. The natural consequence

was the loss of steam and the reduction of the speed of the vessel at the worst possible moment. The dramatic drop in the speed was perfectly reflected in the radiograms that *Richmond* received every few seconds – 'My speed 22 knots, my speed 14 knots, my speed 8 knots, my speed 4 knots, my speed zero!'[67] At 0952 hours, *Salt Lake City* suffered two more 203mm hits from *Maya* in quick succession. They slammed the port side below the waterline, in the vicinity of the hit from 0903 hours. Apart from tearing a piece out of the bilge keel, cracking a frame and dented plating, which caused some rivets to leak, they did not bring any significant complications.[68]

Salt Lake City's troubles coincided with a torpedo attack by Japanese destroyers. At 0949 hours, *Wakaba* fired five Long Lances, and five minutes later, *Hatsushimo* released six more, taking into account the heavy cruiser's change in course and speed. Seeing thick smoke coming from her funnels, the Japanese were mistakenly convinced that their 203mm shells had severely damaged her, and it was only a matter of time before she went down. For this reason, *Maya*, *Nachi* and *Tama*, already placed on the left flank of TG-16.6, ceased fire by 0951 hours to save their ammunition from depletion. At this stage, the Japanese also reported scoring at least two hits on destroyers at the rear of the enemy formation, and they were credited to *Tama*.[69]

After receiving information about the complete loss of steam in *Salt Lake City*'s boilers, Rear Admiral McMorris was prepared for the worst. He ordered the crew to await a signal from the skipper to abandon the cruiser. The sailors hastily put on life jackets, wondering which side of the ship would sink and how to increase their chances of survival in the icy water. They knew that there was only little chance of being rescued by friendly warships. Captain Rodgers also had no illusions about the fate of *Salt Lake City* if she lost speed in this phase of the battle. As a last resort, he suggested to the TG-16.6 commander that the 14th Destroyer Squadron should be used to launch a torpedo attack that could distract the enemy from the cruiser.[70] Fortunately for the Americans, the Long Lances fired by the 1st Torpedo Squadron were inaccurate. It seemed that the enemy had no more torpedoes. Ultimately, TG-16.6 avoided this deadly Japanese weapon by maintaining distance and zigzagging.

Captain Ralph Riggs of the 14th Destroyer Squadron had no objection to helping *Salt Lake City*, and he also wanted to prove to the Japanese that the US Navy would fight to the bitter end. However, his men were aware of all the possible dangers. At 0954 hours, the destroyers *Bailey*, *Coghlan* and *Monaghan* changed course to 270 degrees. Proceeding at a speed of 32 knots, they began a daring approach towards the 21st Cruiser Squadron. Three minutes later, a plan for a torpedo attack on the enemy heavy cruisers was radioed. The Americans knew they did not have much time to act, as they had attracted the attention of the entire opposing formation. By 1000 hours, they found themselves only 13,000m from *Maya*. Massive columns of water were constantly rising around the leading *Bailey*. Colourful markers seen by the American crews meant that the Japanese heavy and light cruisers had joined the action. Although Rear Admiral McMorris ordered the destroyers to charge on the enemy formation at 36 knots, they were no match for the much larger and better-armed warships in a direct artillery duel.[71]

Looking at the charge of the enemy destroyers on the port side, just before 1000 hours, *Maya* and *Nachi* opened fire for the last time in the battle. Observers in the 1st Torpedo Squadron confirmed through binoculars that the American heavy cruiser was burning and leaving an extensive oil trail behind. In such a situation, the Japanese no longer had any doubts that they should concentrate fire on the remaining three destroyers, which were obviously trying

Salt Lake City dead in the water and screened by *Dale*. (Navasource)

to launch a torpedo attack in the final phase of the engagement. *Abukuma* and the destroyers were already on the same side as the 21st Cruiser Squadron, and the entire group could respond with its artillery fire, gradually proceeding southwest.[72]

The three American destroyers must have aroused the admiration of the Japanese as they were determined to get as close as possible to fire their torpedoes against all odds. Eventually, at 1001 hours, *Bailey* was hit by a 203mm projectile from *Maya*. Lieutenant (jg.) Stan Hogshead wrote down his recollections from those moments:

As the word for the torpedo attack was announced to all hands, there was absolute total silence as we stared at each other and wondered if we could possibly survive it. I didn't and I don't think anyone else did either. Typically, a torpedo attach is made at maximum speed and torpedoes are not launched until you are as close as you can possibly get which greatly increases the possibility of hits. Speed was increased to around 34 or 35 knots and we turned toward our enemy. The range began to close rapidly. Soon we were hearing the sounds of enemy shells landing close to us--a kerchunk sort of sound. Then a very large close explosion, it came from the compartment just forward of us, where the ship's stores, food, was kept, and the galley was located. Then another explosion occurred just aft of us and almost immediately water started coming in and soon reached shoe top level. All this time we were getting off a salvo every 12 to 15 seconds from our two forward guns as they were the only ones who could bear on the target. We were in a very perilous situation, and I stopped to pray to God for protection. As the range continued to close, we shook hands with other, wished us all God's protection, and then the lights went out. We had lost all power, and were slowing steadily, 20 knots, 15 knots, 10 knots, then 5 and finally stopped. Our Captain ordered the signal hoisted "My speed zero". As the 32 degree temperature water continued to rise around our feet, I felt certain that my time had come. The water was numbing cold. We tried to stuff a couple of life jackets in the crack in the bulkhead where the water was seeping in, and that was able to stop most of it, but it continued to slowly rise until it was just below our knees. There were lulls during this period and I was able to keep a rough diary of the events of that morning. I still have it among my memoirs.[73]

Five men were killed as a result of this hit, and the commander of the 14th Squadron, fearing that the destroyer would receive further blows that would put her out of action, ordered to accelerate preparations for the attack. Therefore, at 1003 hours, *Bailey* fired five torpedoes from about 9,000m. Lieutenant (jg.) Hogshead recalled the salvo in the following words:

Finally the distance between the enemy and us had closed to only 9500 yards and at that range, it is considered almost impossible for a heavy cruiser to miss her target. It is like looking down the barrel of a rifle. Well, the cruiser didn't miss, as we shall see in a moment. At 9500 yards, our torpedoes were fired. All were observed to run normally. At least one torpedo struck home and the enemy immediately turned to break off the engagement. Within minutes, our own damage control party under the leadership of Lt. Ralph Moreau was able to get the ship underway again and it was then reported that the SALT LAKE CITY had also gotten underway. Were we safe at last? No one knew, but we had turned from the battle area, about 600 miles from the Komandorski Islands toward Dutch Harbor about 1200 miles away.[74]

Just after firing the torpedoes, *Bailey* received another 203mm hit from *Maya*. The shell penetrated the hull below the waterline near the engine room, which was soon flooded. The destroyer significantly slowed down. Once all the 'fish' were in the water, Captain Riggs ordered the destroyers to immediately change the course to the port side and rejoin the rest of the group. The enemy artillery fire was so furious that *Coghlan* and *Monaghan* did not have a chance to fire torpedoes. The former destroyer was also struck in the upper deck, yet without any casualties or severe damage. All three units survived the deadly barrage and returned to TG-16.6 while setting up an additional smokescreen, which was considered huge luck by the Americans.[75]

While the American destroyers dared to challenge the Japanese cruisers, *Salt Lake City*'s gunners fought to the end, using up the last shells to support their ships. The damage control team sorted out the contaminated fuel supply and fired up all boilers in just four minutes. Thus, by 1000 hours, the cruiser had reached a stable speed of 15 knots. At 1007 hours, TG-16.6 was on an easterly course. *Richmond*, which approached *Salt Lake City*, set up an extra smokescreen to cover the retreat of the destroyers. It was the time when the Americans saw two formations of enemy ships heading southwest at high speed. At 1008 hours, *Salt Lake City* ceased fire. Although the men could hear shells splashing the water nearby, these were the last salvos of the battle. When TG-16.6 ultimately held fire four minutes later, the silhouettes of the Japanese warships were noticeably smaller. By then, *Salt Lake City* had reached 18 knots, and the damaged *Bailey* was retreating at 25 knots with only one operational turbine. Surprisingly, at 1030 hours, the destroyer stopped for a moment due to damage to the feed water pressure line and a temporary loss of electric power, but the damage control team quickly dealt with this problem. *Coghlan* assisted her sister until her gyro was repaired. Without needing to tow *Bailey*, both destroyers limped behind the rest of the group, slowly heading for Adak.[76]

On the other hand, Japanese historians consider 1017 hours to be the end of the battle of the Komandorski Islands when *Maya* and *Abukuma* ceased fire. *Bailey*'s torpedoes were spotted by the 21st Cruiser Squadron and the 1st Torpedo Squadron, which dodged them without any significant problems. Just 13 minutes later, the visual contract with the American task force was lost, and the retreat west continued.[77]

Battle of the Komandorski Islands – Summary
アッツ島沖開戦のまとめ
Attsu-tō oki Kaisen no Matome

The battle of the Komandorski Islands, which lasted approximately three and a half hours, ended without a decisive victory for either side. Theoretically, it was a Japanese tactical success, they damaged three enemy warships, including *Salt Lake City*, and suffered no significant damage in their task force. However, from a strategic point of view, it was a considerable American victory.[78] Without losing any ships, Rear Admiral McMorris performed his operational plan by preventing the crucial enemy convoy from reaching Attu. From a perspective of the Pacific War until the spring of 1943, the battle of the Komandorski Island was also the longest naval artillery engagement between two independent groups of warships without intervention from air or submarines.

Many historians assessed after the war that the Japanese decision to abandon the further pursuit of TG-16.6 had far-reaching consequences for their defeat in the battle. Essentially, it was described as a failure to secure a decisive victory despite the numerical superiority and, thus, missing a chance to deliver the convoy to Attu. In reality, Vice Admiral Hosogaya aborted the mission much earlier, at 0903 hours, when he ordered *Usugumo* and *Sankō Maru* to return to Paramushiru.[79] He made this decision based on a more detailed observation of the battlefield and before receiving information about the critical stock of ammunition for 203mm guns. Due to the efficient evasive manoeuvres of TG-16.6, it seemed that the artillery exchange, which had been going on for over two and a half hours at that point, would not bring a decisive result. Although the Japanese could still score hits with their shells or torpedoes in the final phase, Vice Admiral Hosogaya understood that he would sink one enemy heavy cruiser at best. Even though *Nachi*'s crew misled him regarding the stock of ammunition,[80] it must be stated that he could not pursue the enemy team for too long due to limited fuel supplies. What seems most important, however, is that bombers from Adak and Amchitka could appear in the area at any time, changing the situation in favour of the Americans. Convoy No. 21 "RO" had utterly lost the element of surprise. Even if TG-16.6 could not single-handedly stop its advance towards Attu, the commander of the Fifth Fleet would never risk exposing

three transports and valuable warships to enemy air strikes. The safe return of all vessels to the Kuril Islands was his priority. After heading southwest for over two hours, at 1230 hours, he detached the 1st Torpedo Squadron from the Main Force to protect the transports. Although two Catalinas still tracked *Asaka Maru* and *Sakito Maru* between 1215 and 1305 hours, the American bombers did not attack in the following hours.[81] The entire Japanese task force returned to Paramushiru by 1800 hours the next day without further complications.[82]

The Japanese estimated enemy losses quite accurately. They claimed medium/heavy damage to the Pensacola-class heavy cruiser (over five confirmed 203mm hits), slight damage to the Omaha-class light cruiser (one 203mm hit, which set the ship on fire), and medium damage to one and minor damage to the second destroyer (at least one 203mm hit).[83] Seeing thick smoke from *Salt Lake City* through binoculars, as well as traces of oil and a sudden drop in her speed, the Japanese had good reason to believe that the enemy ship would probably sink. Their own losses were limited to two hits received by *Tama* and five by *Nachi*, which did not threaten either vessel.[84] As for the latter cruiser, the damage can be summarised as light/medium, as the Americans only affected the combat capability of Vice Admiral Hosogaya's flagship. Japanese sources also quote 14–15 men killed and 21–27 wounded.[85] The reconnaissance seaplane catapulted by *Nachi* could not be recovered during the artillery engagement and she tracked the retreating enemy team for some time after the battle. Finally, the aircraft proceeded to Attu, where it made an emergency landing. The local garrison rescued the crew and, after some time, returned to the heavy cruiser.[86]

Immediately after the end of the battle, TG-16.6, minus *Bailey* and *Colghan*, assumed a formation and continued the retreat to the east. Unexpectedly, at 1051 hours, *Salt Lake City*'s radar made contact with unidentified vessels at approximately 18,000m, bearing at the rear of the group. The Americans' instinct was that the enemy had turned back to deal the decisive blow to them. A combat alert was sounded. The crews were nervously running on the decks, waiting for further orders. However, after a while, it turned out that the initial radar contact was a mistake. Everyone could breathe a sigh of relief, and the guns were lowered.[87] At about 1400 hours, friendly bombers (13 B-24s and eight B-25s from Adak and three B-25s and eight P-38s from Amchitka) passed overhead, which were heading for the area indicated by one of the Catalinas following the Japanese ships. Once they arrived on the spot, the crews learned that the enemy was 100 miles farther west. Thus, the B-25s and P-38s returned to base due to shrinking fuel supplies. The B-25s that took off from Adak bombed Attu on the return route and eventually landed on Amchitka.[88]

Meanwhile, Rear Admiral McMorris sent a report of the morning's engagement to Rear Admiral Kinkaid. He also suggested sending *Salt Lake City* and *Bailey* to Adak, while the rest of the group was advised to approach Holtz Bay to torpedo any enemy vessels attempting to reach Attu during the night. The Americans counted on support from bombers stationed at Adak. However, Kinkaid soon stated that the Japanese had submarines and reconnaissance planes in the area, so TG-16.6 was instructed to return to Adak. Once the task force reached the island, *Salt Lake City*, *Monaghan,* and *Coghlan* set off for Dutch Harbor the next day at around 2000 hours. *Richmond*, *Bailey* and *Dale* anchored in Kuluk Bay by midnight on 29 March. The crews loaded additional food, fuel and ammunition supplies, and wounded men were provided with medical assistance. The American toll in the battle of the Komandorski Islands totalled seven killed, seven badly wounded and 13 slightly injured men.[89]

Damage sustained by *Bailey* during the battle. (NH&HC)

The Naval War College's post-war analysis includes valuable information from *Salt Lake City*'s report regarding the assumptions about the abandoned Japanese pursuit after TG-16.6 in order to sink the severely damaged heavy cruiser.[90] This included fear of a massive attack of bombers, exhaustion of ammunition supplies, or severe damage to one of Hosogaya's warships that the Americans overlooked during the battle. The report assessed that the Japanese should have been generally satisfied with the battle result, as they had managed to divert the American attention from the convoy, which was unlikely to reach Attu once detected west of the island.[91]

Contrary to the Americans, the Navy General Staff was strongly dissatisfied with the result of the battle of the Komandorski Islands, which was considered a strategic defeat of the *Nippon Kaigun*. Having double numerical superiority in cruisers, Vice Admiral Hosogaya failed to carry out a vital convoy mission to Attu and did not destroy the enemy task force. The naval engagement with the Americans was thoroughly analysed in terms of errors and wrong decisions made by the commander of the Fifth Fleet, including an overall assessment of the use of artillery and torpedo weapons by Japanese ships. When Vice Admiral Hosogaya ordered the convoy to return to Paramushiru, he made the safest decision possible, but at the same time, he emphasised that he was highly dissatisfied with giving up the pursuit of the enemy. The first general report on the battle (No. 25) was sent to Tokyo just after midnight on 28 March. In addition to information about aborting the convoy mission to Attu and a naval artillery duel with the enemy task force, it justified the failure to secure a decisive victory over TG-16.6. Regardless of the official information provided to the Imperial Headquarters, the Fifth Fleet also independently looked for the reasons for its defeat in the battle of the Komandorski Islands. Owing to comprehensive

study and interviews with officers, the Japanese pointed out the following causes:

1. Insufficient preparation for naval engagement due to bad weather conditions the day before the battle.
2. Incorrect identification of the enemy vessels resulted in the ineffectiveness of *Nachi*'s and *Maya*'s artillery fire in the initial phase of the battle.
3. The distance between the two formations sharply reduced during the pursuit phase, and the failure of the artillery turrets (*Nachi*) caused gunners great difficulties in finding the best angle to shoot at the enemy.
4. When the Americans headed south at about 0900 hours, Hosogaya's task force lost the advantage in the position it had achieved during the pursuit phase.
5. After reducing the distance to the American formation to approximately 14,000m, the ideal one to destroy the enemy with 203mm guns, Hosogaya decided to abandon the further pursuit.
6. Information about the enemy's situation at the end of the battle was insufficient, and the command should have double-checked the early assessments.
7. The 1st Torpedo Squadron could not keep up with the heavy cruisers for most of the battle and, thus, did not cooperate effectively with the rest of the task force.[92]

The points mentioned above cover most of the mistakes made by the Japanese during the naval engagement with TG-16.6. The battle of the Komandorski Islands was fought in unfavourable circumstances for the Fifth Fleet after several days of struggling with weather and waiting for *Usugumo* and *Sankō Maru* to arrive at the rendezvous point. Vice Admiral Hosogaya had little choice but to leave one of the three transports behind, so he decided to wait for her in a safe position south of the Komandorski Islands; this was what he was thinking. He could not have realised that the US Navy intelligence had known his movements from the beginning, and the Japanese convoy had an illusory chance to reach Attu without any obstacles once TG-16.6 appeared in the area. The Fifth Fleet did not have radar at its disposal but was not completely surprised by the enemy, as the Japanese observers noticed part of Rear Admiral McMorris' formation as early as possible. Indeed, the biggest mistake in the initial phase of the battle was ignoring *Inazuma*'s first warning, which indicated that a US Navy warship might have been spotted. Even if Vice Admiral Hosogaya had grave doubts about the ship's identification, he should have ordered his crews to take battle stations until the situation was fully clarified.

Meanwhile, only an hour after the first contact did the Japanese realise they had met the American task force. Importantly, they had a significant numerical superiority over the enemy. In just a few minutes, Vice Admiral Hosogaya made the right decision to head east to cut off TG-16.6's retreat route towards Adak. Still, the Japanese crews, unprepared for the naval engagement and the pursuit, could not secure victory in the further course of the battle. The Fifth Fleet made too many mistakes during that day.

Firstly, the heavy cruisers were entirely unprepared for artillery fire, and by an unfortunate coincidence, two of the three available seaplanes were irreparably damaged. Superior firepower in the first phase could have contributed to a quick victory for the Japanese, primarily since the gunners from *Nachi* were slowly finding the correct angle and distance to the target. Due to the distance from the detected ships in the TG-16.6 formation, the fire of the Japanese heavy cruisers was initially focused on *Richmond*. After

The burial of two American officers from *Salt Lake City* killed during the battle. (NH&HC)

a few minutes, they concentrated on *Salt Lake City* and continued their effort to sink her. However, as the first hits received by *Nachi* showed, the American heavy cruiser thwarted Hosogaya's plans by putting his flagship out of the fight for approximately 30 minutes, giving the entire group more time to escape.

Secondly, due to the earlier instruction to conserve fuel, the 1st Torpedo Squadron had great difficulty to readjust to a new condition and keep up with the 21st Cruiser Squadron: *Abukuma* and her destroyers were excluded from the first phase of the battle. Even when they reached 32 knots, they could not coordinate their actions with the heavy cruisers, so the Japanese were unable to take advantage of their numerical superiority and secure a favourable result. Taking a position on both flanks of the American formation could result in the enemy being caught in the crossfire, but dividing the task force into three smaller groups weakened its firepower.

Third, the hasty sending of the transport ships north immediately after the correct identification of the American warships certainly did not give Vice Admiral Hosogaya more operational freedom. He still had to protect the vulnerable transports from TG-16.6 and the enemy's attempt to break through towards the convoy. The prolonged artillery duel also put the entire task force in massive danger. The American bombers could appear overhead at any point in the battle. Thus, the commander of the Fifth Fleet aimed for a quick and decisive victory in the unexpected naval engagement.

American and Japanese historians tended to assess the actions taken by the 1st Torpedo Squadron critically. However, given the instructions received from the commander of the Fifth Fleet and the distance to Rear Admiral McMorris' formation, it must be stated that Rear Admiral Mori had limited options to contribute to the battle's result. The deadliest Japanese weapon, the Long Lance, was ineffective in the pursuit of American ships, which constantly changed course, and their escape route could not be predicted. The destroyers *Wakaba* and *Hatsushimo* had the best chance of scoring torpedo hits at the very end of the battle. Still, an unexpected engine failure on *Salt Lake City* was repaired within a few minutes, entirely thwarting the plans of the Japanese torpedo officers to administer the *coup de grâce* to the damaged heavy cruiser.

Unlike the Americans, the Japanese catapulted one reconnaissance seaplane, which could provide valuable support during the exchange of fire. However, directing artillery became significantly challenging as TG-16.6 set up a thick smokescreen. Additionally, communication issues between the commander of the Fifth Fleet and the seaplane crew made it impossible to determine the actual technical condition of *Salt Lake City* at the very end of the battle.

In their analysis of the effectiveness of artillery fire, the Japanese were generally critical of their own performance and considered it the main reason for jeopardising the victory. In addition to the reasons mentioned above, the *Maya*'s gunnery officer, Lieutenant Commander Futagami Enzō, admitted during the official evaluation hearing (*Kaigun hanseikai*) that his loaders got confused in the heat of the battle and did not distinguish between high-explosive and armour-piercing 203mm shells. This mistake had far-reaching consequences for the damage to enemy vessels. Thus, it can be assumed that with the correct selection of ammunition and a dose of luck, *Maya*, the only ship that scored hits on *Salt Lake City*, could have sunk the enemy's heavy cruiser or put her out of action for the entire battle.[93] On the other hand, the Japanese evaluation committee positively assessed the performance of the American task force, which maintained the appropriate distance during the escape and scored several hits against *Nachi* in the early stage of the battle.[94]

Acceding to this assessment, it is worth adding that the Japanese advantage in large-calibre guns was alleviated due to the very active participation of American destroyers, as evidenced by the number of shells fired by each warship of both task forces as shown in Table 26.[95]

Table 26: Number of shells fired by the American and Japanese task forces during the battle of the Komandorski Islands.					
	203mm	152mm	140mm	127mm	AA
Nachi	707				276
Maya	904				9
Tama			135		
Abukuma			96		
Hatsushimo				6	
Wakaba					
Ikazuchi				13	
Salt Lake City	832				95
Richmond		271			24
Bailey				482	
Coghlan				750	
Monaghan				235	48
Dale				728	

In the summary of the battle, it is worth adding that apart from the initial misidentification of the enemy convoy, Rear Admiral McMorris made no significant mistakes and saved his group, particularly *Salt Lake City*, from destruction. The Americans were also lucky in the final phase when the Japanese could have quickly finished off the damaged heavy cruiser, but they decided to retreat to the southwest. The General Staff severely criticised Vice Admiral Hosogaya for the lack of decisiveness and non-aggressive stance. Once Captain Jō Ei'ichirō delivered the news about the negative result of the battle of the Komandorski Islands directly to Emperor Hirohito, the Navy General Staff drew up consequences for the commander of the Fifth Fleet.[96] On 31 March, he was replaced by Vice Admiral Kawase Shirō, who was supposed to ensure that the *Nippon Kaigun* would not make any further critical mistakes in the Aleutian Islands campaign. Surprisingly, Rear Admiral Mori escaped responsibility for the outcome of the naval engagement with the Americans. At the beginning of June, he had to turn the command of the 1st Torpedo Squadron over to Rear Admiral Kimura Masatomi due to the sudden deterioration of his health. During medical examinations, he was diagnosed with an intracranial bleed, which prevented his active participation in the North Pacific campaign.[97]

An interesting fact in the analysis of the battle of the Komandorski Islands was a potential alternative scenario, which assumed a more favourable outcome for the Japanese. The Naval War College officers conducted a war game given the enemy would attack with greater determination, use all the ammunition for the heavy cruisers and make fewer errors than in reality. In this scenario, after 50 turns, Rear Admiral McMorris would lose *Salt Lake City*, but Vice Admiral

Rear Admiral Kimura Masatomi. (NDL)

Hosogaya would also pay a price for a more active pursuit. After all, he would have to sacrifice the light cruiser at the head of the formation, described as Kuma-class (*Tama*). In any case, the battle would not have ended with a decisive victory for the Fifth Fleet. Therefore, the possibility of destroying the entire TG-16.6 remained solely an option in the Japanese operational plans despite having numerical superiority.[98]

7
CONCLUSION

結論
Ketsuron

The battle of the Komandorski Islands was the culmination of the aerial and naval struggle for the Aleutian Islands. Since the seizing of Attu and Kiska in early June 1942, the Japanese attempted to actively oppose the American strategy of regaining both islands. Once Convoy No. 21 "RO" failed to reach Attu and the Fifth Fleet could not take advantage of its superiority at sea, the Japanese lost their last upper hand in the North Pacific campaign. Consequently, they had to give up sending bigger convoys to Attu with reinforcements and supplies, preparing on a limited scale for the enemy landing. The forces gradually gathered by TF-16 on Adak and Amchitka were a herald of a larger offensive operation in the near future. Concerns about the American colossal material superiority, initially raised by the *Nippon Kaigun*'s planners, became a bitter reality. If the Japanese Navy wanted to preserve its combat potential during the further stage of the war, it could no longer risk losing valuable warships on transport missions in the North Pacific, far from air bases in the Kuril Islands. Starting from the end of February, and especially after the battle of the Komandorski Islands, submarines took over the role of delivering supplies to the Attu and Kiska garrisons. They had a better chance to get to the Aleutians from the Kuril Islands and maintain the communications between Kiska and Attu. However, the submarines' size severely constrained their transport capabilities. Nonetheless, the *Nippon Kaigun* often used them to ship specialised supplies or officers by mid-June.[1]

The Aleutian Islands campaign from 3 June 1942 to 27 March 1943 was undoubtedly the period of equal rivalry between the Japanese and the Americans. The latter profited from their advantages through various strategic initiatives and secured the approach to reclaiming Attu and Kiska. Once the struggle in the North Pacific turned to unquestioned domination by the Americans, the Japanese could only prepare for the worst.

These two volumes have depicted the aerial and naval aspects of the Aleutian Islands campaign, influencing a different perception of the research questions presented in the introduction.

Compared to the parallel campaigns of the Pacific War, it must be assessed that the struggle for the Aleutian Islands had secondary strategic importance. As shown, Operation AL was not designed to divert American attention from Operation MI and force them to disperse their forces since the primary plans of the Combined Fleet and Navy General Staff envisaged destroying the main potential of the US Navy in the Pacific. Yet, seizing the western part of the Aleutian Islands was an equally important task from the point of view of the long-term defence of the home islands. Still, it certainly did not overshadow the ultimate goal of the *Nippon Kaigun*, which wanted to take advantage of its strategic initiative to push back the Allies from East Asia. Due to the defeat of Admiral Yamamoto's plans concerning Midway, his attention focused on Guadalcanal in the following months. From August 1942 to February 1943, Japanese Navy and Army planners sacrificed most of the available manpower and supplies to retake the island from the enemy.

Although the fighting for the 'hell island' took place in a theatre of war much further away than the Aleutian Islands, the Guadalcanal campaign become a crucial litmus paper for assessing the overall war situation.[2] Giving up control over the island to the Americans meant a complete loss of strategic initiative and the need to go on the deep defence, a nightmare that the *Nippon Kaigun* wanted to avoid at all costs in 1941. Even after the evacuation from Guadalcanal in February 1943, the Japanese Navy committed to halting the enemy's advance up the Solomon Islands archipelago and thus, still considered the South Pacific as the priority front.

The Aleutian Islands campaign was the main topic of deliberations at the headquarters of both sides only for a short period. The North Pacific became the centre their attention immediately after the battle of Midway, but immediately lost its significance when the Japanese secretly advanced to Guadalcanal and significantly progressed in the construction of the airfield on the island in early July 1942. The seizing of Attu and Kiska by enemy troops was a great shock for the American military and civilians. The US Navy in its first instinct intended to move aircraft carriers to the North Pacific to challenge the projected Japanese advance towards Alaska. At that time, the *Nippon Kaigun* also kept their remaining available aircraft carriers east of the Kuril Islands in anticipation of the enemy's attempt to retake Attu and Kiska. It seemed that one braver decision by CINCPAC or the Combined Fleet could have led to another decisive naval battle. In reality, however, neither the Americans nor the Japanese were ready for such a risk. Once confirming that the opposing side was not planning large-scale offensive operations in the North Pacific, the aircraft carriers were withdrawn to safe bases, foreseeing their participation in other strategic initiatives.

The secondary strategic importance of the Aleutian Islands campaign can also be reflected by numbers. Unlike the struggle for Guadalcanal, both sides engaged few warships, planes and soldiers in the North Pacific over 10 months. While the Americans enjoyed quite large forces within 11 AF and could count on building up the garrisons, the naval command and TF-8/TF-16 suffered from a constant lack of warships. Some of the vessels were also sent to the South Pacific during the decisive stage of the fighting. On the contrary, the Japanese struggled with the urgent need to reinforce the Attu and Kiska garrisons from the very beginning of the campaign. They did not have a fully operational airfield on either island, which negatively impacted the air defence and the setting up of any air unit that could complete on equal footing with the enemy bombers and fighters. Equally, the Fifth Fleet, although theoretically superior to TF-8/TF-16 for most of the campaign, eventually turned out to be unable to adequately protect the shipping routes to the Aleutian Islands.

In connection with the above findings, the question automatically arises whether the Japanese should have occupied Attu and Kiska after the disastrous defeat at the battle of Midway? The answer remains not clear. In the strategic situation in June 1942, it seemed that this was a necessary step that gave the Japanese Army and Navy a sense of at least partial control over the North Pacific area. It was not until the advanced stage of the Aleutian Islands campaign when both sides realised that control over the entire chain did not imply an easier approach to Japan's home islands. The lack of appropriate infrastructure, the harsh climate most of the year, as well as the distances between bases made a potential American aircraft carrier strike along the northern route highly unlikely. The Japanese were well aware of these factors. Still, they were afraid that after the expansion of naval and air bases in the western part of the Aleutians, the US Navy would gain a risky, but open space in the later stage

Japanese soldiers with the national flag, the *Hi no Maru*, at the beginning of the Aleutian Islands campaign. (NHK)

of the conflict. Surprisingly, given the internal rivalry between the Japanese Army and Navy, the capture of Attu and Kiska and their subsequent defence at all costs were equally supported by the Army and the Navy General Staff. Beside the threat of further carrier raids on Tokyo, the reason for this was a justified fear of establishing American-Soviet military cooperation aimed directly against Japan. Although Tokyo and Moscow had been bound by the Neutrality Pact since April 1941, the Japanese expected that the Soviets would respect the treaty as long as it was to their favour. As the events of August 1945 proved, these forecasts were not far from the truth, especially once the Americans convinced Stalin to join the war with Japan. Had the Navy General Staff not pressed for the capture of Attu and Kiska, the Japanese admirals and generals would have thought that *Nippon Kaigun* had completely overlooked the defence of the North Pacific and had given the enemy a chance to encircle Japan.

If the Aleutian Islands campaign was a natural consequence of Japan's geostrategic position during the Pacific War, the final point should consider whether the *Nippon Kaigun* (with the support of the *Nippon Rikugun*) used its limited resources effectively to secure the northern flank and prepare for the defence of Attu and Kiska in 1943. The analysis of the campaign presented in these volumes allows the author to answer this question negatively. Although the Fifth Fleet was not defeated and retained full combat capability, within the crucial 10 months the Japanese made too many mistakes, which led to the cutting-off of the Attu and Kiska garrisons at the end of March 1943. By the time the Americans captured Adak, the Imperial Headquarters had much greater opportunities to build up the Japanese bases in the Aleutians. Instead, the higher command made the wrong decision to withdraw from Attu and delayed the construction of a new airfield on Kiska. The directive to defend both islands until the spring thaw of 1943 contained too short-sighted orders since the Japanese could repel enemy attacks much longer by sending relatively small forces to the chain. This claim is based on the performance of the floatplane fighters, which effectively dealt with the subsequent 11 AF raids until October 1942. They eventually lost due to the lack of spare parts and crucial supplies. If Kiska's defenders had a fully operational airfield or at least a runway for fighters, the American bombers would not have felt invulnerable during the missions over the enemy bases. The greater involvement in the Aleutian Islands campaign required only the explicit consent of the Navy General Staff to establish a fighter air group in the North

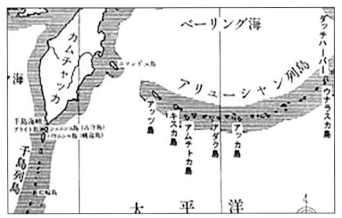

Japanese map of the Aleutians as the northern approach toward Japan. (Haisen no Rekishi)

Americans disembarking supplies in the Aleutians. (Dmitri Kessel/Life Pictures)

Pacific and to express the readiness to replenish its combat losses regularly. Even 10 operational Japanese Navy fighters could have had a colossal impact on the defence of Kiska and Attu, at least until the end of 1942.

There is no doubt that the Guadalcanal campaign occupied much of the attention of the Imperial Headquarters. However, when the officers in Tokyo learned about the American capture of Amchitka in late January 1943, they suddenly realised the gravity of the situation in the North Pacific. Due to the limited number of transports and warships, the Japanese could not make up for lost time in just a few weeks, especially when enemy bombers already had fighter support, and the US Navy increased its patrol missions in the western part of the Aleutians. From the Japanese point of view, it may have appeared that the strategic position of the garrisons on Kiska and Attu had unexpectedly deteriorated in late January and early February 1943. In reality, this was only the consequence of neglecting the North Pacific campaign for over seven months. Although the Imperial Headquarters initially advocated the seizing of the western Aleutians, it perceived the North Pacific campaign as a potential war of attrition. The high command in Tokyo wanted to avoid sending additional soldiers and equipment to the chain, as they were essential elsewhere. In this respect, the Japanese military leadership was highly inconsistent. It accepted successive failed offensives to reconquer Guadalcanal while purposely limiting the help to halt the American advance in a much less engaging theatre of war. This way of thinking narrowed down Japanese options to the defence of two isolated islands, ignoring other possibilities. For example, the Fifth Fleet and the North Sea Garrison Force could have occupied the Semichi Islands to establish a new observation outpost and a safer seaplane base.

The author's goal is not to convince readers that the Japanese could win the Aleutian Island campaign with better planning. It was quite the opposite. Eventually, they had to yield to the enemy's numerical superiority in the longer term. Still, the Japanese decision to withdraw from competing at sea near the Aleutian Islands at the end of March 1943 was a direct consequence of past mistakes and inaction. Even the Fifth Fleet had a clear advantage over TG-16.6 during the convoy mission to Attu but was not able to turn to its favour. Although a decisive victory over Rear Admiral McMorris's task force would not automatically facilitate the safe arrival of Convoy No. 21 "RO" at its destination, as the summary of the battle had shown, the Japanese would have another opportunity to reinforce the Attu garrison in the next two or three weeks. There is also a high probability that a *Nippon Kaigun* victory in the battle of

the Komandorski Islands would have prolonged the preparations for Operation Landcrab, until the Americans had deployed additional warships to the North Pacific and had achieved naval superiority.[3] Additionally, if the Japanese had built airfields on Attu and Kiska with at least a small fighter wing in the first months of the campaign, their positions in the Aleutians would not have been lost so fast, just over a year since both islands had been conquered.[4]

Above all, the author wants to strongly agree with B. Paul's words that during the Aleutian Islands campaign, the weather was a more formidable enemy than the opposing side.[5] His book contains fantastic personal stories, including refreshing views on everyday stationing in the North Pacific. Reading Paul's work, one can realise that 'the long hours of daylight at the height of summer and the short daylight hours of deep winter could interfere with sleep patterns' or that 'the Aleutian area didn't get as much food attention as it should've,' depending mainly on canned and mostly frozen rations.[6] Most importantly, however, one can learn that the winter of 1942–43 in the Aleutians was the worst in 34 years,[7] which massively impacted the struggle between the Americans and the Japanese, giving the latter an upper hand in the defence of Attu and Kiska. Therefore, once analysing the Japanese strategy in the North Pacific, the author is tempted to claim that the weather was their greatest enemy, yet the biggest ally at the same time.

The first contact with the Aleutian Islands was certainly a big shock for the soldiers unfamiliar with the desolate and rugged landscape. There are disproportionately more American diaries and testimonies concerning the stationing and everyday life in the bases on the chain. However, the Japanese perspective on the same matter still remains unknown for Western historians. It worth mentioning that service in the Aleutians was for the Japanese men an equally traumatic experience, even for people who had experienced the harsh climate of the Kuril Islands. Most Japanese documents and accounts of the North Pacific campaign focus on military aspects. Still, Sugiyama Kira, a famous *Nippon Rikugun* photographer, described ordinary life in the Aleutians in his diary in picturesque words, which attracted the author's attention despite his awareness

American personnel sheltering near a wrecked aircraft on the Aleutian Islands. (Dmitri Kessel/Life Pictures)

of local environmental conditions. Apart from garrison duties, Sugiyama perfectly captured the specificity of the duty in the chain, showing how it could be rich in new experiences and observations. Although the impression was drafted soon after the landing on Attu, it remains valid regardless of the season:

A transport ship departing the island.

The transport ship, now completely unloaded, began to slowly drift away from Attu. Using the provided photographic film, I tried to record as precisely as possible the silhouette of the ship and a local muddy hill. While walking around the area, I captured some soldiers who seemed to be working on the construction of military facilities. I recorded a film with an Eyemo camera that was to be used for Japanese newsreels, and if I added all the recordings made so far, I would have a lot of material.

There was no nature at all in the newsreel recorded by the Eyemo camera. In my long life as a cameraman, it was the first time I did my job without any self-confidence. Since it was extremely challenging to convey all the impressions about this swampy hill in the video, I added some commentary. Without using my surname, I marked the time and signed it with my first name. For this reason, when my recording was first published in the newspaper [as a still from the film], it was credited as "Army Photojournalist Kira's shot".[8]

Towards Annihilation and Total Defeat: The Aleutian Islands Campaign from March to July 1943
絶滅及び完敗に向けて、昭和18年3月から同年6月までアリューシャン作戦
Zetsumetsu oyobi Kampai ni mukete, Shōwa 18-nen 3-gatsu kara 6-gatsu made no Aryūshan Sakusen

The result of the battle of the Komandorski Islands encouraged the Americans to continue preparations for the planned invasion of Attu in May, which gained even more significance in the following weeks. Thanks to the further expansion of the airfields at Adak and Amchitka and the bringing of additional aircraft, 11 AF could finally consider conducting regular raids on Kiska. Although the weather conditions in the Aleutians were as unpredictable as ever, the slowly approaching spring allowed for sending as many as 83 bombing missions by 21 April. By the end of the month, 640 tons of bombs had been dropped on enemy military facilities.[9]

CINCPAC determined that during the landing on Attu, Rear Admiral Kinkaid would enjoy the support of one escort carrier, three battleships, three heavy cruisers, three light cruisers, a dozen destroyers and many other auxiliary vessels. By then, TF-16 was to ensure that no Japanese reinforcements reached the island and, starting in mid-April, a tight blockade was ordered. A few days later, TG-16.6 went to sea on a combat patrol and also for routine gunnery drills. In the afternoon of 25 April, Rear Admiral McMorris's task force, comprising the light cruisers *Richmond*, *Detroit*, *Santa Fe*, and the destroyers *Caldwell*, *Bancroft*, *Coghlan*, *Frazier*, *Edwards*, and *Gansevoort*, was ordered to bombard Holtz Bay and Chichagof Bay the next day.[10] Thus, on the morning of 26 April, TG-16.6 closed to Attu and shelled at the enemy's positions for less than 30 minutes. Apart from a few Japanese planes sighted from *Richmond*, no activity was reported. Although the American ships opened fire from a distance of only 8,000m, the crews later admitted that the enemy's artillery positions were well camouflaged, which made it difficult to estimate the result of the bombardment except for a few probable hits on anti-aircraft gun batteries.[11] Rear Admiral McMorris believed that his group could have achieved much better results if only the weather conditions had allowed the reconnaissance seaplanes to be catapulted. Photos of Attu taken several days later showed a couple of shell craters in the vicinity of identified military facilities. Still, it was assessed that the bombardment could not have caused much damage to the defenders.[12]

By the end of April, the Americans had gathered 19,067 military and 7,811 naval personnel on Adak. The island quickly became the main operational base in the western Aleutians. In the meantime, the US Army and US Navy built up their positions in Amchitka, bringing there 10,260 and 903 men respectively. A much more important fact was that the Seabees completed the construction of a new 1,500m runway for bombers. The resources and infrastructure available at forward bases were sufficient to launch an invasion of Attu in the coming days.[13]

American preparations for the landing, including preliminary staff studies, lasted five months. The Western Defense Command estimated in mid-March 1943 that the Japanese garrison on Attu comprised approximately 1,350 men, mostly from anti-aircraft artillery and construction units, armed with infantry weapons. Rear Admiral Kinkaid was more cautious in his calculations and indicated fewer than 1,600 men with a similar organisation. The TF-16 command was also confident that the Fifth Fleet had failed to send any convoy towards the island from March to May. This prediction was accurate. However, the Americans made a significant mistake in identifying the Japanese forces. At the beginning of May, Colonel Yamasaki's garrison numbered approximately 2,650 men. It would have been 20 percent bigger if the convoy from Paramushiru scheduled for mid-May had managed to reach the island before the enemy landed.

According to Captain Yamamoto Chikao's recollections, the 1st Section of the Navy General Staff did not believe in the American invasion of Attu practically until the very end, and certainly not in May 1943. At that time, they were convinced that the enemy would first try to capture Kiska.[14] The Fifth Fleet and the *Nippon Rikugun* even planned to launch a counterattack against Amchitka at the end of April or the beginning of May, but initial plans stalled. Based on Lieutenant Commander Genda's testimony, it is known that once the airfields on Attu and Kiska were constructed, the *Nippon Kaigun* intended to send its fighters to both islands around mid-July. Until that time, the defenders were to rely on floatplane fighters.[15]

The light cruiser *Santa Fe*. (Navasource)

This unrealistic plan could not come true for one reason – the Americans were going to launch Operation Landcrab soon. Approximately 15,000 men, organised as part of Task Force 51, were initially scheduled to set off from Cold Bay on 3 May. However, terrible weather conditions delayed their departure. Ultimately, the landing date on Attu was rescheduled from 7 to 11 May. Eventually, the Americans appeared on the island beneath the cover of thick fog, landing in Massacre Bay and Holtz Bay. They smoothly secured the bridgeheads on the northern and southern parts of the island. The Japanese immediately noticed the presence of the invasion fleet. They withdrew to previously prepared positions inland and warned the Fifth Fleet and Tokyo, asking for help in the defence.

The first day of Operation Landcrab did not indicate any major problems with seizing Attu. It quickly turned out that the Japanese were dug-in to their positions much more robustly than initially expected. Artillery fire of warships, providing support for infantry, could not destroy well-hidden bunkers. On 12 May, an arduous American advance on land began, bringing heavy losses to the defenders and attackers daily due to harsh weather. Japanese soldiers fought fiercely for every foot of ground but eventually had to retreat gradually towards the main camp under the pressure of the stronger enemy.[16]

However, the real drama of the defenders took place several thousand kilometres away, as the critical decisions were made over their heads. Upon learning of the invasion of Attu, the Combined Fleet began the concentration of its forces near Yokosuka on 15 May to prepare for a possible sortie. Aircraft carriers *Zuikaku*, *Shōkaku* and *Zuihō*, the heavy cruisers *Mogami*, *Kumano* and *Suzuya*, the light cruisers *Agano* and *Ōyodo*, and seven destroyers were already there.

Two days later, the commander of the Combined Fleet, Admiral Koga Mineichi, set off from Truk towards Tokyo Bay, leading the battleships *Musashi*, *Kongō* and *Haruna*, the aircraft carrier *Hiyō*, the heavy cruisers *Tone* and *Chikuma*, and five destroyers. An important part of his journey was the transport of Admiral Yamamoto's ashes, who had been killed a month earlier in an American ambush over Bougainville.

The *Nippon Kaigun* expected the enemy invasion fleet to consist of four or five fleet carriers and numerous screening warships. The idea of giving the US Navy a decisive sea battle blossomed in the minds of the Japanese. Unexpectedly, on 18 May, the Imperial Headquarters, after six days of detailed analyses and considering the opinions of the Army General Staff and the Navy General Staff, presented a preliminary opinion that the chances of regaining Attu were slim. The Combined Fleet command learned of these arrangements while en route to the home islands, but Admiral Koga continued his advance north. A day later, Emperor Hirohito became personally involved in the matter. He urged the Fifth Fleet to rescue the Attu garrison and queried the Combined Fleet about the actual strategic situation. Theoretically, the Fifth Fleet was ready for action on 20 May, when virtually all of its forces were gathered at Paramushiru, including heavy cruisers *Nachi*, *Maya*, *Haguro* and *Myōkō*, seaplane tender *Kimikawa Maru*, light cruisers *Abukuma*, *Tama* and *Kiso*, 10 destroyers and a dozen auxiliary vessels. On the same day, Hirohito visited the Imperial Headquarters office and observed the decision-making process. In his presence, the *Nippon Kaigun* and the *Nippon Rikugun* agreed that the Attu garrison would be partially evacuated by submarines within the possibilities, and the Kiska garrison would be withdrawn in several rounds by submarines, destroyers and

American infantry move a casualty by stretcher during the retaking of Attu. (National Park Service)

transports. The Army and Navy officers were not satisfied with that arrangement. Still, at the same time, they felt convinced that 2,000 men could not be rescued by risking too many crucial warships in a premature confrontation with the Americans.

On 20 May, the Imperial Headquarters sent disastrous news to the Northern Army regarding the rejection of plans to send reinforcements to Attu. Lieutenant General Higuchi and his staff were shocked and asked for a justification for this decision. In the afternoon of the next day, Lieutenant General Hata Hikosaburō, Deputy Chief of the Army General Staff, personally went to Paramushiru to convey detailed arrangements. They had a conversation in a strained atmosphere, but both agreed that nothing could be done to change the Imperial Headquarters' vision. Lieutenant General Hata swore he supported the demand to send relief to the Attu garrison and argued with opposing officers. At the same time, he tried to shift the responsibility to the *Nippon Kaigun*, recalling that its command prioritised the South Pacific campaign and, thus, it could not support the operations in the North Pacific. Army officers claimed they could not force the Navy to change its position.

As a consequence, by citing the Imperial Headquarters' order requiring the Nippon Kaigun and Rikugun to cooperate closely in defence of the Aleutian Islands, the latter resigned from asking for assistance for the Attu garrison in exchange for the *Nippon Kaigun*'s unconditional consent to participate in the evacuation of the Kiska garrison. The price for saving at least part of the Northern Army was abandoning the defenders of Attu, considering the evacuation was utterly unfeasible. Lieutenant General Higuchi later wrote that once he agreed to such a deal with the Navy, he felt deep down in his heart that he had let Colonel Yamasaki and his men die without any help.[17]

The same evening, the commander of the Northern Army sent a telegram to Colonel Yamasaki, sincerely apologising to him for the fact that the Imperial Headquarters and the Army General Staff decided not to support the Attu garrison based on meticulous considerations. In response, Lieutenant General Higuchi received information that in such a case, the defenders would change their tactics from surviving subsequent assaults to a decisive action that would inflict massive losses on the enemy. Colonel Yamasaki also claimed that he could break American morale in a way other than defeating them on the island. Given the circumstances, he believed that his soldiers would sacrifice their lives and that their souls would

A mortar team shelling Japanese positions on Attu. (National Park Service)

save the nation. It is unknown whether Lieutenant General Higuchi expected this type of answer, but it significantly facilitated further decisions. On 23 May, the commander of the Northern Army sent another dispatch to Attu, summarising the findings of recent days – the Army and Navy explored all options and, despite the sincere desire to evacuate the soldiers from Attu, it was officially decided that the best solution would be to inflict tremendous losses on the enemy. Lieutenant General Higuchi also expressed hope that Colonel Yamasaki was ready to show the true spirit and glory of the *Nippon Kaigun* through an 'honourable defeat' (*gyokusai*).[18]

This term, used for the first time during the Pacific War, may raise various questions for English-speaking readers. From the point of view of Japanese culture, which is full of ambiguous words and undefined phrases, *gyokusai* has a special meaning. It is a suicidal defence without the possibility of surrendering to the opponent. The Imperial Headquarters and Lieutenant General Higuchi still needed Hirohito's formal consent to sacrifice the Attu garrison. They received it on 24 May. At the same time, they were severely criticised for leading to a situation where the brave soldiers had to die to cover up the military leadership's incompetence. The next day, Colonel Yamasaki thanked the Emperor for sanctioning the 'honourable defeat'. Once he read his words, he no longer doubted that his offer to sacrifice his men was in the best interest of the entire nation.

While the Imperial Headquarters made decisions regarding the fate of the Attu garrison, the Americans pushed the remaining defenders into a small pocket near Chichagof Bay. On 25 May, a group consisting of the light cruisers *Abukuma* and *Kiso* and eight destroyers set off from Paramushiru to counterattack the enemy invasion fleet and provide supplies to the fighting troops. The Army knew it was a gesture of goodwill rather than actual help from the Navy. The destroyers *Kamikaze* and *Numakaze* tried to reach the island on 28 May, but they were ordered to return to Paramushiru

Admiral Koga Mineichi. (NARA)

Colonel Yamasaki Yasuyo. (NDL)

due to bad weather. A day later, the Combined Fleet also cancelled the rescue mission. Little could be done then, especially in opposition to the Imperial Headquarters' orders.

After midnight on 29 May, when a group of approximately 800 Japanese soldiers remained alive with little stock of ammunition and food, Colonel Yamasaki felt that this was the time to fulfil the promise of an 'honourable defeat'. After listening to his last speech, those who were unable to continue the fight committed suicide, while the rest silently slipped into the darkness towards the enemy positions. The order to attack was passed, and a moment later, the Japanese charged like an avalanche, shouting 'banzai' and running directly under the machine guns. This was certainly not the Americans' first experience of this Japanese infantry charge. Still, they were surprised by the tsunami of the fanatical samurais who had nothing to lose. The psychological effect of this suicidal attack must have been devastating since the Japanese managed to use the initiative to break through the first line of defence, causing a momentary panic. A chaotic bayonet fight broke out, where survival was determined more by luck than by tactics. There were no safe positions or perimeters. The last charge, however, quickly lost its momentum. With every passing metre, the Japanese soldiers dispersed in several different directions.

The Americans finally woke up and began to use their numerical and fire superiority. It was the end for Colonel Yamasaki and his men. Regardless of their true samurai fighting spirit, they knew they would be methodically surrounded and killed. The fighting continued until the following evening when the last Japanese positions were secured. Operation Landcrab ended with the annihilation of the Attu garrison. According to various estimates, the defenders lost from 2,351 to 2,638 men. In any case, it was roughly 99 percent of Colonel Yamasaki's detachment.[19] Only 28 private soldiers were taken prisoner, including some who were seriously injured or had suffered a complete nervous breakdown and were, therefore, unable to commit suicide.

Despite the clear victory, the Americans also suffered heavy losses during the battle of Attu. The capture of the island resulted in 549 dead, 1,148 wounded and 2,132 injured soldiers.[20] Although the first Japanese 'honourable defeat' resulted from poor strategic planning rather than deliberate tactics, it was a genuine warning before the subsequent landing operations on the isolated islands. The battle of

Attu opened a new chapter in the Pacific War, which largely shaped the contemporary vision of this conflict by public.

After capturing Attu and Shemya as part of Operation Landcrab, the Americans began the final stage of the Aleutian Islands campaign, namely the reconquest of Kiska. In addition to the regular bombing raids by 11 AF, the US Navy decided to engage its warships to bombard the completely isolated island. The shelling was carried out on 6 July, and in the following days, individual US Navy vessels tried to make the defenders' lives miserable.

However, the Japanese learned a valuable lesson from the mistakes made during preparations for the defence of Attu. On 27 May, before the annihilation of Colonel Yamasaki's garrison, the *Nippon Kaigun* ordered the commencement of an evacuation from Kiska, codenamed Operation KE. By 26 June, submarines managed to rescue 820 wounded soldiers and civilian workers of the Army and Navy from the island.[21] The price for such a bold undertaking was the loss of *I-7*, *I-9* and *I-24*.[22]

The second round of Operation KE was announced on 28 June. The *Nippon Kaigun* faced the even more difficult task of evacuating almost 5,200 men under tremendous time pressure. According to Navy planners, the operation's success or spectacular failure depended on the 'cautious surprise'. Namely speaking, the Japanese envisaged relying on radars to observe the waters surrounding Kiska and planned to approach the island beneath the thick fog, accepting even zero visibility. The evacuation involved 11 submarines and the Screen Force, comprised of the light cruisers *Abukuma* and *Kiso*, 11 destroyers, and two auxiliary ships. After the first unsuccessful attempt to reach the island, on 22 July, the Japanese ships, personally led by Vice Admiral Kawase and reinforced by the light cruiser *Tama*, left Paramushiru and set course for Kiska. Meteorological forecasts indicated that on 25 July, the nearby waters would be covered with thick fog, providing excellent cover for the convoy. However, due to terrible weather conditions in the following days, the date of the operation was slightly postponed. Finally, before noon on 28 July, Vice Admiral Kawase's task force reached Kiska and dropped anchor. Using *Daihatsu* landing craft, which made multiple trips between the shore and the ships, 5,183 soldiers and civilian army workers were evacuated in just 55 minutes.[23] Soldiers left all their weapons and unnecessary equipment to rapidly board the landing crafts and use their capacity to the maximum. Every minute of presence at Kiska was a mortal danger for the warships. Finally,

The bodies of the Japanese soldiers killed during the last attack. (Wikimedia Commons)

the Japanese decided to scuttle their *Daihatsu* to expedite the final steps of the evacuation. Once the observers reported no one was left on the island, the Japanese ships began a hasty retreat westward at 28 knots. The thick fog in the Aleutian Islands was their greatest ally, and all vessels returned safely to Paramushiru between 31 July and 1 August. Operation KE was a complete success. Soon, the Japanese called it the 'Miracle on Kiska' ('*Kisuka no Kiseki*') since no one expected that the Fifth Fleet would be able to return and evacuate the garrison without any losses.[24] The number of men rescued by each ship is shown in Table 27.[25]

Table 27: Summary of men evacuated from Kiska	
Warship	Evacuated men
Abukuma	1,202
Kiso	1,189
Yūgumo	479
Kazagumo	478
Akigumo	463
Asagumo	476
Usugumo	478
Hibiki	418

The last episode of the Aleutian Islands campaign was Operation Cottage. The American and Canadian invasion forces occupied the abandoned Kiska on 15 August. Although the attackers had not intercepted any enemy radio traffic for over two weeks, they were unsure whether the Japanese had not camouflaged their positions inland. During the landing, the Americans and Canadians mistook each other for enemies, which led to a tragic friendly fire resulting in 32 killed and 50 wounded soldiers. The Japanese also left numerous mines and booby traps in the local bay and abandoned hideouts, causing additional losses among the enemy infantrymen. In any case, Kiska was captured. Over a year after its loss, the Americans achieved complete victory in the struggle for the Aleutian Islands.

The North Pacific campaign from April to August 1943, outlined in the last pages of this volume, fascinates and frightens the author simultaneously, as the fate of the 'twin Japanese garrisons' was vastly different. The tragedy of the 'honourable defeat' of Attu and the 'Miracle on Kiska' certainly deserves a more detailed study. The potential book, a natural continuation of this work, will fill in the gaps in the Japanese perspective on the bloody and blurry events of the less-known theatre of the Pacific War.

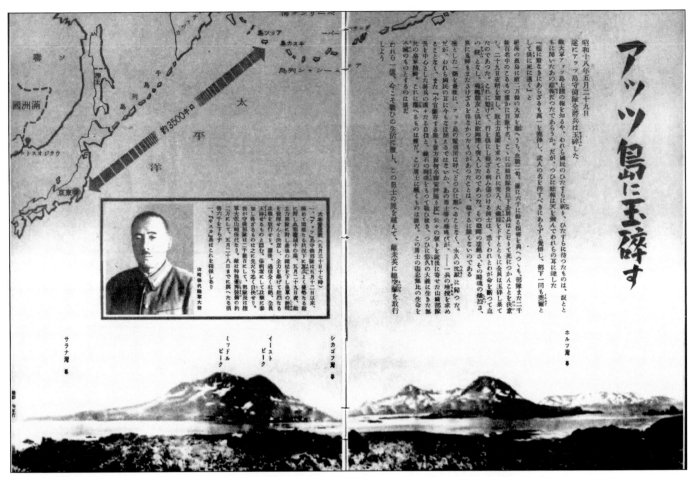

The photos from the Japanese Weekly Photographic Review showing the 'honourable defeat' on Attu. (JACAR)

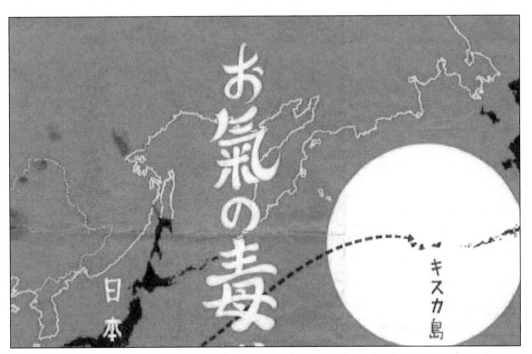

The American propaganda leaflet dropped on the Japanese soldiers on Kiska saying, 'I am so sorry for you'.
(Wikimedia Commons)

BIBLIOGRAPHY

Japan Center for Asian Historical Records
アジア歴史資料センター—(*Ajia Rekishi Shiryō Sentaa*)
JACAR: Ref. A06031087100: Weekly Photographic Magazine No. 276 (in Japanese)
JACAR: Ref. C05023367800: Public Business Trip (Public Business Trip, Overseas) (2) (in Japanese)
JACAR: Ref. C14121137400: Aleutian Campaign Daily Calendar, S17.09 (in Japanese)
JACAR: Ref. C14121137500: Aleutian Campaign Daily Calendar, S17.10 (in Japanese)
JACAR: Ref. C14121137600: Aleutian Campaign Daily Calendar, S17.11 (in Japanese)
JACAR: Ref. C14121137700: Aleutian Campaign Daily Calendar, S17.12 (in Japanese)
JACAR: Ref. C14121137800: Aleutian Campaign Daily Calendar, S18.01 (in Japanese)
JACAR: Ref. C14121138400: Aleutian Campaign Daily Calendar, S18.02 (in Japanese)
JACAR: Ref. C14121138500: Aleutian Campaign Daily Calendar, S18.03 (in Japanese)
JACAR: Ref. C14121138600: Aleutian Campaign Daily Calendar, S18.04 (in Japanese)
JACAR: Ref. C14121138700: Aleutian Campaign Daily Calendar, S18.05 (in Japanese)
JACAR: Ref. C14121138800: Aleutian Campaign Daily Calendar, S18.06 (in Japanese)
JACAR: Ref. C14121138900: Aleutian Campaign Daily Calendar, S18.07 (in Japanese)
JACAR: Ref. C14121139000: Aleutian Campaign Daily Calendar, S18.08 (in Japanese)
JACAR: Ref. C14121147900: Campaign Until the Evacuation from the Aleutians (…) Prospects (in Japanese)
JACAR: Ref. C14121148000: Campaign Until the Evacuation from the Aleutians (…) Imperial Headquarters' Leadership in Campaign (in Japanese)
JACAR: Ref. C14121148100: Campaign Until the Evacuation from the Aleutians (…) Combined Fleet's Leadership in Campaign (in Japanese)
JACAR: Ref. C14121148100: Campaign Until the Evacuation from the Aleutians (…) Northern Force's Leadership in Campaign (in Japanese)
JACAR: Ref. C14121148500: Campaign Until the Evacuation from the Aleutians (…) Battle of the Komandorski Islands (in Japanese)
JACAR: Ref. C14121148600: Campaign Until the Evacuation from the Aleutians (…) The Enemy Capture of Attu Island (in Japanese)
JACAR: Ref. C14121148700: Campaign Until the Evacuation from the Aleutians (…) Evacuation from Kiska (in Japanese)
JACAR: Ref. C14121148800: Campaign Until the Evacuation from the Aleutians (…) Screening Convoys (in Japanese)
JACAR: Ref. C16120635400: S18.03.19–03.31, Pacific War Outline of Progress (5)
JACAR: Ref. C08051628400: S17.08–S17.10, 5. Kū Action Report (1) (in Japanese)
JACAR: Ref. C08051628500: S17.08–S17.10, 5. Kū Action Report (2) (in Japanese)
JACAR: Ref. C08051628600: S17.08–S17.10, 5. Kū Action Report (3) (in Japanese)
JACAR: Ref. C08051676900: S17.11–S18.04, 452. Kū Action Report (1) (in Japanese)
JACAR: Ref. C08051677000: S17.11–S18.04, 452. Kū Action Report (2) (in Japanese)
JACAR: Ref. C08051677100: S17.11–S18.04, 452. Kū Action Report (3) (in Japanese)
JACAR: Ref. C08030082200: S17.08–S17.10, 1. Torpedo Squadron Action Report (3) (in Japanese)
JACAR: Ref. C08030082300: S17.08–S17.10, 1. Torpedo Squadron Action Report (4) (in Japanese)
JACAR: Ref. C08030082600: S17.11.01–S17.11.28, 1. Torpedo Squadron Detailed Action Report (1) (in Japanese)
JACAR: Ref. C08030082700: S17.11.01–S17.11.28, 1. Torpedo Squadron Detailed Action Report (2) (in Japanese)
JACAR: Ref. C08030082800: S17.11.01–S17.11.28, 1. Torpedo Squadron Detailed Action Report (3) (in Japanese)
JACAR: Ref. C08030082900: S17.11.01–S17.11.28, 1. Torpedo Squadron Detailed Action Report (4) (in Japanese)
JACAR: Ref. C08030083200: S17.12.01–S12.02.28, 1. Torpedo Squadron Detailed Action Report (1) (in Japanese)
JACAR: Ref. C08030083300: S17.12.01–S12.02.28, 1. Torpedo Squadron Detailed Action Report (2) (in Japanese)
JACAR: Ref. C08030083400: S17.12.01–S12.02.28, 1. Torpedo Squadron Detailed Action Report (3) (in Japanese)
JACAR: Ref. C08030083700: S18.03.01–S18.05.31, 1. Torpedo Squadron Action Report (1) (in Japanese)
JACAR: Ref. C08030083800: S18.03.01–S18.05.31, 1. Torpedo Squadron Action Report (2) (in Japanese)
JACAR: Ref. C08030083900: S18.03.01–S18.05.31, 1. Torpedo Squadron Action Report (3) (in Japanese)
JACAR: Ref. C08030084000: S18.03.01–S18.05.31, 1. Torpedo Squadron Action Report (4) (in Japanese)
JACAR: Ref. C08030084900: S18.07.22–S18.08.31, 1. Torpedo Squadron Action Report (1) (in Japanese)
JACAR: Ref. C08030085000: S18.07.22–S18.08.31, 1. Torpedo Squadron Action Report (2) (in Japanese)
JACAR: Ref. C08030085100: S18.07.22–S18.08.31, 1. Torpedo Squadron Action Report (3) (in Japanese)
JACAR: Ref. C08030085200: S18.07.22–S18.08.31, 1. Torpedo Squadron Action Report (4) (in Japanese)
JACAR: Ref. C08030747700: S16.11–S18.05, Warship Nachi War Diary with charts (1) (in Japanese)
JACAR: Ref. C08030747800: S16.11–S18.05, Warship Nachi War Diary with charts (2) (in Japanese)
JACAR: Ref. C08030752300: S17.07.06–S17.12.03, Destroyer Inazuma Action Report, part 1 (1) (in Japanese)
JACAR: Ref. C08030752400: S17.07.06–S17.12.03, Destroyer Inazuma Action Report, part 1 (2) (in Japanese)
JACAR: Ref. C08030752500: S17.07.06–S17.12.03, Destroyer Inazuma Action Report, part 1 (3) (in Japanese)
JACAR: Ref. C08030752600: S17.07.06–S17.12.03, Destroyer Inazuma Action Report, part 1 (4) (in Japanese)

JACAR: Ref. C08030752800: S17.12.09–S18.08.22, Destroyer Inazuma Action Report, part 2 (1) (in Japanese)

JACAR: Ref. C08030752900: S17.12.09–S18.08.22, Destroyer Inazuma Action Report, part 2 (2) (in Japanese)

JACAR: Ref. C08030753000: S17.12.09–S18.08.22, Destroyer Inazuma Action Report, part 2 (3) (in Japanese)

JACAR: Ref. C08030753100: S17.12.09–S18.08.22, Destroyer Inazuma Action Report, part 2 (4) (in Japanese)

JACAR: Ref. C08030753200: S17.12.09–S18.08.22, Destroyer Inazuma Action Report, part 2 (5) (in Japanese)

JACAR: Ref. C08030753300: S17.12.09–S18.08.22, Destroyer Inazuma Action Report, part 2 (6) (in Japanese)

JACAR: Ref. C08030272100: S17.09.15–S17.09.30, 51. Base Force War Diary (in Japanese)

JACAR: Ref. C08030272200: S17.10.01–S17.10.31, 51. Base Force War Diary (in Japanese)

JACAR: Ref. C08030272300: S17.11.01–S17.11.30, 51. Base Force War Diary (in Japanese)

JACAR: Ref. C08030272400: S18.02.01–S18.02.28, 51. Base Force War Diary (in Japanese)

JACAR: Ref. C08030272500: S17.03.01–S18.03.31, 51. Base Force War Diary (in Japanese)

JACAR: Ref. J21022438200: Shin Sekai Asahi Newspaper 1940.12.08 (in Japanese)

National Institute for Defense Studies
防衛研究所 (*Bōei Kenkyūsho*)

NIDS: Hokutō Aryūshan 28, Aleutians Campaign Record, Kiska Attu Islands (in Japanese)

NIDS: Hokutō Aryūshan 30, Aleutians Campaign Record, Kiska Attu Islands (in Japanese)

NIDS: Hokutō Aryūshan 31, Aleutians Campaign Record, Kiska Attu Islands (in Japanese)

NIDS: Hokutō Aryūshan 34, Northern Front Campaign Record, Aleutians Islands Invasion Record, Shōwa 20.08 (in Japanese)

NIDS: Hokutō Aryūshan 35, Aleutians Campaign Record (in Japanese)

NIDS: Daitōa Sensō Hondo 60, Aleutians Campaign, Attu Island Killed in Action Study Report, Shōwa 18 (in Japanese)

National Archives
国立公文書館 (*Kokuritsu Kōbunshokan*)

KKS: 情00058100: American Navy Minister A/A, Japanese Army Anti-Aircraft Fire in the Aleutians (4 April 1943)

KKS: 情00056100: Naval Battle in the North Pacific, San Francisco Broadcast

National Records and Administration Records

NARA: ADV INTEL CTR, NOPAC: Memo on investigation of landing strip possibilities, Agattu

NARA: Patwing 4, 8/11/41 to 11/1/42 and Fleet Air Wing, 11/1/42 to 9/2/45

NARA: COM FLT AIR WING 4, War Diary, 11/1-30/42, 12/1-31/42, 1/1-31/42, 2/1-28/43, 3/1-33/43

NARA: COMNORPACFOR: Evacuation of Kiska by Japanese – 1943

NARA: COMNORPACFOR: Evacuation of KISKA by Japs, supplementary report

NARA: COMNOWESTSEAFRON, War Diary, 10/1-31/42, 11/1-30/42, 12/1-31/42, 1/1-31/43, 2/1-28/43, 3/1-31/43

NARA: COMTASKFOR 8 War Diary, 9/1-30/42, 10/1-31/42, 11/1-30/42, 12/1-31/42, 1/1-31/43, 2/1-28/43

NARA: COMTASK-GROUP 8.6, War Diary, 9/1-30/42, 10/1-31/42, 11/1-30/42, 12/1-31/42, 1/1-31/43, 2/1-28/43, 3/1-31/43

NARA: COMTASK-GROUP 8.6, Sinking of Jap Maru, night of 2/19-20/43

NARA: COMTASK-GROUP 16.6, War Diary, 3/1-31/43, 4/1-30/43

NARA: COMTASKFOR 16, War Diary, CTF-8 - 3/1-15/43, CTF-16 - 3/16-31/43

NARA: Task Force 16.6, US Pacific Fleet, USS Richmond (F): Action Report – Engagement with Japanese Force to Southward of Komandorski Islands – 26 March, 1943

NARA: USS Detroit: Bombardment of Attu Island, 4/26/43

NARA: USS Arthur Middleton, Action Reports, Jan 24-27, 1943

NARA: USS Dale, Act Rep, Dive Bombing of USS DALE, 2/1/43 (Enc A)

NARA: USS Dale, Act Rep, Day Surface Engagement, 3/26/43

NARA: USS Dale, War Diary, 2/1-28/43, 3/1-31/43

NARA: USS Indianapolis, War Diary, 8/1-31/42, 9/1-30/42, 10/1-31/42, 11/1-30/42, 12/1-31/42, 1/1/43 to 2/28/43, 3/1-31/43

NARA: USS Kalk, War Diary, 10/17/42 to 3/31/43

NARA: USS Gato, Apr 1942 - Dec 1942

NARA: USS S-28, May 1942 - Oct 1942

NARA: USS Ramsay, War Diary, 1/1-31/43, 2/1-28/43, 3/1-31/43

NARA: USS Tuna, Apr 1942 - Dec 1942

NARA: USS Vega, Jap Aerial Attacks on Amchitka Is, Aleutians, Jan 24, 25 & 27, 1943

The George C. Marshall Foundation Library

PoGCM: 3-311 To Lieutenant General John L. De Witt September 3, 1942

PoGCM: 3-324 To Lieutenant General John L. De Witt September 11, 1942

PoGCM: 3-351 To Lieutenant General John L. De Witt October 2, 1942

PoGCM: 3-513 Informal and Off-the-Record Statement to the American Society of Newspaper Editors February 13, 1943

PoGCM: 3-542 Memorandum for Record March 3, 1943

PoGCM: 3-555 To Lieutenant General John L. De Witt March 17, 1943

Hoover Library Archive

Theobald papers

USSBS Interrogations

Interrogation Nav No. 21, USSBS No. 98, Aleutian Campaign Seaplane Operations, The Naval Battle of The Komandorski Islands, and The Defense of The Kuriles

Interrogation Nav No. 25, USSBS No. 102, Planning and Operations and Defense of the Kuriles, November 1942-August 1945

Interrogation Nav No. 93, USSBS No. 439, Aleutian Campaign, The Japanese Historical Account of the Naval Battle fought off the Komandorski Islands, March 1943

Unpublished Documents and Reports

Breslin, C.B., *World War II in the Aleutians: The Fundamentals of Joint Campaigns* (Newport: Naval War College, 1994)

Demobilisation Office Records Section, *Japanese Monograph No. 46a: Aleutian Islands Operation Records* (in Japanese) (Tokyo: Unpublished Monograph, 1949)

JBE-R: Lieutenant W.S.M. Johnson, *History of the Eleventh Fighter Squadron, from 16 January 1941 to 1 January 1944* (unpublished work, 1945)

Naval War College, *Naval Engagement off Komandorski Islands, March 26, 1943*

Second Demobilisation Office, *Japanese Monograph No. 88: Japanese Navy Aleutian Islands Operation* (in Japanese) (Tokyo: Unpublished Monograph, 1947)

Steele, J.M., *War Plans and Files of the Commander-in-Chief, Pacific Fleet, "Nimitz Gray Book"*, vol. 2-3, 1 September 1942 – 30 June 1943 (New York: American Naval Records Society, 2010)

The Joint Army-Navy Assessment Committee, *Chronological List of Japanese Merchant Vessel Losses*, February 1947

US Department of the Interior, *World War II in the Aleutians* (Anchorage: National Park Service, 1991)

Books, Articles and Memoires

Agawa, H., *Evacuation from Kiska, Private Notebook* (in Japanese) (Tokyo: 1990)

Bōei Kenshūsho Senshishitsu (ed.), *Senshi Sōsho vol. 21: Army Operations in the Northern Area (1) Honourable defeat on Attu* (in Japanese) (Tokyo: Asagumo Shimbusha, 1968)

Bōei Kenshūsho Senshishitsu (ed.), *Senshi Sōsho vol. 29: Navy Operations in the Northern Area* (in Japanese) (Tokyo: Asagumo Shimbusha, 1969)

Bōei Kenshūsho Senshishitsu (ed.), *Senshi Sōsho vol. 39: Imperial Headquarters Navy Section, Combined Fleet (4) 3rd Stage Initial Period* (in Japanese) (Tokyo: Asagumo Shimbusha, 1970)

Bōei Kenshūsho Senshishitsu (ed.), *Senshi Sōsho vol. 66: Imperial Headquarters Army Section (6) Until S18.06* (in Japanese) (Tokyo: Asagumo Shimbusha, 1973)

Bōei Kenshūsho Senshishitsu (ed.), *Senshi Sōsho vol. 98: History of Submarines* (in Japanese) (Tokyo: Asagumo Shimbusha, 1979)

Campbell, J., *Naval Weapons of World War Two* (Naval Institute Press: Annapolis, 1985)

Chihaya, M., *Concept of Nippon Kaigun Strategy* (in Japanese) (Purejitentosha: Tokyo 1982)

Chihaya, M., *Nippon Kaigun's Arrogance Syndrome* (in Japanese) (Purejitentosha: Tokyo 1982)

Craven, W.F., Cate, J.L., *The Army Air Forces in World War II, vol. 4, The Pacific: Guadalcanal to Saipan, August 1942 to July 1944* (Chicago: University of Chicago Press, 1948)

D'Albas, A., *Death of a Navy: Japanese Naval Action in World War II* (Johannesburg: Robert Hale, 1957)

Dull, P.S., *A Battle History of the Imperial Japanese Navy, 1941-1945* (Annapolis: Naval Institute Press, 1978)

Friedman, N., *Naval Radar* (Conway Maritime Press: Greenwich, 1981)

Garfield, B., *The Thousand-Mile War: World War II in Alaska and the Aleutians* (Chicago: University of Chicago Press, 2001, sup. ed.)

Handō, K., Yokoyama, K., Hata, I., *Pacific War: Japanese Navy Battlefield and Lessons* (in Japanese) (Tokyo: 2003)

IIata, I. (ed.), *Comprehensive Encyclopaedia of the Nippon Kaigun and Rikugun* (in Japanese) (Tokyo: Tōkyō Daigaku Shuppankai, 2005)

Hata, I., Izawa, Y., Shores, C., *Japanese Naval Air Force Fighter Units and Their Aces, 1932–1945* (London: Grub Street, 2011)

Hays, O., Jr., *Alaska's Hidden War: Secret Campaigns on the North Pacific Rim* (Fairbanks: University of Alaska Press, 2004)

Herder, B.L., *The Aleutians 1942-43: Struggle for the North Pacific* (Oxford-New York: Osprey Publishing, 2019)

Ichikawa, H., *Kiska: The Glory of the Japanese Navy* (in Japanese) (Tokyo: 1983)

Ikeda, K., *Heavy Cruiser Maya* (in Japanese) (Tokyo: 1986)

Ishibashi, T., *The Battle of the Komandorski Islands,* in: "Sekai no Kansen" 1979, No 272 (in Japanese), pp. 139–145.

Japanese Monograph No. 88, Aleutian Naval Operation March 1942–February 1943

Jō, E. *Emperor's Aide-de-camp, Jō Ei'ichirō Diary* (in Japanese) (Tokyo: 1982)

Johnson, R.L., *Aleutian Campaign, World War II: Historical Study and Current Perspective* (Fort Leavenworth: Unpublished Master's Thesis, 1992)

Kaigun Heigakkō (ed.), *Volume 279: Japanese Naval Academy History, Vol 2: Taishō 9-nen–Shōwa 20-nen* (in Japanese) (Tokyo: 1978)

Kaigun Rekishi Hozonkai, *History of the Japanese Navy,* vols. 1-10 (in Japanese) (Tokyo: 1995)

Katsume, J., *Japanese Navy's Submarines: Their Development and Complete War Records* (in Japanese) (Tokyo: Dai Nippon Kaiga, 2010)

Lacroix, E., Wells, L., *Japanese Cruisers of the Pacific War* (Naval Institute Press: Annapolis, 1998)

Lorelli, J.A., *The Battle of the Komandorski Islands* (Annapolis: Naval Institute Press, 1984)

MacGarrigle, G.L., *Aleutian Islands: The U.S. Army Campaigns in WWII* (Washington: U.S. Army Center of Military History, 1992)

Mori, T., *Japanese Cruisers: Illustrated Monographs of Warships' Mechanisms* (in Japanese) (Tokyo: 1993)

Morison, S.E., *Aleutians, Gilberts and Marshalls, June 1942 – April 1944,* vol. 7 of History of United States Naval Operations in World War II (Annapolis: Naval Institute Press, 2011, sup. ed.)

Nakazawa, T., *Vice Admiral Nakazawa Memories* (in Japanese) (Tokyo: Kankōkai, 1978)

O'Hara, V.P., *The U.S. Navy Against the Axis: Surface Combat, 1941-1945* (Annapolis: Naval Institute Press, 2007)

Office of Naval Intelligence, *United States Navy Combat Narrative: The Aleutians Campaign, June 1942-August 1943* (Washington: Naval Historical Center Department of the Navy, 1993)

Olson, M.K., *Tales From a Tin Can: The USS Dale from Pearl Harbor to Tokyo Bay* (London: Zenith Press, 2010)

Paul, B., *Awaiting the Sun, WWII Veterans Remember the Aleutians* (Atglen: Schiffer Publishing, 2022)

Perras, G.R., *Stepping Stones to Nowhere,* The Aleutian Islands, Alaska, and American Military Strategy, 1867–1945 (Annapolis: Naval Institute Press, 2003)

Piegzik, M.A., *Aleutians 1942–1943* (in Polish) (Warszawa: Bellona, 2022)

Rearden, J., *Forgotten Warriors of the Aleutian Campaign* (Missoula: Pictorial Histories Publishing Company, 2005)

Rekishi Gunzō, Pacific War Series: Vol. 16, Takao-class Heavy Cruisers (in Japanese) (Tokyo: 1997)

Ritter, J.T., *From Texas to Tinian and Tokyo Bay: The Memoirs of Captain J. R. Ritter, Seabee Commander during the Pacific War, 1942-1945* (Denton: University of North Texas Press, 2019)

Rottman, G.L., *World War II Pacific Island Guide* (Westport-London: Greenwood Publishing Group, 2002)

Shōguchi, Y., *Kiska – Miraculous Evacuation* (in Japanese) (Tokyo: 2012)

Shōguchi, Y., *Kiska – the Evacuation Commander* (in Japanese) (Tokyo: 2009)

Stern, R.C., *Big Gun Battles: Warship Duels of the Second World War* (Barnsley: Seaforth Publishing, 2015)

Sugiyama, K., *Aleutians War Diary* (in Japanese) (Tokyo: 1999)

Takamatsunomiya, N., *Takamatsunomiya Diaries*, vol. 4 (in Japanese) (Tokyo: Chūō Kōronshinsha, 1996)

Takemoto, S., *Navy Enlisted Man: Cruiser Nachi* (in Japanese) (Tokyo: 1971)

Todaka, K. (ed.), „*Shōgen roku*": *Kaigun Hanseikai, vol. 3* (in Japanese) (Tokyo: 2012)

Toll, I.W., *The Conquering Tide: War in the Pacific Islands, 1942-1944* (New York: W.W. Norton, 2015)

Ugaki, M., *War Diary*, vol. 1–2 (in Japanese) (Tokyo: PHP Kenkyūsho, 2019)

Wheeler, G.E., *Kinkaid of the Seventh Fleet: A Biography of Admiral Thomas C. Kinkaid* (Washington: Naval Historical Department, Department of the Navy, 1994)

Yamamoto, C., *Imperial Headquarters Navy Section* (in Japanese) (Tokyo: 1974)

Online Sources

807th Battalion History, part 2: Adak Island, https://www.nps.gov/articles/aleu-807th-history-pt-2.htm [accessed on 12 Dec 2023]

ADAK Historical Guide, <https://adak-ak.gov/sites/default/files/fileattachments/community/page/2269/hguide10.pdf> [accessed on 11 Dec 2023]

Japanese blog on the Aleutian Islands campaign, <https://korechialeutian.blogspot.com/2021/06/3-al.html>, [accessed on 10 Nov 2023]

Memories of Lieut. (jg.) Stan Hogshead, USS BAILEY DD-492, "March 26th, 1943", <https://ussslcca25.com/uss_bailey.htm> [accessed on 21 Nov 2023]

Tatsuguchi Nobuo Diary: Attsu-tō no Gyokusai (in Japanese), < http://ohmura-study.net/331.html> [accessed: 12 Dec 2023].

Vice Admiral Charles Horatio McMorris, USN, <http://www.ussmcmorris.org/vadm_mac.html> [accessed: 12 Dec 2023].

Website on airfields in the Aleutian Islands:<http://www.airfields-freeman.com/AK/Airfields_AK.htm#ftglenn>, [accessed on 20 Nov 2023]

World War II National Historic Landmarks: The Aleutian Campaign, <http://npshistory.com/publications/nhl/world-war-ii-aleutian.pdf> [accessed on 10 Nov 2023]

NOTES

Chapter 1

1 JACAR: Ref. C14121148800: Campaign Until the Evacuation from the Aleutians (…) Screening Convoys (in Japanese), p. 1; SS vol. 29 (in Japanese), pp. 449–452.

2 Wheeler wrote that Admiral Kings and Admiral Nimitz were also dedicated to planning the North African campaign in the second part of 1942. Thus, besides the Guadalcanal campaign, the Americans had other priorities than the Aleutians. See Wheeler, *Kinkaid of the Seventh Fleet*, p. 299.

3 Even after the battle of the Komandorski Island Rear Admiral Kinkaid felt a bit frustrated that TG-16.6 did not sink any Japanese ships in the engagement, as he wanted to keep the offensive spirit among his men. See Wheeler, *Kinkaid of the Seventh Fleet*, p. 317.

4 The 12. Air Fleet (*Dai 12. Kōkū Kantai*), assigned to defend the North Pacific area and Hokkaido, was not established until 18 May 1943. Its commander was the commander of the Northern Fleet.

5 Paul, *Awaiting the Sun*, p. 20.

6 Paul, *Awaiting the Sun*, pp. 25, 27.

7 Paul, *Awaiting the Sun*, p. 25.

8 K. Sugiyama, *Aleutians War Diary* (in Japanese), Tokio 1999, pp. 72–73.

9 ONI, *The Aleutians Campaign*, p. 65.

10 NARA: COMTASK-GROUP 16.6: War Diary, 4/1-30/43, pp. 17–18.

11 NARA: USS Detroit: Bombardment of Attu Island, 4/26/43, pp. 1–5.

12 ONI, *The Aleutians Campaign*, p. 66.

13 ONI, *The Aleutians Campaign*, p. 67.

14 Bōei Kenshūsho Senshishitsu (ed.), *Senshi Sōsho vol. 21: Army Operations in the Northern Area (1) Honourable defeat on Attu* (in Japanese) (Tokyo: Asagumo Shimbusha, 1968), p. 268.

15 Bōei Kenshūsho Senshishitsu (red.), *Senshi Sōsho vol. 39: Imperial Headquarters Navy Section, Combined Fleet (4) 3rd Stage Initial Period* (in Japanese), Tokyo 1970, p. 200.

16 NIDS: Hokutō Aryūshan 31, Aleutians Campaign Record, Kiska Attu Islands (in Japanese).

17 SS vol. 21 (in Japanese), pp. 411–412.

18 SS vol. 21 (in Japanese), p. 421.

19 The Japanese figure of 2,638 men is based on Army and Navy documents, while the American figure of 2,351 men is based on counting the found bodies.

20 Herder, *The Aleutians*, p. 85.

21 JACAR: Ref. C14121148700: Campaign Until the Evacuation from the Aleutians (…) Evacuation from Kiska (in Japanese), p. 4; Some Japanese sources also says about 873 men. See SS vol. 98 (in Japanese), p. 244.

22 JACAR: Ref. C14121148700: Campaign Until the Evacuation from the Aleutians (…) Evacuation from Kiska (in Japanese), p. 1.

23 JACAR: Ref. C14121148700: Campaign Until the Evacuation from the Aleutians (…) Evacuation from Kiska (in Japanese), pp. 11–12.

24 JACAR: Ref. C08030085000: S18.07.22–S18.08.31, 1. Torpedo Squadron Action Report (2) (in Japanese), p. 16.

25 JACAR: Ref. C14121148700: Campaign Until the Evacuation from the Aleutians (…) Evacuation from Kiska (in Japanese), p. 12.

26 JACAR: Ref. C16120635400: S18.03.19–03.31, Pacific War Outline of Progress (5), p. 17.

27 SS vol. 29 (in Japanese), p. 477.

28 NARA: USS Dale, Act Rep, Day Surface Engagement, 3/26/43, p. 2.

29 NARA: Task Force 16.6, US Pacific Fleet, USS Richmond (F): Action Report – Engagement with Japanese Force to Southward of Komandorski Islands – 26 March, 1943, pp. 5–6; NARA: Destroyer Squadron 14, USS Bailey, Action Report of Enemy Engagement March 26, 1943, Komandorski Islands, p. 2.

30 Lorelli, *The Battle of the Komandorski Islands*, pp. 66–67.

31 NARA: Task Force 16.6, US Pacific Fleet, USS Richmond (F): Action Report – Engagement with Japanese Force to Southward of Komandorski Islands – 26 March, 1943, p. 6.

32 SS vol. 29 (in Japanese), p. 479.

33 JACAR: Ref. C08030083800: S18.03.01–S18.05.31, 1. Torpedo Squadron Detailed Report (2) (in Japanese), p. 6.

34 Lorelli, *The Battle of the Komandorski Islands*, p. 68.

35 Interrogation Nav No. 31, USSBS No 205, Transports at the Battle of the Komandorskis.

36 JACAR: Ref. C08030083800: S18.03.01–S18.05.31, 1. Torpedo Squadron Detailed Report (2) (in Japanese), pp. 6–7.

37 SS vol. 29 (in Japanese), p. 479.

38 Other American reports mentioned identifying 'two NACHI-class CA's, two KUMA-class CL's and four DD's'. NARA: USS Dale, Act Rep, Day Surface Engagement, 3/26/43, p. 2

39 Lorelli, *The Battle of the Komandorski Islands*, p. 69.

40 NARA: Task Force 16.6, US Pacific Fleet, USS Richmond (F): Action Report – Engagement with Japanese Force to Southward of Komandorski Islands – 26 March, 1943, p. 7.

41 NARA: Task Force 16.6, US Pacific Fleet, USS Richmond (F): Action Report – Engagement with Japanese Force to Southward of Komandorski Islands – 26 March, 1943, p. 8.

42 SS vol. 29 (in Japanese), pp. 480–481.

43 SS vol. 29 (in Japanese), pp. 480–481.

44 SS vol. 29 (in Japanese), p. 485.

45 K. Ikeda, *Heavy Cruiser Maya* (in Japanese), Tokyo 1986, p. 157.

46 S. Takemoto, *Navy Enlisted Man: Cruiser Nachi* (in Japanese), Tokyo 1971, pp. 162-163. With several boilers turned off, only one generator supplied the ship with energy. However, it had insufficient power to work with all the gunnery turrets. In combat alert conditions, to ensure reliability, one generator provided voltage to one half of the ship and the other to the second half. During a sudden switch to the second half, when the boilers did not yet have the pressure to connect the generator, and when there was too much load from the electric motors (turrets), *Nachi* experienced a power failure.

47 NARA: Task Force 16.6, US Pacific Fleet, USS Richmond (F): Action Report – Engagement with Japanese Force to Southward of Komandorski Islands – 26 March, 1943, p. 10.

48 Ikeda, *Heavy Cruiser Maya* (in Japanese), p. 157.

49 Most of the source evidence and circumstantial evidence resulting from distance calculations indicate that *Salt Lake City* scored those hits. American accounts, although they also mention *Richmond*, mostly attribute the hit to the heavy cruiser. Japanese reports and studies have added a bit more confusion to this narrative, as they contain information about a certain hit received from a destroyer. Japanese officers also claimed that it could not have been a shell larger than 6-inch (155mm), which theoretically suggested *Richmond*. Ultimately, it was confirmed that the shell was fired by *Salt Lake City*, based on the information about a blue marker, which was mentioned by both Lieutenant Commander S. Hashimoto and Lieutenant Commander K. Miura in two separate interviews. This was the colour used by the American heavy cruiser during the battle to distinguish her 8-inch (203mm) AP shells. Some Japanese historians also support the claim that *Salt Lake City* should be credited for scoring the hit on *Nachi*. See: Interrogation Nav No. 25, USSBS No. 102, Aleutian Campaign and Defense of the Kuriles Planning and Operations from November 1942 to August 1945; Interrogation Nav No. 21, USSBS No. 98, Aleutian Campaign Seaplane Operations, The Naval Battle of The Komandorski Islands, and The Defense of The Kuriles; SS vol. 29 (in Japanese), pp. 481–486; Lorelli, *The Battle of the Komandorski Islands*, pp. 79–81; T. Ishibashi, *The Battle of the Komandorski Islands,* in: "Sekai no Kansen" 1979, No 272 (in Japanese), p. 141.

50 SS vol. 29 (in Japanese), p. 482.

51 Takemoto, *Cruiser Nachi* (in Japanese), p. 163; Ishibashi, *The Battle of the Komandorski Islands* (in Japanese), p. 141.

52 SS vol. 29 (in Japanese), p. 482.

53 Ikeda, *Heavy Cruiser Maya* (in Japanese), p. 157.

54 JACAR: Ref. C08030083800: S18.03.01–S18.05.31, 1. Torpedo Squadron Detailed Report (2) (in Japanese), p. 12.

55 NWC, *Naval Engagement off Komandorski Islands, March 26, 1943*, p. 14.

56 NARA: Task Force 16.6, US Pacific Fleet, USS Richmond (F): Action Report – Engagement with Japanese Force to Southward of Komandorski Islands – 26 March, 1943, p. 10.

57 Ikeda, *Heavy Cruiser Maya* (in Japanese), p. 158.

58 Lorelli, *The Battle of the Komandorski Islands*, pp. 90–91.

59 SS vol. 29 (in Japanese), appendix 6.

60   Lorelli, *The Battle of the Komandorski Islands*, p. 92.

61   SS vol. 29 (in Japanese), appendix 6.

62   JACAR: Ref. C14121148500: Campaign Until the Evacuation from the Aleutians (…) Battle of the Komandorski Islands (in Japanese), p. 8; JACAR: Ref. C08030083800: S18.03.01–S18.05.31, 1. Torpedo Squadron Detailed Report (2) (in Japanese), p. 13. *Abukuma* reported as soon as at 0735 hours that enemy shells were falling about 200m abeam, but at 0751 hours she sent a cable informing about the concentration of enemy fire.

63   SS vol. 29 (in Japanese), pp. 489–490.

64   NWC, *Naval Engagement off Komandorski Islands, March 26, 1943*, p. 15.

65   NARA: Task Force 16.6, US Pacific Fleet, USS Richmond (F): Action Report – Engagement with Japanese Force to Southward of Komandorski Islands – 26 March, 1943, p. 10.

66   SS vol. 29 (in Japanese), p. 489.

67   JACAR: Ref. C14121148500: Campaign Until the Evacuation from the Aleutians (…) Battle of the Komandorski Islands (in Japanese), p. 8.

68   JACAR: Ref. C08030083800: S18.03.01–S18.05.31, 1. Torpedo Squadron Detailed Report (2) (in Japanese), p. 15.

69   Lorelli, *The Battle of the Komandorski Islands*, p. 105.

70   NWC, *Naval Engagement off Komandorski Islands, March 26, 1943*, p. 16.

71   SS vol. 29 (in Japanese), appendix 6.

72   JACAR: Ref. C14121148500: Campaign Until the Evacuation from the Aleutians (…) Battle of the Komandorski Islands (in Japanese), p. 8.

73   SS vol. 29 (in Japanese), appendix 6.

74   JACAR: Ref. C08030083800: S18.03.01–S18.05.31, 1. Torpedo Squadron Detailed Report (2) (in Japanese), p. 16.

75   JACAR: Ref. C14121148500: Campaign Until the Evacuation from the Aleutians (…) Battle of the Komandorski Islands (in Japanese), p. 8.

76   NWC, *Naval Engagement off Komandorski Islands, March 26, 1943*, p. 17.

77   NARA: Task Force 16.6, US Pacific Fleet, USS Richmond (F): Action Report – Engagement with Japanese Force to Southward of Komandorski Islands – 26 March, 1943, p. 13.

78   Lorelli, *The Battle of the Komandorski Islands*, p. 113.

79   NARA: USS Salt Lake City (CA-25) Gunfire Damage 15 May, 1944: Bering Sea, 26 March 1943, pp. 2–3.

80   NWC, *Naval Engagement off Komandorski Islands, March 26, 1943*, p. 17.

81   SS vol. 29 (in Japanese), p. 492.

82   Ishibashi, *The Battle of the Komandorski Islands* (in Japanese), p. 142.

83   JACAR: Ref. C14121148500: Campaign Until the Evacuation from the Aleutians (…) Battle of the Komandorski Islands (in Japanese), p. 10.

84   SS vol. 29 (in Japanese), pp. 492–493.

85   JACAR: Ref. C08030083800: S18.03.01–S18.05.31, 1. Torpedo Squadron Detailed Report (2) (in Japanese), pp. 19–20.

86   NARA: Destroyer Squadron 14, USS Bailey, Action Report of Enemy Engagement March 26, 1943, Komandorskis Islands, p. 4.

87   NARA: Task Force 16.6, US Pacific Fleet, USS Richmond (F): Action Report – Engagement with Japanese Force to Southward of Komandorski Islands – 26 March, 1943, p. 14.

88   Ishibashi, *The Battle of the Komandorski Islands* (in Japanese), p. 142.

89   SS vol. 29 (in Japanese), pp. 493, 495, 499.

90   JACAR: Ref. C08030083800: S18.03.01–S18.05.31, 1. Torpedo Squadron Detailed Report (2) (in Japanese), pp. 21–22.

91   Lorelli, *The Battle of the Komandorski Islands*, p. 118. Japanese sources do not describe the fourth hit in detail.

92   Lorelli, *The Battle of the Komandorski Islands*, p. 123.

93   NARA: USS Salt Lake City (CA-25) Gunfire Damage 15 May, 1944: Bering Sea, 26 March 1943, p. 5.

Chapter 2

1   SS vol. 29 (in Japanese), p. 494.

2   Lorelli, *The Battle of the Komandorski Islands*, p. 128.

3   NARA: Destroyer Squadron 14, USS Bailey, Action Report of Enemy Engagement March 26, 1943, Komandorskis Islands, p. 5.

4   JACAR: Ref. C08030083800: S18.03.01–S18.05.31, 1. Torpedo Squadron Detailed Report (2) (in Japanese), p. 24.

5   Memories of Lieut. (jg.) Stan Hogshead, USS BAILEY DD-492, "March 26th, 1943", https://ussslcca25.com/uss_bailey.htm, Accessed on 21.11.2023.

6   Memories of Lieut. (jg.) Stan Hogshead, USS BAILEY DD-492, "March 26th, 1943", https://ussslcca25.com/uss_bailey.htm, Accessed on 21.11.2023.

7   NARA: Task Force 16.6, US Pacific Fleet, USS Richmond (F): Action Report – Engagement with Japanese Force to Southward of Komandorski Islands – 26 March, 1943, p. 15.

8   ONI, *The Aleutians Campaign*, pp. 58–59.

9   JACAR: Ref. C08030083800: S18.03.01–S18.05.31, 1. Torpedo Squadron Detailed Report (2) (in Japanese), p. 25.

10   This view dominates in the Japanese and American historiography.

11   SS vol. 29 (in Japanese), p. 501.

12   According to Lieutenant Commander Hashimoto Japanese heavy cruisers had a supply of 1,100 shells for 203mm guns. Based on data on projectiles fired during the battle (the summary table is provided later in the text), it is possible to estimate the consumption of ammunition. In total, *Nachi* fired approximately 64 percent and *Maya* about 82 percent of their stocks. For comparison, *Salt Lake City* fired 85 percent of her 203mm shells. Interrogation Nav No. 25, USSBS No. 102, Planning and Operations and Defense of the Kuriles, November 1942-August 1945; Morison, *Aleutians*, p. 32.

13   NARA: COM FLT AIR WING 4, War Diary, 3/1-33/43, p. 33; Cloe, *The Aleutian Warriors*, p. 359.

14   JACAR: Ref. C14121148500: Campaign Until the Evacuation from the Aleutians (…) Battle of the Komandorski Islands (in Japanese), pp. 11–12.

15   SS vol. 29 (in Japanese), p. 501.

16   *Tama* was probably hit by the destroyers. SS vol. 29 (in Japanese), p. 501; Interrogation Nav No. 93, USSBS No. 439, Aleutian Campaign, The Japanese Historical Account of the Naval Battle fought off the Komandorski Islands, March 1943.

17   The number of killed and wounded varies depending on the document. JACAR: Ref. C08030747800: S16.11–S18.05, Warship Nachi War Diary with charts (2) (in Japanese), p. 29; JACAR: Ref. C16120635400: S18.03.19–S18.03.31, Pacific War Outline of Progress (5) (in Japanese), p. 16; JACAR: Ref. C14121148500: Campaign Until the Evacuation from the Aleutians (…) Battle of the Komandorski Islands (in Japanese), p. 12; Interrogation Nav No. 93, USSBS No. 439, Aleutian Campaign, The Japanese Historical Account of the Naval Battle fought off the Komandorskis Islands, March 1943.

18   JACAR: Ref. C08030747800: S16.11–S18.05, Nachi (2) (in Japanese), s. 29; Interrogation Nav No. 21, USSBS No. 98, Aleutian Campaign Seaplane Operations, The Naval Battle of The Komandorski Islands, and The Defense of The Kuriles.

19   Lorelli, *The Battle of the Komandorski Islands*, pp. 144–145.

20   NARA: COMTASKFOR 16, War Diary, CTF-8 - 3/1-15/43, CTF-16 - 3/16-31/43, p. 56.

21   NARA: Task Force 16.6, US Pacific Fleet, USS Richmond (F): Action Report – Engagement with Japanese Force to Southward of Komandorski Islands – 26 March, 1943, p. 17–22.

22   This question was commonly asked among the American officers. Captain Jonathan T. Ritter wondered in his memoires why the Japanese fleet did not annihilate the American task force and left the area. See J.T. Ritter, *From Texas to Tinian and Tokyo Bay: The Memoirs of Captain J. R. Ritter, Seabee Commander during the Pacific War, 1942-1945* (Denton: University of North Texas Press, 2019), p. 63.

23   NWC, *Naval Engagement off Komandorski Islands, March 26, 1943*, p. 18.

24   SS vol. 29 (in Japanese), pp. 502–503.

25   K. Todaka (ed.), „*Shōgen roku*": Kaigun Hanseikai, vol. 3 (in Japanese), Tokyo 2012, p. 329.

26   SS vol. 29 (in Japanese), pp. 506–512.

27   ONI, *The Aleutians Campaign*, p. 64; SS *vol. 29* (in Japanese), pp. 500–501.

28   E. Jō, *Emperor's Aide-de-camp, Jō Ei'ichirō Diary* (in Japanese), Tokyo 1982, p. 256.

29   H. Ichikawa, *Kiska: The Glory of the Japanese Navy* (in Japanese), Tokyo 1983, p. 64.

30   NWC, *Naval Engagement off Komandorski Islands, March 26, 1943*, p. 70.

31   *Rekishi Gunzō, Pacific War Series: Vol. 16, Takao-class Heavy Cruisers* (in Japanese), Tokyo 1997.

32   The muzzle velocity of Japanese 203mm AP shells was 835m/s, whereas the muzzle velocity of American 8-inch AP shells was 760m/s. The range of the American shells was 27,480m. See J. Campbell, *Naval Weapons of World War Two*, Annapolis 1985, pp. 127–131.

33   Lorelli, *The Battle of the Komandorski Islands*, p. 181.

34   Interrogation Nav No. 21, USSBS No. 98, Aleutian Campaign Seaplane Operations, The Naval Battle of The Komandorski Islands, and The Defense of The Kuriles.

35   N. Friedman, *Naval Radar*, Greenwich 1981, pp. 147–148.

36 JACAR: Ref. C08030272500: S17.03.01–S18.03.31, 51. Base Force War Diary (in Japanese), pp. 3–4.
37 Tatsuguchi Nobuo Diary: Attsu-tō no Gyokusai (in Japanese).
38 JACAR: Ref. C14121148500: Campaign Until the Evacuation from the Aleutians (…) Battle of the Komandorski Islands (in Japanese), p. 3.

Chapter 3
1 JACAR: Ref. C08051677100: S17.11–S18.04, 452. Kū Action Report (3) (in Japanese), pp. 16–25; JACAR: Ref. C08030083700: S18.03.01–S18.05.31, 1. Suirai Sentai Senji Nisshi (1) (in Japanese), p. 17.
2 JACAR: Ref. C08030019200: S16.12.01–S19.06.30: Dai 5 Kantai Senji Nisshi AL Sakusen (3) (in Japanese), p. 22.
3 JACAR: Ref. C08030083700: S18.03.01–S18.05.31, 1. Suirai Sentai Senji Nisshi (1) (in Japanese), p. 19.
4 JACAR: Ref. C14121148500: Campaign Until the Evacuation from the Aleutians (…) Battle of the Komandorski Islands (in Japanese), p. 5.
5 SS vol. 29 (in Japanese), pp. 474–477.
6 NARA: Task Force 16.6, US Pacific Fleet, USS Richmond (F): Action Report – Engagement with Japanese Force to Southward of Komandorski Islands – 26 March, 1943, p. 3.
7 Gray Book, vol 3, p. 230.
8 PoGCM: 3-542 Memorandum for Record March 3, 1943.
9 Craven, Cate, The Pacific: Guadalcanal to Saipan, pp. 378–379.
10 Gray Book, vol 3, p. 235.
11 Perras, Stepping Stones, p. 122.
12 Gray Book, vol 3, p. 242–243.
13 Naming changed along with the changes in TF-16.
14 NARA: COMTASK-GROUP 16.6, War Diary, 3/1-31/43, pp. 11–17.
15 NARA: COMTASKFOR 16, War Diary, CTF-8 - 3/1-15/43, CTF-16 - 3/16-31/43, p. 22.
16 Morison, Aleutians, p. 23.
17 Lorelli, The Battle of the Komandorski Islands, p. 59.
18 NARA: COMTASK-GROUP 16.6, War Diary, 3/1-31/43, pp. 21–22.
19 NARA: COMTASKFOR 8, War Diary, 1/1-31/43, pp. 10–11. Kinkaid arrived Kodiak Island late in the afternoon of 3 January. He was welcomed by Generals Buckner, Butler, Charles H. Corlett and Rear Admiral Theobald.
20 G.E. Wheeler, Kinkaid of the Seventh Fleet: A Biography of Admiral Thomas C. Kinkaid, Washington 1994, p. 294.
21 Wheeler, Kinkaid of the Seventh Fleet, pp. 296–297.
22 NARA: COMTASKFOR 8, War Diary, 1/1-31/43, p. 12.
23 SS vol. 29 (in Japanese), p. 392.
24 SS vol. 29 (in Japanese), p. 391.
25 NARA: COMTASK-GROUP 8.6, War Diary, 1/1-31/43, pp. 14–15; NARA: USS Indianapolis, War Diary, 1/1/43 to 2/28/43, pp. 12–14. The group departed on 10 January.
26 NARA: Loss of USS WORDEN (Enc A-B), 1/17/1943, COMTASKFOR 8, War Diary, 1/1-31/43, p. 45.
27 NARA: COMTASKFOR 8, War Diary, 1/1-31/43, pp. 32–33.
28 Wheeler, Kinkaid of the Seventh Fleet, p. 305.
29 NARA: COM FLT AIR WING 4, War Diary, 1/1-31/43, pp. 20–25.
30 Cloe, The Aleutian Warriors, p. 254.
31 Craven, Cate, The Pacific: Guadalcanal to Saipan, p. 375.
32 NARA: COMTASKFOR 8, War Diary, 1/1-31/43, p. 46.
33 B. Paul, Awaiting the Sun, WWII Veterans Remember the Aleutians (Atglen: Schiffer Publishing, 2022), p. 128.
34 JACAR: Ref. C14121137800: Aleutian Campaign Daily Calendar, S18.01 (in Japanese), p. 4. More details about the American base on Amchitka were learned on 5 February. NIDS: Aleutians Campaign Record, Kiska Attu Islands (in Japanese).
35 NARA: USS Vega, Jap Aerial Attacks on Amchitka Is, Aleutians, Jan 24, 25 & 27, 1943, pp. 2–3.
36 JACAR: Ref. C14121137800: Aleutian Campaign Daily Calendar, S18.01 (in Japanese), p. 5.
37 JACAR: Ref. C14121137800: Aleutian Campaign Daily Calendar, S18.01 (in Japanese), p. 6.
38 NARA: COMTASKFOR 8, War Diary, 1/1-31/43, p. 66.
39 NARA: COMTASKFOR 8, War Diary, 1/1-31/43, p. 69.
40 Dale crew reported about four attacking planes. NARA: USS Dale, Act Rep, Dive Bombing of USS DALE, 2/1/43 (Enc A)
41 JACAR: Ref. C14121138400: Aleutian Campaign Daily Calendar, S18.02 (in Japanese), pp. 1–5.
42 JACAR: Ref. C14121137800: Aleutian Campaign Daily Calendar, S18.01 (in Japanese); JACAR: Ref. C14121138400: Aleutian Campaign Daily Calendar, S18.02 (in Japanese); NARA: USS Arthur Middleton, Action Reports, Jan 24-27, 1943; NARA: USS Vega, Jap Aerial Attacks on Amchitka Is, Aleutians, Jan 24, 25 & 27, 1943.
43 Cloe, The Aleutian Warriors, p. 258.
44 NARA: COMTASKFOR 8, War Diary, 2/1-28/43, p. 35.
45 SS vol. 29 (in Japanese), pp. 382, 388–389.
46 The report from 7 February indicated the airstrip on Amchitka was 1,000m long and 100m wide. The Japanese estimated that the enemy would bring his first fighters by the end of the month. JACAR: Ref. C08030272400: S18.02.01–S18.02.28, 51. Base Force War Diary (in Japanese), p. 4.
47 SS vol. 29 (in Japanese), p. 402.
48 JACAR: Ref. C14121148000: Campaign Until the Evacuation from the Aleutians (…) Imperial Headquarters' Leadership in Campaign (in Japanese), p. 1; SS vol. 29 (in Japanese), pp. 417–419.

Chapter 4
1 Bōei Kenshūsho Senshishitsu (ed.), Senshi Sōsho vol. 66: Senshi Sōsho vol. 66: Imperial Headquarters Army Section (6) Until S18.06 (in Japanese), Tokyo 1973, pp. 141–145.
2 NARA: COMTASKFOR 8, War Diary, 2/1-28/43, p. 39.
3 NARA: COMTASKFOR 8, War Diary, 2/1-28/43, p. 39.
4 JACAR: Ref. C14121138400: Aleutian Campaign Daily Calendar, S18.02 (in Japanese), p. 7.
5 NARA: COMTASK-GROUP 8.6, Sinking of Jap Maru, night of 2/19-20/43, p. 1.
6 ONI, The Aleutians Campaign, pp. 26–27.
7 NARA: COMTASKFOR 8, War Diary, 2/1-28/43, pp. 44–45.
8 JACAR: Ref. C14121148100: Campaign Until the Evacuation from the Aleutians (…) Northern Force's Leadership in Campaign (in Japanese), p. 2.
9 SS vol. 29 (in Japanese), pp. 446–447.
10 NIDS: Aleutians Campaign Record, Kiska Attu Islands (in Japanese); SS vol. 29 (in Japanese), pp. 440–441.
11 JACAR: Ref. C14121138500: Aleutian Campaign Daily Calendar, S18.03 (in Japanese), p. 4.
12 NARA: ADV INTEL CTR, NOPAC: Memo on investigation of landing strip possibilities, Agattu, pp. 1–9.
13 NARA: COMTASKFOR 8 War Diary, 1/1-31/43; NARA: COMTASKFOR 8 War Diary, 2/1-28/43; NARA: COMTASKFOR 8 War Diary, 3/1-31/43; NARA: COM FLT AIR WING 4, War Diary, 1/1-31/43; NARA: COM FLT AIR WING 4, War Diary, 2/1-28/43; NARA: COM FLT AIR WING 4, War Diary, 3/1-33/43.
14 NARA: COMTASKFOR 8, War Diary, 2/1-28/43, pp. 10–12.
15 Some primary Japanese sources claim that the airfield was completed only in 40 percent. JACAR: Ref. C14121148100: Campaign Until the Evacuation from the Aleutians (…) Northern Force's Leadership in Campaign (in Japanese), p. 2.
16 SS vol. 29 (in Japanese), p. 458.
17 SS vol. 29 (in Japanese), p. 457.
18 Japanese documents provide contradictory information regarding the size of the Kiska garrison. In March 1943, there were about 3,000 men on the island, while on 10 June, during the first round of evacuation, there were already 5,639 men. It is also known that after 27 March 1943 no major convoy reached Kiska. Even if the first calculation does not include about 1,170 civilian employees of the Army and Navy, there remains a difference of approximately 1,800 soldiers. However, the numbers included in the summary of the evacuation from Kiska remain the most reliable source and thus, they were quoted in the book. JACAR: Ref. C14121148500: Campaign Until the Evacuation from the Aleutians (…) Battle of the Komandorski Islands (in Japanese), p. 2; Bōei Kenshūsho Senshishitsu (ed.), Senshi Sōsho vol. 98: History of Submarines (in Japanese), Tokyo 1979, p. 242.
19 PoGCM: PoGCM: 3-311 To Lieutenant General John L. De Witt September 3, 1942.
20 Herder, The Aleutians, p. 51.
21 NARA: COMTASKFOR 8 War Diary, 12/1-31/42, p. 23.

Chapter 5

1 Based on the TF-8 report, it can be concluded that the Americans knew exactly the schedule of Convoy "D" and that after the bombardment of Attu, the Shemya landing operation was initially postponed by three days and then cancelled. NARA: COMTASKFOR 8 War Diary, 12/1-31/42, p. 10.
2 Gray Book, vol 2, pp. 383–384.
3 NARA: COMTASKFOR 8 War Diary, 12/1-31/42, p. 12.
4 NARA: COMTASKFOR 8 War Diary, 12/1-31/42, p. 23.
5 NARA: COMTASKFOR 8 War Diary, 12/1-31/42, p. 31.

Chapter 6

1 JACAR: Ref. C14121137700: Aleutian Campaign Daily Calendar, S17.12 (in Japanese), p. 2; JACAR: Ref. C08051676900: S17.11–S18.04, 452. Kū Action Report (1) (in Japanese), p. 17.
2 The Japanese were convinced that these were three 'large reconnaissance planes'. JACAR: Ref. C14121137700: Aleutian Campaign Daily Calendar, S17.12 (in Japanese), p. 2.
3 NARA: COMTASKFOR 8 War Diary, 12/1-31/42, p. 36.
4 NARA: COMTASKFOR 8 War Diary, 12/1-31/42, p. 43.
5 SS vol. 29 (in Japanese), p. 354.
6 NARA: COMTASKFOR 8 War Diary, 12/1-31/42, p. 46.
7 NARA: Patwing 4, p. 120; NARA: COMTASKFOR 8 War Diary, 12/1-31/42, p. 51.
8 Cloe, *The Aleutian Warriors*, p. 251.
9 JACAR: Ref. C14121137700: Aleutian Campaign Daily Calendar, S17.12 (in Japanese), p. 4.
10 NARA: COMTASKFOR 8 War Diary, 12/1-31/42, p. 54.
11 Morison, *Aleutians*, p. 17.
12 NARA: USS Indianapolis, War Diary, 12/1-31/42, p. 5.
13 NARA: COMTASKFOR 8 War Diary, 12/1-31/42, p. 58.
14 JACAR: Ref. C08051676900: S17.11–S18.04, 452. Kū Action Report (1) (in Japanese), p. 22.
15 NARA: COMTASKFOR 8 War Diary, 12/1-31/42, s. 64.
16 The Japanese claimed they shot down two and damaged one B-24. JACAR: Ref. C14121137700: Aleutian Campaign Daily Calendar, S17.12 (in Japanese), p. 5.
17 Cloe, *The Aleutian Warriors*, p. 248.
18 NARA: COMTASKFOR 8 War Diary, 12/1-31/42, p. 64.
19 NARA: USS Indianapolis, War Diary, 12/1-31/42, p. 9.
20 NARA: COMTASKFOR 8 War Diary, 12/1-31/42, p. 70, 76.
21 According to the Japanese documents, only three floatplane fighters were damaged. JACAR: Ref. C08051676900: S17.11–S18.04, 452. Kū Action Report (1) (in Japanese), p. 29; Cloe, *The Aleutian Warriors*, p. 248.
22 Cloe, *The Aleutian Warriors*, p. 248.
23 JACAR: Ref. C08051676900: S17.11–S18.04, 452. Kū Action Report (1) (in Japanese), p. 31.
24 NARA: COMTASKFOR 8 War Diary, 12/1-31/42, p. 75.
25 The Japanese did not lose a single plane that day and claimed two P-38s shot down. JACAR: Ref. C08051676900: S17.11–S18.04, 452. Kū Action Report (1) (in Japanese), p. 33.
26 NARA: COMTASKFOR 8 War Diary, 12/1-31/42, s. 76.
27 Garfield, *Thousand-Mile War*, pp. 204–205.
28 NARA: COMTASKFOR 8 War Diary, 12/1-31/42; NARA: COM FLT AIR WING 4, War Diary, 12/1-31/42; HLA: Theobald Papers, The Planes Used in Kiska Mission.
29 Four men were killed due to the attack. JACAR: Ref. C14121137700: Aleutian Campaign Daily Calendar, S17.12 (in Japanese), p. 6.
30 The Joint Army-Navy Assessment Committee, *Chronological List of Japanese Merchant Vessel Losses*, February 1947, p. 37.
31 PoGCM: 3-453 To Private Allen T. Brown December 17, 1942.
32 NARA: COMTASKFOR 8 War Diary, 9/1-30/42, p. 96.
33 JACAR: Ref. C08051628500: S17.08–S17.10, 5. Kū Action Report (in Japanese), pp. 33–34.
34 Garfield, *Thousand-Mile War*, p. 178.
35 NARA: COMTASKFOR 8 War Diary, 9/1-30/42, s. 96.
36 Garfield, *Thousand-Mile War*, p. 179.
37 JACAR: Ref. C14121137400: Aleutian Campaign Daily Calendar, S17.09 (in Japanese), p. 5, JACAR: Ref. C08051628500: S17.08–S17.10, 5. Kū Action Report (2) (in Japanese), p. 36.
38 JACAR: Ref. C08030272100: S17.09.15–S17.09.30, 51. Base Force War Diary (in Japanese), p. 2.

39 JACAR: Ref. C08030272100: S17.09.15–S17.09.30, 51. Base Force War Diary (in Japanese), p. 6.
40 SS vol. 29 (in Japanese), p. 332.
41 Some publications indicate that the Fifth Fleet promised to send only five floatplane fighters. *Maru Special* (in Japanese), p. 49.
42 SS vol. 29 (in Japanese), pp. 332–333.
43 NARA: COMTASKFOR 8 War Diary, 9/1-30/42, p. 175.
44 JACAR: Ref. C08051628500: S17.08–S17.10, 5. Kū Action Report (2) (in Japanese), p. 41.
45 SS vol. 29 (in Japanese), p. 342.
46 NARA: COMTASKFOR 8 War Diary, 9/1-30/42, p. 175.
47 JACAR: Ref. C08051628500: S17.08–S17.10, 5. Kū Action Report (2) (in Japanese), pp. 43–44.
48 JACAR: Ref. C14121137400: Aleutian Campaign Daily Calendar, S17.09 (in Japanese), p. 8.
49 NARA: COMTASKFOR 8 War Diary, 9/1-30/42, p. 193.
50 JACAR: Ref. C08051628600: S17.08–S17.10, 5. Kū Action Report (3) (in Japanese), p. 7.
51 NARA: COMTASKFOR 8 War Diary, 9/1-30/42, p. 208.
52 JACAR: Ref. C08051628600: S17.08–S17.10, 5. Kū Action Report (3) (in Japanese), p. 9.
53 NARA: COMTASKFOR 8 War Diary, 9/1-30/42, p. 208.
54 JACAR: Ref. C14121137400: Aleutian Campaign Daily Calendar, S17.09 (in Japanese), p. 9.
55 SS vol. 29 (in Japanese), p. 336.
56 JACAR: Ref. C08051628600: S17.08–S17.10, 5. Kū Action Report (3) (in Japanese), p. 9.
57 JACAR: Ref. C08051628600: S17.08–S17.10, 5. Kū Action Report (3) (in Japanese), p. 16, 18.
58 NARA: COMTASKFOR 8 War Diary, 9/1-30/42, p. 217.
59 JACAR: Ref. C14121137400: Aleutian Campaign Daily Calendar, S17.09 (in Japanese), p. 9.
60 JACAR: Ref. C08051628600: S17.08–S17.10, 5. Kū Action Report (3) (in Japanese), p. 29.
61 SS vol. 29 (in Japanese), p. 358.
62 SS vol. 29 (in Japanese), p. 358.
63 PoGCM: 3-351 To Lieutenant General John L. De Witt October 2, 1942.
64 SS vol. 29 (in Japanese), p. 362.
65 SS vol. 29 (in Japanese), pp. 335–337.
66 NARA: COMTASKFOR 8 War Diary, 10/1-31/42, p. 5.
67 JACAR: Ref. C08051628600: S17.08–S17.10, 5. Kū Action Report (3) (in Japanese), p. 24. The floatplane fighters reported seven B-24s and two P-39s over Kiska.
68 JACAR: Ref. C14121137400: Aleutian Campaign Daily Calendar, S17.09 (in Japanese), p. 10.
69 NARA: COMTASKFOR 8 War Diary, 10/1-31/42, p. 5.
70 NARA: COMTASKFOR 8 War Diary, 10/1-31/42, p. 11.
71 JACAR: Ref. C08051628600: S17.08–S17.10, 5. Kū Action Report (3) (in Japanese), p. 33.
72 NARA: COMTASKFOR 8 War Diary, 10/1-31/42, p. 27.
73 JACAR: Ref. C08051628600: S17.08–S17.10, 5. Kū Action Report (3) (in Japanese), p. 35; JACAR: Ref. C14121137400: Aleutian Campaign Daily Calendar, S17.09 (in Japanese), p. 10.
74 SS vol. 29 (in Japanese), p. 343.
75 NARA: COMTASKFOR 8 War Diary, 9/1-30/42; NARA: COMTASKFOR 8 War Diary, 10/1-31/42; HLA: Theobald Papers, The Planes Used in Kiska Mission.
76 NARA: COMTASKFOR 8 War Diary, 10/1-31/42, p. 45.
77 JACAR: Ref. C14121137500: Aleutian Campaign Daily Calendar, S17.10 (in Japanese), p. 1.
78 NARA: COMTASKFOR 8 War Diary, 10/1-31/42.
79 JACAR: Ref. C14121137500: Aleutian Campaign Daily Calendar, S17.10 (in Japanese), pp. 2–3.
80 NARA: COMTASKFOR 8 War Diary, 10/1-31/42, p. 151.
81 NARA: COMTASKFOR 8 War Diary, 10/1-31/42, p. 141.
82 JACAR: Ref. C08030082200: S17.08–S17.10, 1. Torpedo Squadron Action Report (3) (in Japanese), pp. 23–24.
83 JACAR: Ref. C141211374500: Aleutian Campaign Daily Calendar, S17.10 (in Japanese), p. 4.
84 JACAR: Ref. C08030082200: S17.08–S17.10, 1. Torpedo Squadron Action Report (3) (in Japanese), p. 6.
85 NARA: COMTASKFOR 8 War Diary, 10/1-31/42; HLA: Theobald Papers, The Planes Used in Kiska Mission. There is no information about the 19

October raid in the TF-8 action report, based on Japanese sources. See: JACAR: Ref. C14121137450O: Aryūshan Kōryaku Sakusen Higoyomi, S17.10 (in Japanese), p. 5.

86   SS vol. 29 (in Japanese), p. 365.

87   SS vol. 29 (in Japanese), p. 369.

88   JACAR: Ref. C08030082300: S17.08–S17.10, 1. Torpedo Squadron Action Report (4) (in Japanese), p. 13.

89   JACAR: Ref. C08030082200: S17.08–S17.10, 1. Torpedo Squadron Action Report (3) (in Japanese), pp. 47–50.

90   JACAR: Ref. C08051628600: S17.08–S17.10, 5. Kū Action Report (3) (in Japanese), p. 46.

91   JACAR: Ref. C14121137450O: Aleutian Campaign Daily Calendar, S17.10 (in Japanese), p. 7; JACAR: Ref. C08030272200: S17.10.01–S17.10.31, 51. Base Force War Diary (in Japanese), p. 1.

92   Detailed information about the organisation of the convoy and the landing on Attu: JACAR: Ref. C08030082300: S17.08–S17.10, 1. Torpedo Squadron Action Report (4) (in Japanese), p. 13.

93   It is unknown whether the Japanese knew at that time that the earlier message about the occupation of Amchitka by the Americans was false, but it should be assumed that it envisaged retaking the island from the enemy's hands.

94   NARA: COMTASKFOR 8 War Diary, 10/1-31/42, pp. 206–221.

95   NARA: COMTASKFOR 8 War Diary, 10/1-31/42, p. 94.

96   NARA: COMTASKFOR 8 War Diary, 10/1-31/42, p. 279.

97   ONI, The Aleutians Campaign, p. 21.

98   NARA: Patwing 4, p. 117.

Chapter 7

1   Herder, The Aleutians, p. 40.

2   JACAR: Ref. C14121137600: Aleutian Campaign Daily Calendar, S17.11 (in Japanese), pp. 2–3.

3   Garfield, Thousand-Mile War, p. 192.

4   NARA: OMTASKFOR 8 War Diary, 11/1-30/42, p. 15.

5   This information was a surprise, yet on 28 October, right before the Japanese reoccupied Attu, a reconnaissance bomber reported that the roof of one of the destroyed buildings near the church had recently been rebuilt. Based on this information, the Americans could have suspected that the enemy had left only a small reconnaissance or meteorological party on the island.

6   It remains unknown how many floatplane fighters were destroyed and slightly damaged during this attack. JACAR: Ref. C14121137600: Aleutian Campaign Daily Calendar, S17.11 (in Japanese), pp. 4–5. The 452nd Kaigun Kōkūtai report (the 5th Kaigun Kōkūtai changed its name on 1 November as part of the reorganisation of naval air forces) does not provide information on losses. JACAR: Ref. C08051676900: S17.11–S18.04, 452. Kū Action Report (1) (in Japanese), p. 1.

7   NARA: COMTASKFOR 8 War Diary, 11/1-30/42, p. 20.

8   NARA: COMTASKFOR 8 War Diary, 11/1-30/42, pp. 24–25.

9   NARA: COM FLT AIR WING 4, War Diary, 11/1-30/42, p. 3

10   NARA: COMTASKFOR 8 War Diary, 11/1-30/42, p. 55.

11   NARA: COMTASKFOR 8 War Diary, 11/1-30/42, p. 58.

12   JACAR: Ref. C08051676900: S17.11–S18.04, 452. Kū Action Report (1) (in Japanese), p. 8.

13   NARA: COMTASKFOR 8 War Diary, 11/1-30/42, p. 60.

14   JACAR: Ref. C14121137600: Aleutian Campaign Daily Calendar, S17.11 (in Japanese), p. 9. The report indicates an army transport ship Kachōsan Maru, but it was actually Cheribon Maru.

15   NARA: COMTASKFOR 8 War Diary, 10/1-31/42; NARA: COMTASKFOR 8 War Diary, 11/1-30/42; NARA: COM FLT AIR WING 4, War Diary, 11/1-30/42; HLA: Theobald Papers, The Planes Used in Kiska Mission.

16   SS vol. 29 (in Japanese), pp. 373–378.

17   SS vol. 29 (in Japanese), p. 377.

18   JACAR: Ref. C08030082700: S17.11.01–S17.11.28, 1. Torpedo Squadron Detailed Action Report (1) (in Japanese), pp. 15–16.

19   Some Japanese diaries confuse the date of this transport. See Tatsuguchi Nobuo Diary: Attsu-tō no Gyokusai (in Japanese), < http://ohmura-study. net/331.html>, [accessed: 12 Dec 2023].

20   JACAR: Ref. C08030082700: S.17.11.01–S17.11.28, 1. Torpedo Squadron Detailed Action Report (1) (in Japanese), pp. 26–36.

21   519 men are mentioned in JACAR: Ref. C08030083200: S.17.12.01–S18.02.29, 1. Torpedo Squadron Detailed Action Report (1) (in Japanese),

p. 13. 570 men are mentioned in JACAR: Ref. C14121137700: Aleutian Campaign Daily Calendar, S17.12 (in Japanese), p. 1.

22   JACAR: Ref. C08030083200: S17.12.01–S18.02.29, 1. Torpedo Squadron Detailed Action Report (1) (in Japanese), p. 6.

23   SS vol. 29 (in Japanese), p. 391.

24   JACAR: Ref. C08030083200: S17.12.01–S18.02.29, 1. Torpedo Squadron Detailed Action Report (1) (in Japanese), pp. 6–7.

25   JACAR: Ref. C08030272300: S17.11.01–S17.11.30, 51. Base Force War Diary (in Japanese), pp. 9–10; SS vol. 29 (in Japanese), pp. 376–380.

ABOUT THE AUTHOR

Michal A. Piegzik has a PhD in Japanese law, working at Edinburgh Napier University as a lecturer in Family Law. He was awarded the Japanese Ministry of Education scholarship for exceptional research results. In 2016–2017 and 2020–2022, he researched Japanese civil law at Tokyo Metropolitan University. The Pacific War is his life's passion which also, remarkably influenced his academic skills and career path. The author of six monographs and 20 articles related to law and history, *The Darkest Hour: The Japanese Naval Offensive in the Indian Ocean*, published by Helion and Company in 2022, was his debut in British historiography.